Eric Laws
Bruce Prideaux
Editors

Tourism Crises:
Management Responses
and Theoretical Insight

Tourism Crises: Management Responses and Theoretical Insight has been co-published simultaneously as *Journal of Travel & Tourism Marketing*, Volume 19, Numbers 2/3 2005.

*Pre-publication
REVIEWS,
COMMENTARIES,
EVALUATIONS . . .*

"This book PROVIDES A WEALTH OF CASE STUDIES demonstrating best practice in crisis management from around the world. It provides both academic and industry excellence and is A MUST READ FOR TOURISM MANAGERS, STUDENTS, AND RESEARCHERS."

Dimitrios Buhalis, PhD
*Programme Leader
MSc in Tourism Marketing
School of Management
University of Surrey*

THHP

The Haworth Hospitality Press®
An Imprint of The Haworth Press, Inc.

New York • London • Victoria (AU)
www.HaworthPress.com

Tourism Crises:
Management Responses
and Theoretical Insight

Tourism Crises: Management Responses and Theoretical Insight has been co-published simultaneously as *Journal of Travel & Tourism Marketing,* Volume 19, Numbers 2/3 2005.

Tourism Crises: Management Responses and Theoretical Insight, edited by Eric Laws and Bruce Prideaux (Vol. 19, No. 2/3 2005). *"COMPREHENSIVE AND TIMELY. . . . CRUCIAL READING for scholars, destination planners, and industry leaders." (Dallen J. Timothy, PhD, Associate Professor, Department of Recreation Management and Tourism, College of Public Programs, Arizona State University)*

Handbook of Consumer Behavior, Tourism, and the Internet, edited by Juline E. Mills, PhD, and Rob Law, PhD (Vol. 17, No. 2/3, 2004). *"WORTHWHILE. . . . RECOMMENDED. . . . The assembled research talent between the covers of this long-overdue (and much-needed) book represents writing from some of the most insightful thinkers in the field." (Andrew J. Frew, PhD, Professor and Chair, IT and Tourism; Director, SITI, Faculty of Business and Arts, Queen Margaret University College, United Kingdom)*

Management Science Applications in Tourism and Hospitality, edited by Zheng Gu, PhD (Vol. 16, No. 2/3, 2004). *"A THOROUGH BLUEPRINT for graduate students and industry executives." (Michael Kwag, PhD, CHA, CHAE, Associate Professor, Boston University)*

Safety and Security in Tourism: Relationships, Management, and Marketing, edited by C. Michael Hall, PhD, Dallen J. Timothy, PhD, and David Timothy Duval, PhD (Vol. 15, No. 2/3/4, 2003). *Examines tourism safety and security issues in light of the September, 2001 terrorist attacks on the United States.*

Wine, Food, and Tourism Marketing, edited by C. Michael Hall, PhD (Vol. 14, No. 3/4, 2003). *"One of the world's foremost researchers in culinary tourism takes the field to a new level. . . ." (Erik Wolf, MA, Director, International Culinary Tourism Association)*

Tourism Forecasting and Marketing, edited by Kevin K. F. Wong, PhD, and Haiyan Song, PhD (Vol. 13, No. 1/2, 2002). *"A valuable resource for policymakers in both the private and public sectors . . . Makes a significant contribution to the field of tourism forecasting by bringing together many different research methodologies with data on tourism flows from around the world." (Pauline J. Sheldon, PhD, Interim Dean and Professor, School of Travel Industry Management, University of Hawaii at Manoa)*

Japanese Tourists: Socio-Economic, Marketing and Psychological Analysis, edited by K. S. (Kaye) Chon, Tustomo Inagaki, and Taji Ohashi (Vol. 9, No. 1/2, 2000). *Presents recent studies on the socioeconomic, marketing, and psychological analysis of Japanese tourists.*

Geography and Tourism Marketing, edited by Martin Oppermann, PhD (Vol. 6, No. 3/4, 1997). *"Casts much light on how insights from geography can be applied to, and gained from, tourism promotion. . . . Well-written, informative, and interesting, and the issues are important." (David Harrison, PhD, Co-ordinator of Tourism Studies, School of Social and Economic Development, University of the South Pacific, Suva, Fiji)*

Marketing Issues in Pacific Area Tourism, edited by John C. Crotts, PhD, and Chris A. Ryan, PhD (Vol. 6, No. 1, 1997). *"A significant volume on the marketing issues that face the region. Nicely complements existing texts and will carve its own distinctive niche as a reference work. . . . Valuable to students of tourism marketing both inside and outside of the Pacific region." (C. Michael Hall, PhD, Professor and Chairperson, Tourism and Services Management, Victoria University of Wellington, New Zealand)*

Recent Advances in Tourism Marketing Research, edited by Daniel R. Fesenmaier, PhD, Joseph T. O'Leary, PhD, and Muzaffer Uysal, PhD (Vol. 5, No. 2/3, 1996). *"This book clearly marks the current advancement in tourism marketing research. . . . Tourism marketing researchers and academics can gain useful insights by reading this text." (Journal of the Academy of Marketing Science)*

Economic Psychology of Travel and Tourism, edited by John C. Crotts, PhD, and W. Fred van Raaij, PhD (Vol. 3, No. 3, 1995). *"A fresh and innovative volume that expands our understanding of consumers in the tourism market. . . . Will be a useful reference for scholars and graduate students working in tourism psychology and marketing." (Dr. Stephen L. J. Smith, Professor, Department of Recreation and Leisure Studies, University of Waterloo, Ontario, Canada)*

Communication and Channel Systems in Tourism Marketing, edited by Muzaffer Uysal, PhD, and Daniel R. Fesenmaier, PhD (Vol. 2, No. 2/3, 1994). *"Loaded with information on a variety of topics that provides readers with a solid background of the topic as well as introduces them to new ideas. . . . A valuable resource." (Robert M. O'Halloran, PhD, Associate Professor, School of Hotel, Restaurant & Tourism, University of Denver)*

Tourism Crises:
Management Responses
and Theoretical Insight

Eric Laws
Bruce Prideaux
Editors

Tourism Crises: Management Responses and Theoretical Insight has been co-published simultaneously as *Journal of Travel & Tourism Marketing*, Volume 19, Numbers 2/3 2005.

The Haworth Hospitality Press®
An Imprint of The Haworth Press, Inc.

New York • London • Victoria (AU)
www.HaworthPress.com

Published by

The Haworth Hospitality Press®, 10 Alice Street, Binghamton, NY 13904-1580 USA

The Haworth Hospitality Press® is an imprint of The Haworth Press, Inc., 10 Alice Street, Binghamton, NY 13904-1580 USA.

Tourism Crises: Management Responses and Theoretical Insight has been co-published simultaneously as *Journal of Travel & Tourism Marketing,* Volume 19, Numbers 2/3 2005.

Cover design by Marylouise Doyle

Library of Congress Cataloging-in-Publication Data

Tourism crises : management responses and theoretical insight / Eric Laws, Bruce Prideaux, editors.
    p. cm.
   "Tourism Crises: Management Responses and Theoretical Insight has been co-published simultaneously as Journal of Travel & Tourism Marketing, Volume 19, Numbers 2/3 2005."
   Includes bibliographical references and index.
   ISBN-13: 978-0-7890-3208-9 (soft cover : alk. paper)
   ISBN-10: 0-7890-3208-2 (soft cover : alk. paper)
   1. Tourism–Management. 2. Crisis management. 3. Travel–Safety measures. I. Laws, Eric, 1945- II. Prideaux, B. (Bruce) III. Journal of travel and tourism marketing.

   G155.A1.L384 2006
   910.68'4–dc22

                                                    2005031478

Indexing, Abstracting & Website/Internet Coverage

This section provides you with a list of major indexing & abstracting services and other tools for bibliographic access. That is to say, each service began covering this periodical during the year noted in the right column. Most Websites which are listed below have indicated that they will either post, disseminate, compile, archive, cite, or alert their own Website users with research-based content from this work. [This list is as current as the copyright date of this publication.]

(continued)

(continued)

Tourism Crises: Management Responses and Theoretical Insight

CONTENTS

ABOUT THE EDITORS

Eric Laws, PhD, is an Adjunct Professor in the Business School of James Cook University in Cairns, Queensland, Australia. He has authored more than 50 refereed journal and conference papers, and four books. He has edited or co-edited eight additional books and three special journal editions. Dr. Laws' research interests include service quality in tourism, the destination impacts of tourism, and the impact of the structured relationships of the tourism industry on tourists' experiences.

Bruce Prideaux, PhD, is Professor of Marketing and Tourism Management at James Cook University in Cairns, Queensland, Australia. He has published more than 100 journal articles, book chapters, and conference papers, and serves on the editorial boards of several journals. He has guest edited special journal issues on themes ranging from cybertourism to drive tourism to crisis management. Dr. Prideaux is actively involved in a number of research organizations, including the Sustainable Tourism Cooperative Research Center and the Marine and Tropical Science Research Facility.

Preface

In recent years the number of crises impacting on the tourism industry appears to have escalated. Perhaps this is result of the industry's growing importance in the global economy or perhaps because of the almost omnipotent power of the mass media to report on crisis. Interest by researchers in crisis and its impact has also grown and this special issue is one attempt to bring together recent research in this area of scholarship. The cases discussed offer analysis, reflection and new agendas for dealing with crisis.

The volume particularly focuses on the British Foot and Mouth crisis, the September 11, 2001 terrorist attack on the United States and the impact of the 2003 SARS crisis. Each of these crises had major impacts at regional, national and international levels. Other papers look at a range of conceptual issues including a typology of crisis terms, crisis communications and the systematic analysis of crisis.

Unfortunately the future will continue to witness new crises that will have adverse impacts on the regional, national and global tourism industry. We hope that the research reported on in this volume will stimulate debate, lead to new methods of coping with crisis, encourage further research and open new areas of crisis research.

Eric Laws
Bruce Prideaux

[Haworth co-indexing entry note]: "Preface." Laws, Eric, and Bruce Prideaux. Co-published simultaneously in *Journal of Travel & Tourism Marketing* (The Haworth Hospitality Press, an imprint of The Haworth Press, Inc.) Vol. 19, No. 2/3, 2005, pp. xix; and: *Tourism Crises: Management Responses and Theoretical Insight* (ed: Eric Laws, and Bruce Prideaux) The Haworth Hospitality Press, an imprint of The Haworth Press, Inc., 2005, pp. xv. Single or multiple copies of this article are available for a fee from The Haworth Document Delivery Service [1-800-HAWORTH, 9:00 a.m. - 5:00 p.m. (EST). E-mail address: docdelivery@haworthpress.com].

Crisis Management:
A Suggested Typology

Eric Laws

Bruce Prideaux

SUMMARY. This paper explores the current state of research on the study of crisis and its management from a tourism perspective. Given the increasing interest in this area of research the authors suggest a typology of terms used to describe research into issues related to tourism crisis. The aim of the paper is to offer a common starting point for discussion but not to attempt to provide prescriptive definitions. *[Article copies available for a fee from The Haworth Document Delivery Service: 1-800-HAWORTH. E-mail address: <docdelivery@haworthpress.com> Website: <http://www.HaworthPress. com> © 2005 by The Haworth Press, Inc. All rights reserved.]*

KEYWORDS. Crisis, definitions, crisis typology

A cursory review of newspaper headlines over any ten-year period since tourism became one of the leading sectors of the international economy will confirm that the industry is subject to a wide range of events, shocks and incidents that disrupt its orderly operation and development. However, despite the frequency of disruptive events tourism scholars have neglected the systematic study of this area of research until comparatively recently. There are a wide range of events that can impact on the tourism industry and this paper will briefly examine the state of research to date before suggesting a typology of terms and their meaning that together encapsulate the current state of research into the origin, impact and management of tourism crises.

The starting point must be an examination of the event or events that generate problems for the tourism industry. An event, in whatever form it occurs, that creates a shock to the tourism industry resulting in the sudden emergence of an adverse situation, is usually referred to as a crisis. Crises can occur at any level of operation including an individual restaurant or a local coach company, a destination, a region, nation or the global tourism industry. In the case of a destination, a crisis is usually characterised by falling visitor numbers followed by a fall in employment, decline in private sector profits and eventually a reduction in government revenue, and possibly cessation of further investment. Crisis events may be internal in origin, such as a strike, or

Eric Laws is Adjunct Professor of Tourism, James Cook University, P.O. Box 6811, Cairns, Queensland, 4870, Australia (E-mail: e.laws@runbox.com). Bruce Prideaux is Deputy Head of the School of Business Studies, James Cook University, P.O. Box 6811, Cairns, Queensland, 4870, Australia (E-mail: Bruce.prideaux@jcu.edu.au).

[Haworth co-indexing entry note]: "Crisis Management: A Suggested Typology." Laws, Eric, and Bruce Prideaux. Co-published simultaneously in *Journal of Travel & Tourism Marketing* (The Haworth Hospitality Press, an imprint of The Haworth Press, Inc.) Vol. 19, No. 2/3, 2005, pp. 1-8; and: *Tourism Crises: Management Responses and Theoretical Insight* (ed: Eric Laws, and Bruce Prideaux) The Haworth Hospitality Press, an imprint of The Haworth Press, Inc., 2005, pp. 1-8. Single or multiple copies of this article are available for a fee from The Haworth Document Delivery Service [1-800-HAWORTH, 9:00 a.m. - 5:00 p.m. (EST). E-mail address: docdelivery@haworthpress.com].

Available online at http://www.haworthpress.com/web/JTTM
© 2005 by The Haworth Press, Inc. All rights reserved.
doi:10.1300/J073v19n02_01

have a cause that lies outside of the tourism industry, as was the case with the September 11, 2001 attack on the USA. The way in which the tourism aspects of these adverse events are managed has only recently begun to attract substantial attention in the tourism literature (Prideaux, Laws & Faulkner, 2003; Hall, Timothy & Duval, 2003; McKercher, 1999; McKercher & Pine, 2005; Sonmez & Graefe, 1998; Sonmez, Apostolopoulos & Tarlow, 1999; Barton, 1994; Beirman, 2003; Mansfeld, 1999; Faulkner, 2001; Faulkner & Vikulov, 2001; Pizam, 2002; Pizam & Smith, 2000; Pizam, Tarlow & Bloom, 1997; Ritchie, 2004).

The term "crisis" is commonly applied in many settings and may include a "mid-life crisis," a monetary crisis, managerial crisis, national crisis, political crisis and so on. The ubiquitous use of this and related terms has resulted in a lack of precision. A crisis is sometimes a state of consciousness where one person's problems may be another's gain. While the term has a utility or "many things to many people" quality it is worth attempting to more precisely define the term in the context of an event or series of events that upset the orderly operation of the tourism industry. Santana (2003) for example notes that the word crisis is derived from the Greek "Krisis" meaning decision or turning point and observes that the word is widely misused. Santana further observes that the literature is divided on the causes of crisis. One view is that crises (Mitroff, Pearson & Pauchant, 1992) are normal accidents while an opposing view is that crises are the results of "wrong" decisions. Lack of precision could be a limiting factor as claimed by Santana but equally the term is used so widely to describe something that disrupts that its broadness can be interpreted as the popular understanding of crisis as something that is out of the ordinary and unexpected. While lacking the precision as a specific word, the term "crisis" can be seen as a word that describes a range of events that disrupt. In this paper the term "crisis" is broadly defined as an event of any magnitude that disrupts the orderly operation of the tourism industry.

The definition of other terms associated with crisis, their cause, impacts and long-term effects is also important as a means of reducing any confusion over the meanings associated with the term. The effect of crisis may be defined narrowly and focus on a specific event that for example has a serious and unplanned consequence on a firm or an individual or may be defined more broadly to describe the effect of a crisis on a wide range of people, institutions, destinations and even society in general. Any attempt to define the many terms that describe the elements of crisis, its management and its impacts remains difficult and meanings will remain open to debate. The alternative, however, is to continue the current situation where the absence of any attempt to introduce a measure of uniformity in the literature is likely to lead to the development of mutually exclusive definitions that will confuse rather than illuminate.

Outside of the tourism literature there is a growing body of research into the causes, impacts and management of a range of shocks including those that are natural in origin as well as those of human origin. A large body of literature has emerged from the study of crises and disasters in disciplines including economics, management, geography, political science, international relations, disaster research, engineering and areas of science. A number of journals including *Risk Analysis, Risk Management, Disaster Planning and Prevention* and *Emergency Planning Digest* focus entirely on crises and disasters that occur in areas that include nature, disease, the international economy, political crises and private sector mismanagement. These and other similar publications recognise that there are a large range of events that cause crisis to occur while also recognising that it is difficult if not impossible to predict a crisis event on an a priori basis. Equally important this literature recognises that there are methodologies for identifying the precursors of crisis situations, for implementing planning that is designed to mitigate the worst impact of crisis and for managing the situation after a crisis has occurred.

One tool that has become an important method for studying and managing crisis is scenarios which is a method used for predicting the cause, impact and cost of a range of possible crisis events and their subsequent evolution. In many fields of study the use of scenarios as the basis for predicting the impact of a range of disruptions is a widely accepted method of planning for crises including environmental, economic, natural and even multiple events. The tourism literature has been extremely slow to investigate the use of scenarios as an alternative to the current forecasting and prediction methodologies (Prideaux, Laws & Faulkner, 2003). Moreover the tourism literature has neglected to investigate the rich range of techniques developed in other fields of research. The risk management literature for example has significant potential to yield models, frameworks and theories that will assist tourism managers to cope with a range of crises. Further, adoption of complexity theory as advocated in the non-tourism literature provides, as demonstrated in the work of Bill Faulkner discussed below, a means of focussing on the multiplex dependencies within the tourism industry, and shows the need to examine the ways in which it interacts with other aspects of society. It is hoped that this paper will provide a benchmark of current understanding, and assist in further developing the theory and practice of crisis management in tourism.

Disruptions to the tourism industry are not new and have in all likelihood been impacting on the tourism industry from the time that pre-modern tourists were visiting the Seven Wonders of the Ancient World, the third century BC equivalent of the contemporary "must see" sights of the modern world. The significant differences between then and now lie in the global scale of tourism, the interconnectedness of its component sub-sectors, and the resultant complexity of the industry. In the past tourism was the exclusive preserve of the leisured wealthy whereas today tourism is an option available to most members of developed nations. Crisis can occur on a scale spectrum that commences with local and ranges through to global. At the local level the crisis may be as simple as a bridge to a scenic place becoming unserviceable resulting in tourists substituting that locality with another attraction. In cases of this type the impact is localised and there is little if any impact nationally. At the regional level the impact of a crisis can be expected to have implications for the region and potentially for the nation. In a recent example the series of four typhoons that struck Florida and other parts of the Caribbean in September 2004 caused significant damage to the regional tourism industry, and if visitor patterns after previous crises of this nature are repeated a percentage of foreign visitors originally intending to visit Florida will substitute other destinations, causing a decline in tourism numbers and revenue for both the region as well as for the nation. On a national level crisis can have a significant impact on the national tourism industry. The 2002 Bali nightclub bombing that killed 202 persons had a significant impact on inbound tourism to Bali and even by mid-2004 the destination had not fully recovered to the level of inbound visitors experienced prior to the bombing.

Globally, crisis can also have significant impacts on tourism flows. The 2003 SARS outbreak in Asia had a significant impact on visitor flows within, into and out of parts of Asia. McKercher and Pine (2005) state that the magnitude of the rebound effect in the post crisis period is in direct proportion to the extent of privation felt by affected individuals. Cooper (2005) observed that Japanese simply stopped travelling to destinations affected by crisis. Crisis that has a global reach is arguably more damaging to tourism than a local or regional crisis. Events such as SARS illustrate the potential impact that would occur if a pandemic of the type last seen with the Spanish Flu of 1918 were to occur. However, there is also scope for crisis that has a local or regional origin to have impacts that reach far beyond the geographic boundaries of the local area or the region. At the time of writing there have been a number of localised outbreaks of bird flu (avian influenza) in parts of Asia. If this disease outbreak can be contained within regional areas there will be few effects on the national tourism sector of the nations most involved (China, Thailand and Indonesia). However, if the bird flu crosses over the species boundary into the human population in a significant way, the impacts will migrate from sub-national economies through to national economies and perhaps even into the global economy (World Health Organisation, 2004). It is pertinent to observe that SARS killed only 774 persons in 2003 (World Health Organisation, 2004) but had an enormous economic impact. In comparison HIV/AIDS killed an estimated 3 million people in 2003 (UNAIDS, 2004) while malaria killed an estimated 1 to 1.5 million in the same year (World Health Organisation, 2003). If the same level of fear were to emerge over malaria that occurred over SARS, the impact on tourism in many tropical countries would be enormous. If predictions of global warming become a future reality the areas that are capable of hosting malaria carrying mosquitos will expand significantly, posing an additional danger for tourism in subtropical countries as well as in the tropics. Global warming would also be expected to cause many weather events that would effect tourism, although when and to what extent cannot be predicted with the current state of scientific knowledge.

The comparison between SARS and HIV/ AIDS of effects of disease on the demand for tourism illustrate another significant but little understood relationship involving perceptions of risk (Prideaux & Master, 2001). While this is an area largely beyond the scope of this paper, the individual traveller's perception of risk or danger is an important factor in the study of crisis. For many tourists the indiscriminate nature of a disease like SARS appears to be more worrying than the indiscriminate nature of malaria in tropical countries or the risk of sexually transmitted diseases such as HIV/AIDS from risky sexual encounters that may be either commercial or from a short holiday romance (Prideaux, Agrusa, Donlon & Curran, 2004). It is apparent that the media has a significant positive role to play in alerting the population to crisis (Fall & Massey, 2005), but conversely, the visual and often graphic nature of contemporary reporting on many occasions exaggerates the scale of the crisis and its impact (Fall & Massey, 2005). In this sense adverse media reporting may have a greater impact on tourism than the crisis (Cooper, 2005).

Prideaux, Laws and Faulkner (2003) recommended a synthesis between risk specification, identification, management, and forecasting. In such a synthesis, forecasting could be based on revised variables determined by risk analysis or forward looking scenarios as an alternative to current forecasting techniques. In a discussion on quantitative risk analysis, Haimes, Kaplan and Lambest (2002, p. 383) observed

that ". . . It is clear that the first and most important step in a quantitative risk analysis (QRA) is identifying the set of risk scenarios. If the number of risk scenarios is large, then the second step must be to filter and rank the scenarios according to their importance." Prideaux et al. (2003, p. 487) noted that "Ranking of risk, where the level of probability of occurrence and the degree of impact can be established, provides data that can then be used as a basis for forecasting." They acknowledged that the possible range of scenarios is large and there is some need to rank risk scenarios by the probability of their occurrence on a scale that must start with highly probable through to improbable. They also noted (Prideaux et al., 2003, p. 485) that ranking must include the flexibility to adjust the scale of probability. "Prior to the September 11 terrorist attack on the USA, an incident of this nature could be described as a highly improbable risk but after the attack the level of risk moved to highly probable."

It is apparent from the papers in this special volume that a wide range of events, shocks and incidents can trigger crisis situations, and that many of these are neither caused by the tourism industry, nor able to be affected in their course of development by the tourism industry. The response by the UK government to the foot and mouth outbreak of 2001 resulted in drastic measures as documented in the papers by Leslie and Black (2005), and Irvine and Anderson (2005). Despite the serious impact on tourism of many of these measures, the needs of tourism were ignored by government as it pursued what it regarded as the great public need to eradicate a serious animal disease. This case also demonstrates the limitations as well as the possible adverse consequences to the tourism industry of government policy based on the needs of a specific sector of the economy (farming). Further, this case underlines the need for a more systemic understanding of crisis management, including more detailed analysis of both stakeholder concerns and the relative strength of different stakeholder groups. Conversely, in areas of potential risk, such as Alpine regions, tourists feel safer when preventive crisis management tools are in place and made obvious by the authorities (Peters & Pikkemaat, 2005).

In some tourism regions the probability of particular crisis events is relatively high. Although the actual timing, location and severity of earthquakes, hurricanes or avalanches cannot be accurately predicted with current technology, it is certainly possible to learn from past crises, to pre-plan emergency procedures, and to mitigate the severity of such events by adopting appropriate building codes, providing alternative escape routes and develop crisis management strategies. From a destination perspective, effective methods of sharing knowledge about crises and the best ways to cope with them amongst all industry organisations (and staff) is critical. As an example, *Crisis–it wont happen to us* (PATA, 2003), prepared by the Pacific Asia Travel Association after a number of crises in Asia, can be seen as collecting and disseminating best practice for member organisations.

Some sectors of the industry, particularly transportation, are relatively prone to problems including strikes, bad weather, and serious accidents. While technical expertise can improve safety or minimise the resultant disruptions, good management is also needed to deal with the needs of those caught up in the situation (Ross, 2005), as well as with the adverse publicity which might result, but as the papers in this volume show, there is an ongoing need to learn from experience. Organisations and individuals within those organisations also suffer as the result of crisis. Organisational responds that are not driven by an ethical perspective may well compound the effects crises upon those who work within the tourism industry.

The development and the consequences of a crisis (if not its origins) may be understood through a systems and complexity approach. This immediately highlights the question of what is being analysed, the crisis itself, or the effects of the crisis on a specified part of the tourism industry. Both levels of analysis are justifiable: as Yin (1989) has pointed out there is a need to describe situations which are not fully understood as a preliminary step to developing theoretical models.

Faulkner (2001) synthesised crisis situations based on research by Fink (1986, p. 20), Keown-McMullan (1997, p. 9) and Weiner and Kahn (1972, p. 21) identified the following key factors:

- A triggering event, which is so significant that it challenges the existing structure, routine operations or survival of the organisation. Trigger events may include political crises, religious or ethnic tensions, economic decline and climate change;
- Characterised by "fluid, unstable, dynamic" situations (Fink, 1986, p. 20);
- High threat, short decision time and an element of surprise and urgency;
- A perception of an inability to cope among those directly affected; and
- A turning point, when decisive change, which may have both positive and negative connotations, is imminent. Keown-McMullan (1997, p. 9) noted that organisations will undergo significant change even when they successfully manage a crisis situation.

The previous discussion highlighted the inadequacy of Newtonian (linear) thinking with its presumption of stability and predictability (Russell & Faulkner, 1999). A typical large scale disruption precipitates complex movements away from the previous relationships which usually tend towards organisation or destination stability and equilibrium. During a crisis situation multiple events and their follow-on affects may prolong the period of disequilibrium unless there is some mechanism that can assist to re-establish a new equilibrium situation. Chaos theory (Russell & Faulkner, 1999; McKercher, 1999) provides an insightful paradigm for the investigation of changing complex situations where multiple influences impact on non-equilibrium systems. In these conditions of uncertainty, fruitful approaches to strategy formulation need to incorporate contingencies for the unexpected. Chaos theory demonstrates that there are elements of system behaviour that are intrinsically unstable and not amenable to formal forecasting. If this is the case, a new approach to forecasting is required. Possible ways forward may include political audits and risk analysis to develop a sense of the possible patterns of events allowing these to be factored into projections of future tourism activity using a series of scenarios. The latter may involve the use of a scenario building approach that may incorporate elements of van der Heijden's (1997) strategic conversion model, elements of the learning organisation approach based on a structured participatory dialogue (Senge, 1990) or elements of risk management described by Haimes et al. (2002). Whichever direction is taken, there are a number of factors that must be identified and factored into considerations of the possible course of events in the future.

Prideaux (2004) has noted that the first and totally unpredictable driver of history is chance which may also be described as chaos or random events. Events of this type cannot be controlled or forecast. Prideaux (2004) identified trends as a possible early cause of crisis that in this case can be examined on a priori basis by scenario techniques. Trends were defined as those sequences of events that can be identified in the present and which, unless remedial action is taken, will cause some magnitude of disruption in the future. Crises and disasters as well as nature were identified as the other major forces that shape the future. In relation to nature he noted that unlike trends, humanity has little control over nature but major natural events such as floods, earthquakes, droughts and global ice ages can have a severe impact on the course of history.

The papers in this special issue highlight the need to develop new techniques that (1) identify probable (and possible) crisis situations (2) assist in predicting the course of future crises, (3) clarify the roles of industry and government agencies which are called upon to deal with crisis situations and (4) identify the various stakeholder groups affected by crisis events. There is also a need to distinguish between crises and disasters, and to agree on a consistent typology for the terms describing tourism crises to enable a dialogue with colleagues researching other aspects of crisis management. The authors offer the following typology as a starting point (see Table 1).

CONCLUSION

This typology is neither exhaustive nor extensive but does aim to encompass the major terms that are associated with crisis. It is hoped that this typology will assist to develop a broad and common understanding of the meaning of

TABLE 1. Typology of Crisis Terms

Term	Meaning
Crisis	1. An unexpected problem seriously disrupting the functioning of an organisation or sector, or nation. 2. A general term for such problems.
Trends	Those sequences of events that can be identified in the present and which, unless remedial action is taken, will cause some magnitude of disruption in the future.
Disaster	Unpredictable catastrophic change that can normally only be responded to after the event, either by deploying contingency plans already in place or through reactive response.
Triggering event	The origin of a crisis. May be of human origin or as a result of natural forces.
Crisis episode	The period during which the crisis occurs.
Crisis pre-planning	Managerial planning to ensure the best possible responses to a crisis including training, role play, and the acquisition and storing of appropriate resources.
Crisis management	Management strategies that commence with pre-crisis planning, are activated to respond to the crisis as it unfolds and are implemented to recover from the crisis.
Crisis reporting	A mechanism to facilitate learning from crisis episodes to further improve crisis pre-planning.
Knowledge sharing	Organisational, industry or regional mechanisms to analyse and share with relevant individuals and bodies.
Turning point	When decisive change, which may have both positive and negative connotations, is imminent.
Crisis scenario	Scenario based planning that may lead to better responses during actual crises.
Organisational learning	Organisations acquire new management strategies and systems to deal with crisis.
Risk	The level of probability of an undesirable event or incident occurring.
Event	A situation which may lead to crisis if not contained.
Incident	A situation which may lead to crisis if not contained.
Trend	Sequences of events that can be identified in the present and which, unless remedial action is taken, will cause some magnitude of disruption in the future.
Crisis communications	The development and implementation of communications strategies: prior to a crisis; during a crisis; and in the post-crisis recovery period.

the many terms associated with crisis. It is likely that the literature will attract additional studies in coming years and rather than each paper arguing at length about the meanings of specific terms this typology will short circuit the discussion allowing authors greater scope to concentrate on the aspects of crisis, their impacts and strategies for recovery, risk and damage minimisation and so on.

REFERENCES

Barton, L. (1994). Crisis management: Preparing for and managing disasters. *Cornell Hotel and Restaurant Administration Quarterly, 35*(2), 59-65.

Beirman, D. (2003). *Restoring tourism destinations in crisis: A strategic marketing approach.* Sydney: Allen & Unwin.

Cooper, M. (2005). Japanese outbound tourism and the SARS and Iraqi crises of 2003. *Journal of Travel and Tourism Marketing,* Special Issue: Crises, 119-133

Fall, L.T., & Massey, J.E. (2005). The significance of crisis communication in the aftermath of 9/11: A national investigation of how tourism managers have re-tooled their promotional campaigns. *Journal of Travel and Tourism Marketing,* Special Issue: Crises, 79-92.

Faulkner, B. (2001). Towards a framework for disaster management. *Tourism Management, 22,* 135-147.

Faulkner, B., & Vikulov, S. (2001). Katherine, washed out one day, back on track the next: A post-mortem of a tourism disaster. *Tourism Management, 22,* 331-344.

Fink, S. (1986). *Crisis management.* New York: Association of Management.

Haimes, Y., Kaplan, S., & Lambest, J.H. (2002). Risk filtering, ranking, and management framework using hierarchical holographic modelling. *Risk Analysis, 22*(2), 383-397.

Hall, C.M., Timothy, D.J., & Duval, D.T. (2003). Security and tourism: Towards a new understanding? In C.M. Hall, D.J. Timothy & D.T. Duvall (Eds.), *Safety and security in tourism: Relationships, management, and marketing* (pp. 1-18). New York: The Haworth Hospitality Press.

Irvine, W., & Anderson, A.R. (2005). The impacts of Foot and Mouth Disease on a peripheral tourism area: the role and effect of crisis management. *Journal of Travel and Tourism Marketing,* Special Issue: Crises, 49-62.

Keown-McMullan, C. (1997). Crisis: When does a molehill become a mountain? *Disaster Prevention and Management, 4*(2), 20-37.

Leslie, D., & Black, L. (2005). Tourism and the impact of the foot and mouth epidemic in the UK: Reactions, responses and realities with particular reference to Scotland. *Journal of Travel and Tourism Marketing,* Special Issue: Crises, 37-48.

Mansfeld, Y. (1999). Cycles of war, terror and peace: Determinants and management of crisis and recovery on the Israeli tourism industry. *Journal of Travel Research, 38*(August), 30-36.

McKercher, B. (1999). A chaos approach to tourism. *Tourism Management, 20*(4), 425-434.

McKercher, B., & Pine, R. (2005). Privation as a stimulus to travel demand? *Journal of Travel and Tourism Marketing,* Special Issue: Crises, 109-118.

Mitroff, I., Pearson, C., & Pauchant, T. (1992). Crisis management and strategic management: Similarities, differences and challenges. In P. Shrivastava, A. Huff & J. Dutton, (Eds.), *Advances in strategic management,* V. 8. JAI Press Inc.

PATA. (2003). *Crisis–it won't happen to us.* Bangkok: Author.

Peters, M., & Pikkemaat, B. (2005). Crisis management in Alpine winter sports resorts–the 1999 avalanche disaster in Tyrol. *Journal of Travel and Tourism Marketing,* Special Issue: Crises, 9-21.

Pizam, A. (2002). Tourism and terrorism. *International Journal of Hospitality Management, 21*(1), 1-3.

Pizam, A., & Smith, G. (2000). Tourism and terrorism: A quantitative analysis of major terrorist acts and their impact on tourism destinations. *Tourism Economics, 6*(2), 123-138.

Pizam, A., Tarlow, P., & Bloom, J. (1997). Making tourists feel safe: Whose responsibility is it? *Journal of Travel Research, 36*(1), 23-28.

Prideaux, B. (2004). *What forces will shape tourism in coming decades? Visions of the future.* Inaugural Professorial Lecture presented on September 16th at Sofitel Hotel Cairns, Australia.

Prideaux, B., Agrusa, J., Donlon, J., & Curran, C. (2004). Exotic or erotic-contrasting images for defining destinations. *Asia Pacific Journal of Tourism Research, 9*(1), 5-18.

Prideaux, B., Laws, E., & Faulkner, B. (2003). Events in Indonesia: Exploring the limits to formal tourism trends forecasting methods in complex crisis situations. *Tourism Management, 24*(4), 511-520.

Prideaux, B., & Master, H. (2001). Health and safety issues effecting international tourists in Australia. *Asia Pacific Journal of Tourism, 6*(2), 24-32.

Ritchie, B.W. (2004). Chaos, crises and disasters: A strategic approach to crisis management in the tourism industry. *Tourism Management, 25,* 669-683.

Ross, G.F. (2005). Tourism industry employee work-stress–A present and future crisis. *Journal of Travel and Tourism Marketing,* Special Issue: Crises, 135-149.

Russell, R., & Faulkner, B. (1999). Movers and shakers: Chaos makers in tourism development. *Tourism Management, 20,* 411-423.

Santana, G. (2003). Crisis management and tourism: Beyond the rhetoric. *Journal of Travel and Tourism Marketing, 15*(4), 299-321.

Senge, P.M. (1990). *The fifth principle: The art and practice of the learning organisation.* New York: Doubleday.

Sönmez, S., Apostolopoulos Y., & Tarlow, P. (1999). Tourism in crisis: Managing the effects of terrorism. *Journal of Travel Research, 38*(1), 13-18.

Sönmez, S., & Graefe A.R. (1998). Influence of terrorism risk on foreign tourism decisions. *Annals of Tourism Research, 25*(1), 112-144.

UNAIDS. (2004). *Report on the global AIDS epidemic–executive summary.* Retrieved November 24, 2004, from UNAIDS website: www.unaids.org/bangkok2004/GAR2004_HTML/ExecSummary_enExecSumm.

van der Heijden, K. (1997). *Scenarios: The art of strategic conversion.* Chichester: Wiley.

Weiner A.J., & Kahn, H. (1972) Crisis and arms control. In C.F. Hermann (Ed.), *International crises: Insights from behaviour research* (p. 21). New York: The Free Press.

World Health Organisation. (2003). *Malaria is alive and well and killing more than 3000 African children every day.* Retrieved November 12, 2004, from WHO website: http://www.who.int/mediacentre/news/releases/2003/pr33/en/.

World Health Organisation. (2004). *Summary of probable SARS cases with onset of illness 1 November 2002 to 31 July 2003.* Retrieved November 12, 2004, from WHO website: http://www.who.int/csr/sars/country/table2004_04_21/en/.

Yin, R.K. (1989). *Case study methods: Design and research.* Newbury Park, CA: Sage.

Crisis Management in Alpine Winter Sports Resorts– The 1999 Avalanche Disaster in Tyrol

Mike Peters
Birgit Pikkemaat

SUMMARY. Alpine tourism destinations must be prepared for environmental hazards such as avalanche disasters. The maintenance of safety and security, and thus the management of crises have become a major issue in Alpine winter resorts. After a short literature review of crisis management models applicable for tourism destinations, the article demonstrates the disaster management process of Galtuer (Austria) in 1999, which suffered one of the severest avalanche disasters ever experienced in the Austrian Alps. The authors investigate security and emergency measures taken in this Alpine resort and discuss failures and success factors in disaster management. The paper reveals that destinations greatly improve their disaster management tools and procedures after having faced a crisis. The final part of the paper identifies key lessons and provides recommendations for future research. *[Article copies available for a fee from The Haworth Document Delivery Service: 1-800-HAWORTH. E-mail address: <docdelivery@haworthpress.com> Website: <http://www.HaworthPress. com> © 2005 by The Haworth Press, Inc. All rights reserved.]*

KEYWORDS. Crisis management, tourism destinations, disasters, hazards, Alpine tourism, avalanche, disaster management plan

INTRODUCTION

In the recent past, events like September 11th, crime and terrorism attacks in the Middle East, natural and environmental disasters such as floods, avalanches and oil spills, have demonstrated how sensitive the tourism industry is to uncertainties of safety and security. Thus, the main question for all branches of economic activity, particularly for tourism, is to bring risk, security and crisis management under control. Given both the size and growth of the global tourism industry, safety and security problems have seen a similar, if not a more significant increase, as the tourism industry particularly is highly vulnerable to internal and external turmoil. Potential crises involve economic downturns, natural hazards (e.g., avalanches, hurricanes, torrential rains, volcanic eruptions), man-made disasters (e.g.,

Mike Peters (E-mail: mike.peters@uibk.ac.at) and Birgit Pikkemaat (birgit.pikkemaat@uibk.ac.at) are affiliated with the Department for General and Tourism Management, Center for Tourism and Service Economics, University of Innsbruck, Universitätsstrasse 15, 6020 Innsbruck, Austria.

[Haworth co-indexing entry note]: "Crisis Management in Alpine Winter Sports Resorts–The 1999 Avalanche Disaster in Tyrol." Peters, Mike, and Birgit Pikkemaat. Co-published simultaneously in *Journal of Travel & Tourism Marketing* (The Haworth Hospitality Press, an imprint of The Haworth Press, Inc.) Vol. 19, No. 2/3, 2005, pp. 9-20; and: *Tourism Crises: Management Responses and Theoretical Insight* (ed: Eric Laws, and Bruce Prideaux) The Haworth Hospitality Press, an imprint of The Haworth Press, Inc., 2005, pp. 9-20. Single or multiple copies of this article are available for a fee from The Haworth Document Delivery Service [1-800-HAWORTH, 9:00 a.m. - 5:00 p.m. (EST). E-mail address: docdelivery@haworthpress.com].

Available online at http://www.haworthpress.com/web/JTTM
© 2005 by The Haworth Press, Inc. All rights reserved.
doi:10.1300/J073v19n02_02

terrorism, crime, war, regional tensions, international conflicts, riots, insurgency), and epidemic diseases and plagues.

A considerable amount of research deals with problems and issues of crisis management within the context of destination management, focusing on political risks, terrorism, and criminal activities (e.g., Leslie, 1999; Pizam & Smith, 2000; Richter, 1999; Ryan, 1993; Sönmez, Apostopoulos & Tarlow, 1999). The majority of surveys carried out in this area are case studies deriving political, managerial, or research implications from crisis analysis (Leslie, 1999; Mansfeld, 1999; Pizam, 2002; Pizam & Smith, 2000; Pizam, Tarlow & Bloom, 1997; Sönmez et al., 1999; Tarlow & Santana, 2002). However, only few research activities have concentrated on crisis management associated with natural disasters in Alpine winter sports resorts.

Initially, the authors provide a short literature review of recent studies dealing with crisis management in tourism and impacts on tourism and tourism destination development. Second, the paper treats natural disasters in Alpine winter sports regions within the last decade. Reactions on both the demand and the supply side are analysed to demonstrate the need for crisis management in Alpine winter sports resorts. Finally, the paper presents crisis management actions taken in the Alpine destination of Galtuer (Austria) and resulting impacts for crisis management and future research.

CRISES AND DISASTERS IN TOURISM DESTINATIONS: TERMS AND DEFINITIONS

Disasters can be defined as "multi-level, complex and damaging systems-related events that unfold over time and space, through an emergent complex interaction of elements involving structures, connections and networks and which are shaped by ideological, economic and social factors to generate impacts on elements of society that change the performance of the 'normal' order of the societal setting" (Smith, 2003, p. 11). Thus, disasters have a multi-level impact and cause physical damage, but also lead to social or long-term ecological changes (Haggett, 2000). A disaster is an unexpected and unavoidable occurrence that has disastrous consequences. While there is no doubt that disasters have negative consequences there is some ambivalence about whether crises have positive and negative impacts (Krystek, 1987). Crises and disasters are closely linked to credence and trust. Most often disasters coincide with trust and communication crises (Dreyer, 2001, p. 9). This is of utmost importance for any tourism destination as the tourism product bundle is characterised by experience and credence qualities of services and by a higher uncertainty of tourists' decision-making processes (Zeithaml, 1991).

A disaster also causes global impacts across distances and over a long period of time. It is obvious that terrorist attacks exert influence on politics, while natural disasters in tourism regions mainly have economic impacts (e.g., arrivals or tourism receipts), and technological changes require the development of new crisis management instruments. These network effects and interrelationships can be interpreted as global and complex (Urry, 2003). Disasters are accompanied by "sudden unpredictable catastrophic changes" (Faulkner, 2001, p. 136) and signify exceptional and hardly controllable events for a company or an enterprise network (e.g., a tourism destination). One stream of disaster research in tourism focuses on the chaos phenomenon to highlight the fact that stable systems always are inherently chaotic (Faulkner & Russel, 1997; Fink, 1986; Prigogine & Stengers, 1985). Table 1 shows potential situations that can trigger a crisis in tourism. Each trigger is illustrated with an example in the field of Alpine tourism in Europe. Due to the political and geographical location of the European Alps, Alpine tourism is not affected by wars, terrorism or epidemics as can be seen below.

As illustrated in Table 1 natural disasters are crises which cannot be anticipated, yet destinations can nevertheless be prepared for crises, e.g., by disposing of preventive crisis management tools for unmanageable crises. Other researchers distinguish between exogenous and endogenous sources of crises with the former leading to unpredictable crises and the latter referring to tourists or suppliers in the destination (Brookfield, 1999; Sonnenberg & Wöhler, 2004). For instance, on the one hand skiers can trigger avalanches by violating ski regulations, and on the other hand suppliers can enforce

TABLE 1. Potential Crisis Triggers in Tourism

Manageable triggers	Examples for Alpine tourism
Financial miscalculation	Huge investments in the field of wellness lead to bankruptcy in many Alpine resorts
Customers' needs are not recognized/ misinterpreted	Small Alpine resorts cannot combine needs of wellness and family guests
Unsatisfactory/no safety and security precautions	No avalanche warning systems/avalanche barriers in mountain areas; cable car accidents
Unqualified employees	Gaps in education and training of local tourism entrepreneurs and employees (e.g., language and communication skills); ski instructors in small destinations have no certified qualifications
No reaction to changes	Avoidance of new information and communication technologies in many SMEs; acceptance of credit cards is relatively low compared to US standards
Unmanageable triggers	
Wars/religious conflicts	
Terrorism/political instability	
Epidemics	
Natural/environmental disasters	Snow avalanches, mudflows in small valleys surrounded by high mountains; North-South transit route
Recession	European Alpine states are welfare states; no currency exchange within Europe necessary
Decreasing income levels	Recession in Germany leads to overnight stay decreases in many Alpine resorts (as the majority of Austrian visitors are Germans); Alpine tourism focuses on a high quality standard: less low-budget accommodations

avalanche disasters due to insufficient or lacking information on avalanche warnings in the winter destination. Social sciences literature discusses a number of crisis management tools to prevent endogenously triggered disasters.

CORE ISSUES IN TOURISM CRISIS MANAGEMENT RESEARCH

In general crisis management comprises activities crucial for handling situations which are dangerous for the (economic) survival of enterprises (Krummenacher, 1981, p. 12). Crisis management in tourism deals with the recognition of crises within the destination and the recovery and rebuilding after the crisis. The latter should focus on restoring a positive image and on preventing a decrease in tourist arrivals. Due to September 11th and the ensuing "Anthrax" affair in the United States, recent acts of crime and terrorism in the Middle East and natural and environmental disasters such as floods, avalanches and/or oil spills, safety and security issues have become a strategic weapon and competitive advantage for a destination's image (Baloglu & Mangaloglu, 2001;

Fuchs & Peters, 2004; Pikkemaat & Weiermair, 2002; Tapachai & Waryszak, 2000). Furthermore, a positive image of a destination supports tourists' decision-making process as it is responsible for "awareness" and "evoked" sets and consequently serves as a differentiating factor among competing destinations (Baloglu & McCleary, 1999; Coshall, 2000; Crompton & Ankomah, 1993; Sönmez & Sirakaya, 2002). Beyond doubt, any form of violence wherever stirred up has a deterrent effect on the destination image. While a natural disaster is likely to impede the short-term flow of tourists, persistent acts of terrorism can damage a destination's image of safety and attractiveness or even destroy its entire tourism industry (e.g., Egypt, Israel, Northern Ireland) (Pizam & Smith, 2000; Sönmez et al., 1999). Thus, profound development and thorough knowledge of crisis management tools seem to be of utmost importance for the success of any tourism destination.

Existing literature on crisis management focuses on specific crisis management phases as well as specific applications. The majority of research concentrates on disasters which have been discussed above and can be interpreted as crises producing negative results (Dreyer, 2001, p. 9; Krystek, 1987). Analysing the management of disasters requires scrutiny of the event itself.

Several crisis management models try to explain the development of crises (Augustine, 1995; Hwang & Lichtenthal, 2000; Klenk, 1989; Turner, 1976). Referring to Smith's three-phase model, a crisis, and thus a disaster, can be mapped on a time continuum reaching from crisis of management, to an operational crisis, up to a crisis of legitimation (Smith, 1990, 2000).

The first phase, the crisis of management phase, is the period which leads to the crisis event and is either characterised by an organisational climate or culture which provokes a crisis or, in the case of natural disasters, by changing natural circumstances (such as pre-earthquakes or strong snowfalls as preconditions for avalanches). The second phase is the operational crisis situation which is determined by a highly complex set of interactions. In the context of organisational crises, clear communication and well-delegated responsibility strongly influence the outcome of the crisis. In the case of natural disasters, the action of stakeholders involved (e.g., rescuers, victims) may have strong influence on the crisis' further development. However, "the aim here is to prevent an escalation of the situation" (Smith, 1990, p. 271). The post-crisis period can be called a crisis of legitimation as government seeks to legitimate measures or to take precautionary measures. Very often a scapegoat is made of somebody, and communication politics deeply influence the image-building processes in crisis situations. The major result of the learning process is to avoid future crisis, which is symbolized by the feedback loop. The ability of crisis managers and stakeholders to clearly communicate with each other is crucial and has to be both bottom-up and top-down oriented in order to prevent disasters and to improve operational or managerial measures (Smith, 1990). Organizational literature states that there is not "one best way" to design the organization of an enterprise (Galbraith, 1977). Thus, the crisis management system can be defined as an open and learning system. The principles of organizational change also imply a dynamic view on crisis management as an "input-throughput-output-system" (Jick, 1993; Mintzberg, 1991; Perich, 1992; Ulrich, 1989). The feedback loop initiates change processes

(improvements and learning) within the three-stage crisis model. This implies the need for detailed management premises to overcome barriers of change (e.g., unwillingness of stakeholders to cooperate within tourism destinations) (Weiermair & Kneisl, 1996).

In an organisation or tourism destination, potential crises or disasters may be avoided by active crisis management. On the one hand, anticipative crisis management may identify trigger variables, e.g., by simulating potential crises, by using scenario techniques or early warning systems; on the other hand, crisis prevention management must be initiated in case anticipative crisis management does not prevent from the upcoming operational crisis (Reinecke, 1997). In the second phase typical crisis symptoms can already be recognised. Thus, it is of prime urgency to assess the crisis early enough and to adopt existing crisis plans within the enterprise or destination unit. Later, in the operational crisis management stage, the goal is to manage the ongoing crisis and to limit damage (Dreyer, 2001).

Other authors have extended their models from four to six phases of crisis management (Augustine, 1995; Dreyer, 2001; Turner, 1976). Dreyer's (2001) model, for example, contains four phases. Starting with the potential phase where anticipative crisis management is needed, the second phase is called latent phase and requires crisis prevention management, the acute third phase involves impulsive crisis management activities, and the fourth and last postprocessing phase is accompanied by recovery measures. Compared to Smith (1990), Dreyer (2001) uses two phases to describe the situation before the disaster occurs, namely the potential and the latent crisis.

Augustine (1995) further refines the phases and distinguishes six phases of crisis management processes. Step one consists of preventing the crisis, step two prepares for the crisis, step three recognizes the crisis, step four blurs the crisis, step five resolves the crisis and step six benefits from the crisis. Linking the work of Augustine (1995) with the model of Smith (1990), it becomes obvious that the first two steps are in line with the crisis of management, step three and four are attributable to the operational crisis, and step five and six are in accordance with the crisis of legitimation.

In the field of tourism research only few studies applied the aforementioned crisis models (Dreyer, 2001; Glaeßer, 2001). One of the most extensive disaster management frameworks in tourism was developed by Faulkner (2001, p. 44) who provides a six-phase process:

1. Pre-event phase: disaster contingency plans, scenarios or probability assessments play a major role in the disaster management strategy.
2. Prodromal phase: the disaster is imminent and warning systems and command centres are established. In this second phase contingency plan actions are initiated.
3. Emergency phase: disaster effects are felt and actions are necessary to protect people or property in the tourism destination.
4. Intermediate phase: short-term and immediate needs of people have to be addressed by emergency and rescue teams. A clear media communication strategy is crucial in this phase.
5. Long-term (recovery) phase: the damaged infrastructure has to be rebuilt and environmentally damaged areas have to be reconstructed.
6. Resolution phase: this phase corresponds to Smith's (1990) feedback loop where existing assessment methods or contingency plans are improved.

Research focus in the field of tourism crisis is put on crisis management of tour operators or tourism destination managers, e.g., following plane crashes (Glaeßer, 2002), terrorist attacks (Blake & Sinclair, 2003; Hollinshead, 2004; Sönmez et al., 1999; Wahab, 1996) or diseases/epidemic outbreaks in target destinations (Noij, 2001; Petty, 1989; Richter, 2003). Only a few contributions refer to crisis management processes in Alpine winter sports resorts (Beritelli & Götsch, 1999). Authors aim to narrow the existing gap in this field of research.

ALPINE WINTER TOURISM CRISES IN THE EUROPEAN ALPS

Today, many avalanches are reported which are caused by downhill skiers or ski touring and 90 percent of all avalanches are triggered by human beings (Engler, 2001). For skiers the attractiveness of the surroundings is a strong motivation to choose a skiing destination (Hudson, 2000). Thus, ski destinations must satisfy an increasingly fragmenting market disposing of more and more specialised facilities and services (Hudson, 2003). This forced many destinations to explore new slopes and to link well-known skiing destinations for guaranteeing variety, scope and quality of slopes (e.g., steep slopes became gradually important in the '80s when high quality strategies were developed by regional tourism planners). In addition, rapid growth of winter tourism in the '60s and '70s has forced many destinations to build tourist facilities in potentially dangerous areas (Hudson, 2000).

Before tourism conquered the Alps, the victims of avalanches were local villagers. However, the number of victims among residents could be reduced by constructing avalanche barriers but nevertheless many severe avalanche catastrophes in the period after World War II were reported. Figure 1 shows the number of victims claimed during the last decade in the Alpine mountain areas of Austria and Switzerland by avalanches. Although the total number of victims during the winter periods 1990 to 2003 is nearly equal for both countries, the number of victims differs significantly from year to year.

For example, in Austria in April 1993 four German skiers and one mountain guide died in the Oetztal Alps; in May 1997 two skiers were buried alive in Pinzgau/Salzburg and in February 1999 a series of avalanches claimed 39 victims in the Paznaun valley/Tyrol (Hauke, 1999, p. 13). The year 1998/99 was one of the hardest winters in terms of avalanches. Continuous snowfalls and strong winds led to an accumulation of extreme snow masses in the Alpine mountains. Beside Austria, France was also affected by several avalanches claiming a total of 22 lives.

At the beginning of winter 2000, not a natural but a technical disaster claimed skiers'

FIGURE 1. Avalanche Victims in Switzerland and Austria

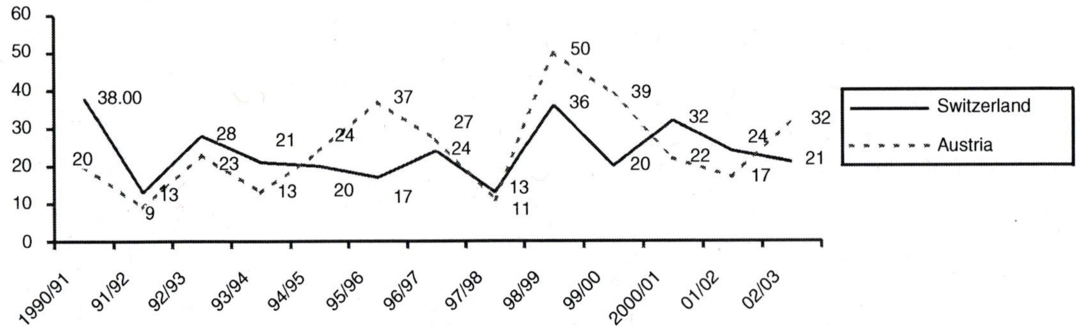

(Source: IKAR, 2004)

lives. In Kaprun, a glacier ski destination, 155 skiers died in a fire in the cable car tunnel. In the mass media, both the avalanche disaster in the Paznaun valley (Tyrol) and the cable car disaster in Kaprun (Salzburg) led to an ongoing discussion on safety and security in Alpine winter sports destinations in Austria. The international press accused the responsible destination managers of having neglected safety and security measures. Today, in terms of overnight stays, both, Galtuer (which is located in the Paznaun valley) and Kaprun compensated the negative effects of the disasters. However, the Kaprun disaster uncovered gaps in the Austrian legislation as no rules or regulations for cable car accidents had been stipulated. As a consequence, a flood of new laws and regulations were declared.

Existing research on Alpine regions and tourism development, especially in Tyrol, does not focus on safety and security issues. A market research analysis on tourists' activities and motivations revealed that safety and security is an important travel decision element for the destination Tyrol, but it does not constitute a key element (IRI, 2001). Regarding the mean value of the items (1 = very important travel motive, 5 = not important travel motive), the most important travel motives in winter for the destination Tyrol are "intensive experience of mountains, snow and sun" (1.4), "doing sports" (1.47) and "security of snow" (1.62) and in summer, "experience of mountain/water/sun" (1.55), "intact and authentic nature/original landscape" (1.69) and "feeling of familiarity and cosiness" (1.73). The answer to the question

on the travel motive ("because I can feel safe/ secure") is appreciably higher in summer (1.95) than in winter (2.25). Another survey on tourists' service quality judgments carried out in 11 winter sports resorts in Austria and Northern Italy interviewed 1,822 winter tourists in 1994/95, analyzing the importance/unimportance of safety and security for various tourist activities of the destination value chain. Interestingly enough, one out of seven safety and security items appears as a satisfier, namely the safety and security dimension belonging to nature and landscape, which was considered a preventive measure for natural disasters (Pikkemaat & Weiermair, 2002).

LESSONS TO BE LEARNT FROM THE CASE STUDY OF GALTUER

In the following discussion the 1999 avalanche disaster in Galtuer is analyzed according to the previously discussed crisis phase models enabling researchers to derive implications for future crisis management in Alpine areas. Galtuer and its more famous neighbouring resort Ischgl are top winter tourism resorts in the Paznaun Valley, Tyrol. The Galtuer avalanche in February 1999, which killed 31 people, was the worst in Austria since 1953 (Mayr, 1999).

Referring to Faulkner's (2001) crisis management scheme, a number of crisis management actions can be observed before, during and after the avalanche disaster. The process description is based on existing data and key interviews conducted in Galtuer.[1]

Step 1: Pre-Event Phase

The main precautions to prevent avalanches in Alpine destinations are security precaution, avalanche barriers and disaster contingency plans. However, many of these avalanche barriers were constructed in the first half of the 20th century and thus were antiquated. In addition, a number of avalanche barriers built since 1950 were state-of-the-art.

Avalanche simulation models have been developed in the past (e.g., simulation model SAMOS), but they calculated worst case simulations with the maximum amount of three days' new-fallen snow. Unfortunately, before the 23rd of February 1999 it was snowing heavily for about 10 days and the amount of fresh-fallen snow was significantly higher than the average assessed during the last 150 years: within one single month 148 inches of new snow fell in Galtuer (Heumader, 2000).

Furthermore, in Alpine regions experts define hazard zones as so-called "red zones." In the case of Galtuer all 31 victims were found in "green zones" defined as safe from avalanche.

Step 2: Prodromal Phase

Due to ongoing snowfall after January 27th, 1999, and new heavy snowfalls after February 16th, several roads to the Paznaun valley were closed or solely opened for a short period of time. As a result, resources in Galtuer were already scarce and the weather was still bad with snow continuing to accumulate and roads blocked. Tourists were getting nervous and evacuated as soon as the roads were passable.

On February 18th, the first discussions about the crisis took place and the first safety measures were taken. One day later an initial crisis management team meeting was called by the district governor and a briefing was given to the central avalanche warning commission in Tyrol. The need for evacuation was discussed by experts and significant differences in opinion were expressed. In Galtuer an initial meeting was arranged to inform tourists and residents. As a consequence, the community feared the worst and asked 15 doctors amongst Galtuer's tourists for help.

Step 3: Emergency Phase

According to Smith (1990), at this stage it can be observed how the "crisis of management" stage turns into the "operational crisis" where actions and processes become extremely complex. On February 23rd at 4 p.m. the main avalanche hit several houses in the centre of the village of Galtuer. The avalanche started at 2,700 meters and its fracture line was about 400 meters wide. The snow depth was between 2.5 and 3.5 meters and a total of 330,000 tons of snow hit Galtuer. About 8,000 locals and 20,000 tourists were in the town at the time the avalanche hit.

Sixty persons were buried by the avalanche. Several emergency actions were taken by local auxiliaries. The most urgent measures were searching for persons buried by the avalanche and medical assistance for wounded. Nevertheless, 31 people lost their lives and 22 were injured. Six residential houses were totally destroyed, seven heavily damaged and eleven lightly damaged. The property damage was estimated at 5.27 million Euros.

During the day, emergency stations were established. Several locations (e.g., tennis centre, hotels) in the village were converted into emergency units and 28 medical practitioners, most of them tourists, volunteered to offer medical/ health services.

Within this phase a small number of locals emerged as leaders and organisers, namely the mayor and the vice-mayor, the director of the tourism board, the chief of the mountain security division in the Paznaun valley, the local doctor and the priest. The crisis management team organised the first rescue procedures and medical assistance. Later that day, emergency accommodation and food supply were arranged by the core emergency team.

Step 4: Intermediate Phase

One day later, on February 24th, a monitoring and communication system was established and all 22 injured persons could be evacuated by helicopters during the day. In addition, several external emergency teams and auxiliaries arrived in Galtuer (700 servicemen of the Federal Armed Forces). It is worth noting that due to ongoing bad weather conditions in Galtuer, the first external auxiliaries arrived fourteen hours after the avalanche disaster occurred. The same day a mass evacuation was initiated with international military help.

The next day (February 25th), about 2,000 residents and tourist were evacuated with military help from NATO. In the following days a mass evacuation started, which was the largest ever in the history of Austria with 2,500 emergency helpers, 47 helicopters, and 782 flight hours and another 8,000 evacuated people.

On Saturday (February 27th), after the last victim was found, the first official press conference was organised in Galtuer with 100 selected journalists flown in by helicopters and another 200 journalists waiting for information in a nearby city outside the valley. Afterwards, Galtuer was not open to the press. International media presence was extremely high and Galtuer had no experience with such a situation. Media communication was poorly managed and a misrepresentation of the catastrophe followed. The next day was proclaimed a day of national mourning.

The focus during the intermediate phase was put on cleaning up the disaster scene as much as possible. However, the auxiliaries tried to hide the damage from new tourists arriving immediately after February 26th.

Step 5: Long-Term (Recovery) Phase

Only a few weeks after the disaster, financial support was provided by donations and government funding. In Galtuer, there were no disagreements about the allocation of the donations.

Communication strategy included a hotline established at the Tyrol tourism board. The Internet was seen as the most appropriate communication channel within the first months after the disaster, but Galtuer tourism entrepreneurs focused on direct contact with guests for conveying the security and safety measures and improvements. Marketing resumed just two weeks after the disaster. In this phase, Galtuer struggled with criticism from the media, and targeted marketing measures were

seen as more efficient than overall broad and unfocused communication.

Step 6: Resolution Phase

It took one year to re-establish routines in the community. The review process which is characteristic of the resolution stage has improved existing products and processes such as disaster contingency plans and risk assessment (e.g., improved scenarios on impacts of potential disasters). Protection measures and improvements in the fields of safety and security have been developed for the resort, e.g., better and more avalanche barriers, improved avalanche protection for the access road to Galtuer, reforestation underneath the fracture line, new weather gauging stations, daily weather forecasts on the Internet, purchase of helicopters, improved emergency supply plans and new emergency precautions such as emergency medicine and psychological supervision of survivors. In addition, a flexible crisis team was established consisting of the mayor and vice-mayor, the chiefs of the fire and mountain security department, and the director of the avalanche security commission.

A number of new services and products developed during the resolution stage and also improved the tourism value chain for customers:

- The "Alpinarium," an avalanche barrier and multifunctional building informs tourists about avalanche disasters in the past. The institution systematically collects data about natural alpine disasters and fosters networking with other institutions in the field of catastrophe management (see: www.alpinarium.at). On the one hand, this new building is an architectural and entertainment attraction for tourists and, on the other hand, it provides safety and security for the centre of Galtuer.
- A non-profit "Alpine Safety and Information Centre" (ASI) was established to promote safety and security in the mountain environment (see: www.alpinesicherheit.com). Its goal is to provide a communication bridge to all participating institutions and local organisations.

- One of their products is ESI, a new internet platform pursuing the goal to overcome geographical barriers and to allow efficient communication among security and emergency units without time constraints. Furthermore, the public part of the platform allows targeted and controlled communication among the crisis management team members, media, and interested stakeholders (e.g., potential tourists). The system was first used at the Olympic winter games 2001 in St. Anton, Austria, to support security management in the destination (see: esis.tirol.gv.at).
- Another product are emergency preparedness checklists which are customised solutions and plans for organisations in mountain regions (e.g., checklists for avalanche accidents, search operations, aircraft accidents).

- Another initiative of the Tyrolean Government was the foundation of the competence centre alpS which internationally links research institutions, non-profit organisations, and businesses in the field of environmental hazards (see: www.alps-gmbh.com). Main objectives are the improvement of security measures, the creation of data bases and efficient and effective up-to-date scenario plans.
- A lack of psychological assistance during the emergency and intermediate disaster phase led to new initiatives, like a psychological emergency unit or training for locals and volunteers where they learn how to care for people in emergency situations.

Besides positive initiatives resulting from the disaster, the review process was characterised by the search for a culprit. All members of the avalanche warning commission were accused of negligent homicide by the state attorney's office. As a result an investigation by the Swiss Avalanche Research Institute followed to settle accusations. Five years later there is still an enormous psychological pressure on the accused who suffer from diseases as a result (e.g., allergies).

To analyze the impact of the disaster on tourism, Table 2 illustrates the development of overnight stays during the period of 1997 to 2003. In Galtuer, the peak winter season starts in December and ends in April. While the figures are relatively stable in December and January, there is an enormous slump in overnight stays directly after the catastrophe in March 1999, as well as in February 2000, one year after the catastrophe. Nevertheless, winter overnight stays steadily improved in the following years.

Faulkner's (2001) scheme seems to be an appropriate framework for analysing complex crisis management steps in Alpine resorts.

CONCLUSIONS

Today, the aforementioned management of the Galtuer catastrophe serves as a prime example for successful crisis management in tourism destinations (Beritelli & Götsch, 1999; Heumader, 2000). However, a number of lessons are learnt and problems should be addressed. The feedback loop as demonstrated in Smith's phase model (1990) led to many important initiatives for the maintenance of safety and security in Alpine regions. Those initiatives were promoted by local and national institutions which mainly focus on knowledge transfer among research institutions and Alpine communities. However, one of the major problems is addressed by Alexander (2002) who points out that there have been 50 years of profound research in the field of disasters, but "what is needed is a better translation of research results into application or instruments for practitioners, which was successfully overcome in the case of Tyrol."

TABLE 2. Overnights Stays Winter 1997-2002 in Galtuer

	1997/98	1998/99	1999/00	2000/01	2001/02	2002/03
December	38.097	38.350	35.824	39.218	38.104	42.235
January	63.983	76.442	60.975	63.222	66.624	72.336
February	82.529	62.570	47.384	62.576	80.495	75.895
March	82.972	33.474	61.973	68.434	86.748	81.861
April	50.729	33.715	33.151	40.791	25.255	41.495
Total	318.310	244.551	239.307	274.232	297.226	313.822

(Source: WKT, 2004)

One main success factor in the crisis management process of Galtuer was the preparedness in the prodromal phase where the general framework for the next phase was established. Thus, in the emergency phase a core group of responsible locals was ready to organize first rescue efforts. The case of Galtuer demonstrates that a competent core contingency team is a key success factor in crisis management processes of destinations.

In the case of Galtuer, one major mistake was made in terms of an effective media strategy. While the media plays a central role in the emergency or in the recovery phase of crisis management (Faulkner, 2001), the media blamed local communities in Galtuer for the disaster and significantly harmed the image of the destination in Germany, where the majority of the tourists comes from. Uncoordinated interviews and fragmented information supported rumours about inefficient warning systems or missing contingency plans and, as a result, a general discussion about guaranteeing tourists' safety and security in Alpine winter sports resorts in Austria was stirred up. To avoid such unpreparedness for the future, the ESIS Internet platform with its communication and content management system was developed after the catastrophe.

In general, tourists and residents in Alpine winter destinations approve of any measures which increase safety or security in the resort despite possible negative external effects (Sonnenberg & Wöhler, 2004, p. 21). For instance, the construction of new avalanche barriers in Galtuer does not negatively affect tourists' satisfaction or locals' wellbeing. On the contrary, the visibility of safety measures may increase the overall satisfaction of destination's stakeholders. In the case of Galtuer, the "Alpinarium" is a successful example of how to design safety and security measures with an additional value for tourists.

It is beyond question that safety and security risks threaten the sustainability of the tourism industry. Consequently, tourists feel safe by existing preventive crisis management tools in the destination. In the long run, safety and risk concerns will become implicit factors of competitiveness (Pikkemaat & Weiermair, 2002). Therefore, Alpine tourism management tools have to be developed, e.g., the

establishment of visible security guides in skiing and hiking areas, published crisis management or contingency plans including crisis management guidebooks. If destination managers miss the opportunity to develop and market management tools for tourists' safety and security in Alpine destinations, competitive disadvantages will arise.

In the past tourism research has concentrated on the crisis' impact on tourist overnight stays but has neglected to analyze success factors of crisis management processes for natural disasters. The case of Galtuer shows that much can be learnt from best practice examples. The paper gives an overview of several crisis management models, but Faulkner's (2001) disaster management framework seems to be most appropriate for systematically analysing disaster management processes in tourism. Nevertheless, crisis management research in tourism may increasingly use models, concepts and experiences from organisational change research and adapt it for special purposes, e.g., natural disasters in tourism. Furthermore, crisis management processes are dynamic learning processes which are determined by a number of variables and which influence the effectiveness and efficiency of learning in a tourism destination. Time, political life cycles and/or stakeholder conflicts can have significant impact on the development of crisis management frameworks.

However, the development of effective crisis management tools and future crisis management research require international knowledge exchange platforms as well as systematic and complete documentations about crisis management processes to benchmark or learn from comparable examples in tourism destinations. Consequently, these data and experiences can be used for the further improvement and application of existing models and frameworks of crisis management processes for Alpine tourism destinations.

NOTE

1. Qualitative interviews with the major, the director of the tourism board and three other locals who were actively involved in the crisis management process were carried out in winter 2003/2004.

REFERENCES

Alexander, D. (2002). Quo vadis emergency preparedness? *Environmental Hazards, 3*(1), 129-131.

Augustine, N.R. (1995). Managing the crisis you tried to prevent. *Harvard Business Review, 1*(4), 147-158.

Baloglu, S., & Mangaloglu, M. (2001). Tourism destination images of Turkey, Egypt, Greece, and Italy as perceived by US-based tour operators and travel agents. *Tourism Management, 22*(1), 1-9.

Baloglu, S., & McCleary, K.W. (1999). A model of destination image formation. *Annals of Tourism Research, 26*(4), 868-897.

Beritelli, P., & Götsch, H. (1999). Krisen-PR bei Tourismusunternehmen-ausgewählte Beispiele und Empfehlungen für die Praxis. *Tourismus Journal, 3*(3), 325-355.

Blake, A., & Sinclair, M.T. (2003). Tourism crisis management: US responses to September 11. *Annals of Tourism Research, 30*(4), 813-832.

Brookfield, H. (1999). Environmental damage: Distinguishing human from geographical causes. *Environmental Hazards, 1*(2), 3-11.

Coshall, J.T. (2000). Measurement of tourists' destination images: The repertory grid approach. *Journal of Travel Research, 39*(3), 85-89.

Crompton, J.L., & Ankomah, P.K. (1993). Choice set propositions in destination decisions. *Annals of Tourism Research, 20*, 461-476.

Dreyer, A. (2001). *Krisenmanagement im Tourismus*. München: Oldenbourg.

Engler, M. (2001). *Die weiße Gefahr, Schnee und Lawinen, Erfahrung-Mechanismen-Risikomanagement*. Sulzberg: Engler Verlag.

Faulkner, B. (2001). Towards a framework for tourism disaster management. *Tourism Management, 22*(1), 135-147.

Faulkner, B., & Russel, R. (1997). Chaos and complexitiy in tourism: In search for a new perspective. *Pacific Tourism Review, 1*(2), 91-106.

Fink, S. (1986). *Crisis management*. New York: American Association of Management.

Fuchs, M., & Peters, M. (2004). Die Bedeutung von Schutz und Sicherheit im Tourismus: Implikationen für alpine destinationen. In H. Pechlaner & D. Glaeßer (Eds.), *Krisen und Strukturbrüche: Perspektiven des Managements von Risiken und Gefahren*. Berlin: Erich Schmidt.

Galbraith, J.R. (1977). *Organization design*. Reading, MA: Addison-Wesley.

Glaeßer, D. (2001). *Krisenmanagement im Tourismus*. Frankfurt Am Main: Peter Lang Verlag.

Glaeßer, D. (2002). Crisis management in air transport and tourism. In P. Keller & T. Bieger (Eds.), *Air transport and tourism* Vol. 44 (pp. 121-142). St. Gallen: AIEST.

Haggett, P. (2000). *The geographical structure of epidemics*. Oxford: Oxford University Press.

Hauke, B. (1999). *Die weiße Gefahr*. München: ERC Fankona Rückversicherungs-AG.

Heumader, J. (2000). The catastrophic avalanche disasters of Galtuer and Valzur on the 23 and 24 of February 1999 in the Paznaun valley/Tyrol. In Interpraevent (Ed.), *International Symposium 2000* Vil. 1 (pp. 397-409). Villach, Austria: ISI.

Hollinshead, K. (2004). Symbolism in tourism: Lessons from "Bali 2002"–Lessons from Australia's dead heart. *Tourism Analysis, 8*(2-4), 267-295.

Hudson, S. (2000). *Snow Business: A study of the international ski industry*. London: Cassel.

Hudson, S. (2003). Winter sport tourism. In S. Hudson (Ed.), *Sport and adventure tourism* (pp. 89-123). New York: The Haworth Press, Inc.

Hwang, P., & Lichtenthal, J.D. (2000). Anatomy of Organizational Crises. *Journal of Contingencies and Crisis Management, 8*(3), 129-139.

IKAR. (2004). Retrieved February 27, 2004, from *www.ikar-cisa.org*.

IRI. (2001). *Gästebefragung Österreich 2000/2001*. Wien: Info Research International.

Jick, T. (1993). *Managing change: Cases and concepts*. Boston: Irwin Inc.

Klenk, V. (1989). Krisen-PR mit Hilfe von Krisenmodellen. *PR-Magazin, 89*(2), 29-36.

Krummenacher, A. (1981). *Krisenmanagement-Zusatzleitfaden zur Verhinderung und Bewältigung von Unternehmenskrisen*. Zürich: Industrielle Organisation.

Krystek, U. (1987). *Unternehmenskrisen: Beschreibung, Vermeidung und Bewältigung überlebenskritischer Prozesse in Unternehmungen*. Wiesbaden: Gabler.

Leslie, D. (1999). Terrorism and tourism: The Northern Ireland situation–a look behind the veil of certainty. *Journal of Travel Research, 38*(1), 37-40.

Mansfeld, Y. (1999). Cycles of war, terror and peace: Determinants and management of crisis and recovery of the Israeli tourism industry. *Journal of Travel Research, 38*(1), 30-36.

Mayr, R. (1999). Die Lawinenkatastrophe vom Februar 1999 (Galtuer, Valzur) aus der Sicht des Katastrophenschutzes. *Wildbach und Lawinenverbau: Lawinenwinter 1999, 64*(141), 1-10.

Mintzberg, H. (1991). The effective organization: Forces and forms. *Sloan Management Review, 32*(2), 54-67.

Noij, E.K. (2001). The global resurgence of infectious diseases. *Journal of Contingencies and Crisis Management, 9*(4), 223-232.

Perich, R. (1992). *Unternehmensdynamik*. Bern/Stuttgart: Haupt.

Petty, R. (1989). Health limits to tourism development. *Tourism Management, 10*(3), 209-212.

Pikkemaat, B., & Weiermair, K. (2002). Safety and security issues–from a tourist destination perspective. In R. Tomljenovic & S. Weber (Eds.), *Reinventing a tourism destination*. Zagreb: University of Zagreb.

Pizam, A. (2002). Tourism and terrorism. *International Journal of Hospitality Management, 21*(1), 1-3.

Pizam, A., & Smith, G. (2000). Tourism and terrorism: A quantitative analysis of major terrorist acts and their impact on tourism destinations. *Tourism Economics, 6*(2), 123-138.

Pizam, A., Tarlow, P., & Bloom, J. (1997). Making tourists feel safe: Whose responsibility is it? *Journal of Travel Research, 36*(1), 23-28.

Prigogine, I., & Stengers, I. (1985). *Order out of chaos: Man's new dialogue with nature.* Hammersmith: Flamingo.

Reinecke, W. (1997). *Krisenmanagement: Richtiger Umgang mit den Medien in Krisensituationen-Ursachen-Verhalten-Strategien-Techniken-Ein Leitfaden.* Essen: Stamm.

Richter, L.K. (1999). After political turmoil: The lessons of rebuilding tourism in three Asian countries. *Journal of Travel Research, 38*(1), 41-45.

Richter, L.K. (2003). International tourism and its global public health consequences. *Journal of Travel Research, 41*(2), 340-347.

Ryan, C. (1993). Crime, violence, terrorism and tourism: An accidental or intrinsic relationship? *Tourism Management, 14*(3), 173-183.

Smith, D. (1990). Beyond contingency planning: towards a model of crisis management. *Industrial Crisis Quarterly, 4*(1990), 263-275.

Smith, D. (2000). On a wing and a prayer? Exploring the human components of technological failure. *Systems Research and Behavioural Science, 17*(6), 543-559.

Smith, D. (2003). *In the eyes of the beholder? Making sense of the system(s) of disaster(s).* Unpublished paper, Centre for Risk and Crisis Management, University of Liverpool Management School, Liverpool.

Sönmez, S., Apostopoulos, Y., & Tarlow, P. (1999). Tourism in crisis: Managing the effects of terrorism. *Journal of Tourism Research, 38*(1), 13-18.

Sönmez, S., & Sirakaya, E. (2002). A distorted destination image? The case of Turkey. *Journal of Travel Research, 41*(2), 185-196.

Sonnenberg, G., & Wöhler, K. (2004). Was bewirkt Sicherheit bzw. Unsicherheit? Prädiktoren der Reisesicherheit. In W. Freyer & S. Groß (Eds.), *Sicherheit im Tourismus: Schutz vor Risiken und Gefahren.* Dresden: FIT-Verlag.

Tapachai, N., & Waryszak, R. (2000). An examination of the role of beneficial image in tourist destination selection. *Journal of Travel Research, 39*(3), 37-44.

Tarlow, P., & Santana, G. (2002). Providing safety for tourists: a study of a selected sample of tourist destinations in the United States and Brazil. *Journal of Travel Research, 40*(4), 424-431.

Turner, B.A. (1976). The organizational and interorganizational development of disasters. *Administrative Science Quarterly, 21*(3), 378-397.

Ulrich, H. (1989). Eine systemischtheoretische Perspektive der Unternehmungsorganisation. In E. Seidel & D. Wagner (Eds.), *Organisation* (pp. 13-25). Wiesbaden: Gabler.

Urry, J. (2003). *Global complexity.* Cambridge: Polity.

Wahab, S. (1996). Tourism and terrorism: Synthesis of the problem with emphasis on Egypt. In A. Pizam & J. Mansfeld (Eds.), *Tourism, crime and international security issues* (pp. 175-186). Chichester: Wiley.

Weiermair, K. & Kneisl, P. (1996). Touristische kooperationen und netzwerke: Basis zur bildung strategischer wettbewerbsvorteile im tourismus. *Tourism Hospitality Management, 2*(1), 121-134.

Zeithaml, V.A. (1991). How consumer evaluation processes differ between goods and services. In C.H. Lovelock (Ed.), *Services marketing* (pp. 39-47). New Jersey: Prentice Hall.

Quantifying the Effects of Tourism Crises:
An Application to Scotland

Juan L. Eugenio-Martin
M. Thea Sinclair
Ian Yeoman

SUMMARY. Effective crisis management requires information about the ways in which tourists of different nationalities respond to different types of crisis. This paper provides a model which can be used to quantify such effects. The model is applied to the case of American, French and German tourism demand in Scotland. The results show that French tourists were particularly affected by the foot and mouth disease crisis. Germans were most severely affected by the September 11 events. Although arrivals from the USA decreased after both crises, receipts were hardly affected. *[Article copies available for a fee from The Haworth Document Delivery Service: 1-800-HAWORTH. E-mail address: <docdelivery@haworthpress.com> Website: <http://www.HaworthPress.com> © 2005 by The Haworth Press, Inc. All rights reserved.]*

KEYWORDS. Forecasting, predictions, foot and mouth disease, September 11

INTRODUCTION

Effective management of tourism crises requires considerable information about the nature of the different types of crises that can occur and the extent and range of their effects. Much of the research that has provided information about tourism crises has concentrated on providing typologies of crises, examining popular perceptions of major events and studying the effects on particular sectors and destinations. The effects of terrorist incidents and political instability have been a particular focus of attention. Research has also been undertaken on the process of crisis management via improved communication strategies and changes in management structures and operations. However, few studies have provided quantitative measures of the impact of crises or forecasts of their impact.

The need for more information about tourism crises has been highlighted by Prideaux, Laws and Faulkner (2003), who showed that investigation of the nature of crises is complex, as multiple events occur concurrently. Thus, for example, a terrorist incident may oc-

Juan L. Eugenio-Martin and M. Thea Sinclair are affiliated with the Christel DeHaan Tourism and Travel Research Institute, Nottingham University Business School, Wollaton Road, Jubilee Campus, Nottingham, NG8 1BB, UK. Ian Yeoman is affiliated with VisitScotland, 23 Ravelston Terrace, Edinburgh EH4 3TP, UK.

The authors would like to thank the referees for their constructive comments on the paper.

[Haworth co-indexing entry note]: "Quantifying the Effects of Tourism Crises: An Application to Scotland." Eugenio-Martin, Juan L., M. Thea Sinclair, and Ian Yeoman. Co-published simultaneously in *Journal of Travel & Tourism Marketing* (The Haworth Hospitality Press, an imprint of The Haworth Press, Inc.) Vol. 19, No. 2/3, 2005, pp. 21-34; and: *Tourism Crises: Management Responses and Theoretical Insight* (ed: Eric Laws, and Bruce Prideaux) The Haworth Hospitality Press, an imprint of The Haworth Press, Inc., 2005, pp. 21-34. Single or multiple copies of this article are available for a fee from The Haworth Document Delivery Service [1-800-HAWORTH, 9:00 a.m. - 5:00 p.m. (EST). E-mail address: docdelivery@haworthpress.com].

cur within a period of financial crisis or political upheaval. In practice it is difficult to separate the effects of the terrorist incident from those that stem from contemporaneous events. Thus, the magnitude of the terrorist incident may be over- or under-estimated.

This paper will illustrate the ways in which quantitative techniques can provide more information about tourism crises by examining the effects of two types of crisis, one internal to a country and one stemming from an external incident. The first case is that of foot and mouth disease which affected the UK from the spring of 2001, and the second is the September 11 terrorist events. Each case will be examined in the context of its effects on American, French and German demand for tourism in Scotland. Analysis of the impact of these events on tourism demand is complicated by ongoing changes in relative prices and exchange rates for pound sterling, the dollar and the euro and incomes in the USA, France and Germany. As all of these events affected tourist arrivals and receipts in Scotland, the magnitudes of the effects of foot and mouth disease and of September 11, in isolation from those of other events, are not evident. The absence of this information is problematic for policy makers who need to know the extent to which the changes in tourism demand from different origins were due to the crises rather than to other economic events. In the absence of such information, policy makers are unable to pursue an effective strategy of tailoring crisis management strategies towards individual origin markets.

The paper will explain and demonstrate an approach that can be used to distinguish the effects of crises on international tourism demand from those of other events that take place simultaneously. A forecasting model will be used to quantify the changes in tourism demand in Scotland from the different origins prior to the occurrence of the crises. The estimated model will then be used to predict the changes in demand that occurred during the ensuing years due to changes in prices, exchange rates and tourists' incomes but in the absence of the crises. By comparing the predicted values with the values of tourism demand that actually occurred, the effects of the crises can be measured. Hence, the results provide the effects on demand of the crisis, relative to the effects of changes in relative competitiveness and tourists' purchasing power. The results show the differences in responses between different origin markets which, in turn, assist government organisations to tailor and target their policies more effectively towards the different destinations.

The next section of the paper will provide a brief overview of some of the main themes in the literature on tourism crises. The following section will provide the model that is used to quantify tourists' responses to the crisis, as well as to other economic changes. The model will be applied to the cases of foot and mouth disease and September 11. The results will be compared for the different types of crisis, as well as for changes in arrivals and receipts in Scotland from the three main international origin markets.

KEY THEMES IN THE LITERATURE

The literature on tourism crises has grown considerably in recent years, particularly in the light of the impacts on destinations of the September 11 events (Goodrich, 2002; Tate, 2002), as well as the impacts of other political events, natural disasters, disease, crime or war (Beirman, 2003). However, the need for more research on the nature of the crises was recognised well before the occurrence of such events. One strand of research was geared towards providing a set of typologies of tourism crises. For example, Meyers (1986) categorised crises into major effects on public perceptions, product failures, sudden changes in the market and changes in top management. Meyers also argued that crises can be caused by problems with financing, industrial relations, take-overs, international events and changes in regulations. Booth (1993) classified crises into those that are gradual, periodic or sudden, where gradual crises threaten parts of the organisation, periodic crises threaten part or all of the organisation and sudden crises threaten the entire organisation. Seymour and Moore (2000) classified crises according to the process by which they occur, terming a crisis that occurs gradually a "python," in contrast to a "cobra" which strikes suddenly.

Crises have also been classified according to their causes. Coombes' (1995) classification was based on stakeholders' perceptions of the crisis as internal or external, resulting from unintentional or intentional decisions. For example, an unexpected crisis within the organisation is both internal and unintentional, whereas terrorism is external and intentional. Other studies that have focussed on the causes of crises include Slatter's (1984) crisis susceptibility model. Further categorisations of crises have also been provided (Pender & Sharpley, 2004). For instance, some researchers have categorised crises according to their severity (Heath, 1994; Augustine, 1995; Argenti, 2002; Prideaux et al., 2003).

Some studies have concentrated on the role that the mass media plays in affecting people's perceptions of crises (Hall, 2002: Glaesser, 2004). Both crises and the media's portrayals of them cause changes in perceptions that affect people's intentions to travel (Sönmez & Graefe, 1998; Seddighi, Nuttall & Theocharous, 2001; Floyd, Gibson, Pennington-Gray & Thapa, 2004) with consequent effects on destinations. Such effects have been examined for destinations ranging from South West England (Coles, 2003), to Malaysia (de Sausmarez, 2004), Nepal (Thapa, 2004) and Bali (Hitchcock, 2001; Henderson, 2003), the Gili Islands (Soemodinoto, Wong & Saleh, 2001) and Lombok (Fallon, 2004) in Indonesia.

Recognition of the magnitude of the effects that crises can inflict on destinations has stimulated research on different approaches that can be used to manage crises. Early contributions include those of Cassedy (1991) who focussed on the strategies that destinations can implement to respond to crises, and Drabek (1995) who examined the operational moves required for crisis response. Young and Montgomery (1998) subsequently emphasized the importance of designing and implementing an effective communications strategy as an integral part of crisis management. A positive communications strategy may enhance the organisation's reputation above its pre-crisis level (Fearn-Banks, 1996). In contrast, an absence of effective communications is likely to instigate belief that the organisation is incompetent or uncaring. In this respect, effective communications channels support the credibility of the organisation (Seymour & Moore, 2000). A

well organised team is required for implementation of the communications system (Barton, 1993; Heath, 1994, 1998), as is an integrated management approach (Heath, 1994). Within this system, top management is expected to play an important role in the organisation and dissemination of information (Sonnenfeld, 1994; Hill & Wetlaufer, 1998).

Communications strategies should form part of a wider crisis management model, as Smith (1990) and Smith and Spipika (1993) pointed out. They identify three states that crisis management must confront, namely crisis of management, operational crisis and crisis of legitimation. As crisis management is concerned with damage limitation in as short a period and by as much as possible, effective management involves regaining control over events (Green, 1992), efficient use of resources and time (Regester & Larkin, 2002) and processes aimed at crisis prevention, mitigation, response and recovery (Rosenthal & Pijnenburg, 1991). These include cultural and religious strategies implemented at the local level (Hitchcock & Darma Putra, forthcoming). Crisis communication management must also ensure that the messages that are communicated at the national and local levels are consistent (Ritchie, Dorrell, Miller & Miller, 2004).

Faulkner (2001) developed a wider crisis management framework, designed for managing tourism disasters. Within the framework, crisis management occurs during six phases: precursors, mobilisation, action, recovery, reconstruction and reassessment and review. The ways in which the framework can be used to assist tourism disaster management and identify appropriate policies were examined by Prideaux (2004) for the case of Australia. He found that the use of an appropriate tourism disaster management framework would provide considerably improved responses to different types of crises. In practice, some government tourism organisations are introducing contingency planning methods relating to different types of crises. For example, VisitScotland, which formulates tourism policy for Scotland, has introduced a range of initiatives covering such issues as communications, short, medium and long term marketing strategies, access, and support for industry recovery, within the context of consultation between representatives from the public and private sectors and relevant experts in the field (Yeoman, Lennon & Black, forthcoming).

One of the key problems confronting the implementation of crisis management frameworks by public or private sector organisations is a lack of accurate information (Ritchie et al., 2004). Information is required not only for fact finding and analysis of the crisis, but should also be a key part of information dissemination and communications strategies designed to mitigate and control the crisis, as well as to assist a process of recovery (Mitroff & Pearson, 1993). As Barton (1993) pointed out, a shortage of such information precludes effective decision-making and a related communications strategy, resulting in real or perceived loss of control of the situation. This, in turn, generates uncertainty among consumers, whose travel demand does not increase until confidence in tourism organisations is re-established.

The information that government and private sector organisations need in order to plan and implement strategies more effectively relates not only to tourism crises but also to other events such as economic changes, that occur simultaneously. McKercher and Hui (2004), for example, found that the confidence of consumers in Hong Kong was affected not only by terrorism but also by economic concerns which can be of a long term nature. As tourism crises are accompanied by other events (Prideaux et al., 2003), it is necessary to disentangle the effects of crises from those of the other events if tourism crisis management and planning are to be undertaken effectively. Some evidence has been obtained about the responses to tourism crises by firms which undertake specific types of tourism activities. These include restaurants (Green, Bartholomew & Murmann, 2004), travel agents (Lovelock, 2003), small and micro tourism businesses (Cushnahan, 2004), hotels (Israeli & Reichal, 2003) and airlines (Ray, 1999; Gillen & Lall, 2003; Alderighi & Cento, 2004). However, little research has been undertaken to quantify the magnitude of the effects of tourism crises with few exceptions, for example, Blake and Sinclair (2003), Blake, Sinclair and Sugiyarto (2003), and Blake et al. (forthcoming). These approaches used a computable general equilibrium model to estimate the effects of crises on macroeconomic variables and on different sectors of the destination economy.

A complementary approach that can be used to quantify the effects of crises, in isolation from those of other economic events, involves forecasting and prediction techniques. Forecasting models have a tradition in tourism analysis and can be based on statistical or econometric methods (Witt & Martin, 1989). The more recent research related to tourism modelling has tended to use econometric methods (Lim, 1997; Song & Witt, 2000; Song, Witt & Li, 2003), among which structural time series modelling is well accepted (Papatheodorou & Song, forthcoming). This paper will use a structural time series model to forecast tourism demand in Scotland up to the occurrence of the crises. Prediction analysis will then be used to predict the levels that tourism demand would have attained in the absence of the crises, so that comparison of actual demand with the predicted values provide quantitative estimates of the effects of the crises. The approach will be explained in detail in the following section of the paper.

PREDICTING THE EFFECTS OF TOURISM CRISES RELATIVE TO OTHER ECONOMIC EVENTS– THE CASE OF SCOTLAND

Tourism is an increasingly important activity within the Scottish economy. In 2002, tourism GDP accounted for 4.7% of Scottish GDP, with a value of around £3,198 million. The average level of employment was 96,500, accounting for 5.3% of total employment in Scotland. Tourism is very seasonal and many resorts rely on the summer season to be profitable. For instance, in 2002, the summer quarter provided 6.4% of GDP and 142,000 people were employed, whereas the winter figures were about half these values, with 3.3% of GDP and an employment level of 66,000. The high level of arrivals in the summer, relative to those in other quarters is relevant to crisis analysis because events such as FMD or September 11 can have particularly significant effects on the profitability of the sector during this period.

The first case of foot and mouth disease (FMD) occurred in the north of England in February 2001 and tourism demand in Scotland was mainly affected from the spring onwards. Recovery was subsequently forestalled by the events of September 11. The analysis of the effects of the two crises on tourism demand focuses on three of the most significant international tourism markets of Scotland, the USA, Germany and France, which accounted for 24.4%, 8.6% and 7.9% of international tourist arrivals, respectively, in 2002.

At first sight, it might appear that FMD and the September 11 events resulted in considerable downturns in American, French and German tourism demand in Scotland. FMD occurred in the first quarter of 2001, followed by the American events in the third quarter. As the main effects of FMD were felt in the second and third quarters of the year, it is useful to compare tourist demand in the second and third quarters of 2001 with demand in the same quarters of preceding years. For instance, the numbers of arrivals from France experienced a 65% downturn in the second quarter and a 53% downturn in the third quarter of 2001, compared with the same quarters of the preceding five years, and receipts experienced decreases of 78% and 39% over the same periods. Comparison of total international arrivals in the fourth quarter of 2001, following the events of September 11, with arrivals in the fourth quarter of 2000 showed a fall of 22%, while receipts decreased by 16%. Since tourism demand had previously been showing an upward trend over time, the decreases were even greater than these figures indicate.

It would be inappropriate, however, to attribute all of the changes in tourism demand to the effects of the crises, as changes in other variables also alter demand. In particular, tourism demand is also known to respond to changes in the competitiveness (relative prices and exchange rates) of the destination relative to tourists' country of origin, as well as to changes in incomes in origin countries. A forecasting model was used to estimate the responsiveness of tourism demand to changes in economic variables that occurred prior to the crises of FMD and September 11. It was then used to predict the levels of tourism demand in Scotland that would have occurred in the presence of changes in prices, exchange rates and income but in the absence of the two crises. These results are known as predicted values. By comparing the predicted values with the values of tourism demand that actually occurred and calculating the differences, we obtain estimates of the magnitudes of the effects of the crises.

The set of variables considered in the forecasting model are the income of the country of origin, the prices and exchange rates of the destination country relative to the country of origin and the prices and exchange rates of an alternative competitive destination relative to the country of origin. Gross domestic product (GDP) is used to measure income, and real exchange rates (RER) are used to measure relative price competitiveness. The real exchange rate (RER) is based on two variables, the consumer price index (CPI) and the nominal exchange rate (ER) between the origin and destination countries, and is given as

$$RER_i = \frac{CPI_{UK}}{CPI_i} ER_i \text{ for country } i.$$

The evolution of tourism demand in Scotland is characterised by a slight trend and marked seasonality. According to Harvey (1989, pp. 93-95), this type of time series is ideally forecast within a structural time series approach, as has been demonstrated in the case of Spain (González & Moral, 1995, 1996) and Barbados (Greenidge, 2001). The main advantage of structural time series models is that they allow for testing alternative error components specifications. It is possible to consider fixed or stochastic components for the seasonality. Error components of the trend can also be decomposed into several parts in order to achieve better understanding of its behaviour over time. The main components are the level of the trend, known as the level component, and its speed of change over time, known as the slope. Both the level and the slope components may be fixed or stochastically specified and the structural time series approach allows for both possibilities. The specification of the structural time series model is:

$$y_t = \varphi y_{t-1} + \mu_{t-1} + \beta_1 GDP_t + \beta_2 RER_t + \\ \beta_3 RERCD_t + \gamma_t + \xi_t \quad (1)$$

where y_t denotes tourism arrivals or tourism receipts, y_{t-1} denotes the autoregressive component of the process and represents tourism in the previous period, and μ_{t-1} is the fixed level of the process. GDP is gross domestic product, RER is the real exchange rate, RERCD is the real exchange rate of the competing destination and $RERCD_i = \dfrac{CPI_{CD}}{CPI_i} ER_i$, for country i. The term γ_t is a fixed seasonal component and ξ_t is the remaining part of the error component.

Structural time series modelling was used for forecasting tourist arrivals and receipts. The model was estimated using quarterly inbound tourism demand data from 1979 onwards obtained from the International Passenger Survey for the UK (Office for National Statistics, 2003). GDP is measured in local currency, seasonally adjusted and at constant prices. GDP, CPI and exchange rates data were obtained from Datastream (2004), where the original sources are the OECD (2003) for GDP and the International Monetary Fund (2003) for the CPI and exchange rates. The forecasting was carried out with a constrained dataset covering the time series until the occurrence of the two crises; i.e., data for price indices, exchange rates and income were included from 1979 until the end of the first quarter of 2001. The estimated equation was then used to predict tourism demand until the end of 2003, using additional quarterly data for prices, exchange rates and income from the second quarter of 2001 until the end of 2003.

RESULTS

The results obtained from estimating equation (1) for the USA, France and Germany, using the constrained dataset, are given in Tables 1 and 2. It can be seen that most of the variables are highly significant and that the results of the diagnostic tests and goodness of fit are appropriate. The signs for the coefficients on GDP were positive and those on the real exchange rate between the origin and destination

TABLE 1. Structural Time Series Model of Tourist Arrivals

	USA	France	Germany
Estimated coefficients of explanatory variables			
ln GDP	1.183**	2.127**	2.340**
	(0.115)	(0.375)	(0.251)
ln RER	−0.672**	−1.384**	−1.144**
	(0.274)	(0.406)	(0.262)
ln RERCD	0.373*	0.783	2.195**
	(0.211)	(0.656)	(1.038)
Estimated coefficients of final state vector			
Level	−7.372**	−16.490**	−19.700**
	(1.817)	(4.659)	(3.275)
AR(1)	−0.110**	−0.389**	−0.301**
	(0.096)	(0.138)	(0.105)
Seasonal1	−0.746**	−0.656**	−0.883**
	(0.063)	(0.062)	(0.063)
Seasonal2	0.272**	0.299**	0.405**
	(0.064)	(0.063)	(0.064)
Seasonal3	−0.001	0.217**	0.125**
	(0.051)	(0.047)	(0.054)
Relative importance of each season			
First quarter	−0.748	−0.439	−0.758
Second quarter	0.274	0.082	0.281
Third quarter	0.745	0.873	1.007
Fourth quarter	−0.271	−0.516	−0.530
Diagnostic tests			
Normality	17.657	4.942	3.420
H(28)	1.415	0.585	0.886
DW	2.033	1.882	2.015
Goodness of fit			
Prediction error variance	0.040	0.165	0.066
R_d^2 (Based on differences)	0.952	0.844	0.937
R_s^2 (Based on diff. around seasonal means)	0.470	0.533	0.496

Note: Standard errors shown in parentheses. *Denotes significance at the 5% level. **Denotes significance at the 10% level.

were negative, as expected. The signs on the coefficients for the real exchange rate for the competing destination were positive, indicating that it is a substitute destination for Scotland. The estimated equations were then used to predict the numbers of arrivals and receipts

TABLE 2. Structural Time Series Model of Tourism Receipts

	USA	France	Germany
Estimated coefficients of explanatory variables			
In GDP	1.710**	1.496**	3.512**
	(0.281)	(0.379)	(0.421)
In RER	−2.546**	−1.251**	−1.893**
	(0.643)	(0.411)	(0.437)
In RERCD	1.408**	1.445**	2.256
	(0.498)	(0.664)	(1.726)
Estimated coefficients of final state vector			
Level	−16.457**	−10.027**	−35.938**
	(4.411)	(4.709)	(5.477)
AR(1)	0.185	−0.282**	0.162
	(0.188)	(0.154)	(0.136)
Seasonal1	−0.870**	−0.790**	−0.995**
	(0.105)	(0.080)	(0.059)
Seasonal2	0.266**	0.249**	0.445**
	(0.107)	(0.081)	(0.060)
Seasonal3	−0.008	0.197**	0.141**
	(0.080)	(0.068)	(0.039)
Relative importance of each season			
First quarter	−0.878	−0.593	−0.854
Second quarter	0.274	0.053	0.304
Third quarter	0.861	0.987	1.136
Fourth quarter	−0.257	−0.446	−0.585
Diagnostic tests			
Normality	16.62	0.368	0.762
H(28)	0.467	0.471	0.915
DW	1.907	1.988	1.948
Goodness of fit			
Prediction error variance	0.155	0.188	0.147
R_d^2 (Based on differences)	0.842	0.850	0.904
R_s^2 (Based on diff. around seasonal means)	0.359	0.557	0.475

Note: Standard errors shown in parentheses. *Denotes significance at the 5% level. **Denotes significance at the 10% level.

that would have occurred in the absence of the crises but in the presence of the changes in income and real exchange rates that occurred during the post-crisis period. The differences between the predicted values of tourism de-mand from each of the origins and the actual values were calculated, providing estimates of the effects of the tourism crises.

The effects of the FMD crisis on the demand for tourism in Scotland by tourists from the three countries are shown in Figures 1-3 and Tables 3 and 4. Figures 1-3 provide both the actual numbers of tourist arrivals (the solid line) and the numbers who, according to the predictions, would have arrived given the changes in prices, exchange rates and income that occurred but in the absence of the crisis (the broken line). Thus, the difference between the numbers of actual arrivals and predicted arrivals (the solid and broken lines) provides an estimate of the effects of the crisis. In the US case, arrivals decreased by 20.6% in the third quarter of 2001 relative to the number predicted to arrive if the crisis had not taken place but given the changes in the other economic variables that occurred in the crisis period. Table 3 also shows that in the case of tourism from the USA, arrivals in the third quarter decreased by 5.3% compared with the previous summer and by 10.3% compared with the average of the five previous quarters. It is interesting to compare the results for arrivals with those for the value of receipts from American tourists, given in Table 4. Although receipts decreased by 28.9% relative to the previous summer and by 0.8% relative to the average of the previous five summers, they were only 4.8% down relative to the predicted value. Thus, the FMD crisis only resulted in a small decrease in total receipts, as average expenditure per capita by the American tourists who visited Scotland increased during the crisis.

Comparison of the American results with those for French tourists shows a very different picture. In this case, both arrivals and receipts decreased dramatically. The number of arrivals fell by over 50% because of FMD. Receipts decreased by 39.3% with respect to the five previous years and by 31.6% (the FMD effect) with respect to the predicted value. Arrivals from Germany were also affected considerably. The number of visitors fell by 25% relative to the average of the previous five summers and by 22% relative to the predicted number. Receipts were affected to a greater extent, with decreases of 40.8% relative to the

FIGURE 1. Actual and Predicted Arrivals from the USA

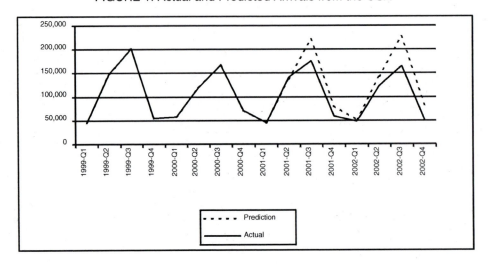

FIGURE 2. Actual and Predicted Arrivals from France

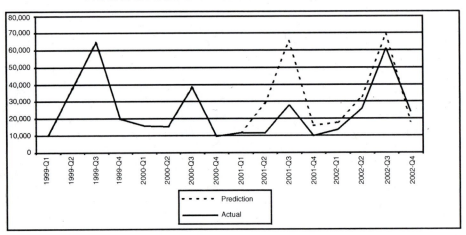

FIGURE 3. Actual and Predicted Arrivals from Germany

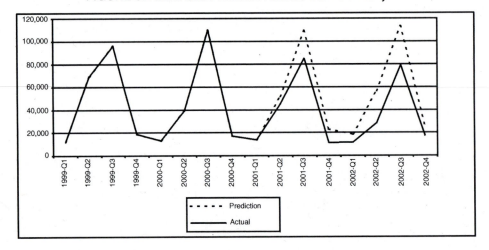

TABLE 3. FMD Effect on the Number of Arrivals in Scotland, 2001

Country		Number of arrivals	Average 5 previous years	Previous year	Prediction year after FMD
USA	Q2	141,097	125,410	119,411	137,723
			15,686	21,685	3,374
			12.5%	18.2%	2.4%
	Q3	175,896	196,158	167,117	221,505
			−20,262	8,779	−45,609
			−10.3%	5.3%	−20.6%
France	Q2	11,494	32,918	15,313	28,727
			−21,424	-3,819	−17,233
			−65.1%	−24.9%	−60.0%
	Q3	27,821	59,444	38,361	65,343
			−31,623	−10,540	−37,521
			−53.2%	−27.5%	−57.4%
Germany	Q2	44,972	57,032	39,072	51,539
			−12,060	5,900	−6,568
			−21.1%	15.1%	−12.7%
	Q3	85,283	113,856	109,961	109,382
			−28,574	−24,679	−24,099
			−25.1%	−22.4%	−22.0%

TABLE 4. FMD Effect on Tourism Receipts in Scotland, 2001

Country		Receipts	Average 5 previous years	Previous year	Prediction year after FMD
USA	Q2	52,868	51,946	43,228	59,587
			922	9,640	−6,719
			1.8%	22.3%	−11.3%
	Q3	96,666	95,922	74,967	101,549
			744	21,699	−4,884
			0.8%	28.9%	−4.8%
France	Q2	1,768	8,173	5,645	6,583
			−6,404	−3,876	−4,814
			−78.4%	−68.7%	−73.1%
	Q3	11,700	19,262	12,401	17,104
			−7,561	−701	−5,404
			−39.3%	−5.7%	−31.6%
Germany	Q2	15,221	19,870	12,435	16,276
			−4,649	2,786	−1,054
			−23.4%	22.4%	−6.5%
	Q3	24,988	42,176	40,527	38,851
			−17,187	−15,539	−13,863
			−40.8%	−38.3%	−35.7%

previous years and 35.7% relative to the predicted value. Overall, therefore, France was most affected by the FMD crisis. Receipts from Germany were also affected but arrivals and receipts did not decrease by as much as those from France. Although arrivals of American tourists were affected by FMD, receipts did not change significantly.

The effects of the September 11 crisis were estimated using the same approach as that applied to the FMD crisis and are given in Tables 5 and 6. To the extent that the FMD crisis affected tourism demand in Scotland beyond the summer, the results in the tables incorporate some of the residual effects of FMD in addition to those of September 11. In the case of American tourist arrivals in Scotland (Table 5), there were immediate negative effects during the fourth quarter, with decreases of 16.3% relative to the average of the five previous years and 26.3% relative to the predicted numbers. In contrast, the numbers of arrivals during the first quarter of 2002 were virtually unaltered. A particularly severe effect occurred in the third quarter of 2002 with decreases of 14.5% relative to the five previous years and

27.3% relative to the predicted number. In the case of receipts, it is once again striking that receipts from the USA were only marginally affected by the crisis.

Arrivals from France were affected severely in the fourth quarter of 2001 but recovered progressively afterwards. Indeed, the number of arrivals in each quarter gradually returned to the situation prior to the crisis, with differences of −37.4%, −23.7%, −20.7% and −11.8% relative to the predicted numbers for each quarter. Germany was the country most affected in relative and absolute terms (except in the third quarter, when the absolute decrease in tourist numbers was similar to the reduction in the number of tourists from the USA). This is reflected in the figures for both the five previous years and the predicted numbers.

The results for tourism receipts (Table 6) show that receipts from American tourists increased compared with the previous five years, but that the predicted values decreased. This is a pertinent example of the usefulness of obtaining predicted values because such values depend on the economic variables that usually affect tourism demand. In this sense, an in-

TABLE 5. September 11 Effect on the Number of Arrivals in Scotland

Country	Quarter	Year after Sept. 11	Average 5 previous years	Previous year	Prediction year after Sept. 11
USA	Q4	59,247	70,790	71,415	80,443
			−11,543	−12,169	−21,196
			−16.3%	−17.0%	−26.3%
	Q1	47,757	44,282	45,219	51,216
			3,475	2,538	−3,459
			7.8%	5.6%	−6.8%
	Q2	123,081	130,943	141,097	142,700
			−7,862	−18,016	−19,619
			−6.0%	−12.8%	−13.7%
	Q3	165,096	193,009	175,896	227,112
			−27,913	−10,800	−62,016
			−14.5%	−6.1%	−27.3%
France	Q4	9,835	17,629	9,619	15,719
			−7,794	216	−5,884
			−44.2%	2.2%	−37.4%
	Q1	13,408	15,999	11,683	17,574
			−2,591	1,725	−4,166
			−16.2%	14.8%	−23.7%
	Q2	25,887	27,550	11,494	32,657
			−1,663	14,393	−6,770
			−6.0%	125.2%	−20.7%
	Q3	61,222	53,163	27,821	69,446
			8,059	33,401	−8,224
			15.2%	120.1%	−11.8%
Germany	Q4	11,246	23,431	17,041	22,960
			−12,185	−5,795	−11,713
			−52.0%	−34.0%	−51.0%
	Q1	11,546	15,750	13,799	18,556
			−4,204	−2,253	−7,010
			−26.7%	−16.3%	−37.8%
	Q2	28,469	53,308	44,972	56,512
			−24,839	−16,503	−28,043
			−46.6%	−36.7%	−49.6%
	Q3	79,240	106,445	85,283	113,391
			−27,205	−6,043	−34,151
			−25.6%	−7.1%	−30.1%

TABLE 6. September 11 Effect on Tourism Receipts in Scotland

Country	Quarter	Year after Sept. 11	Average 5 previous years	Previous year	Prediction year after Sept. 11
USA	Q4	31,028	28,893	30,424	32,552
			2,135	604	−1,524
			7.4%	2.0%	−4.7%
	Q1	17,391	15,724	21,862	18,597
			1,668	−4,471	−1,205
			10.6%	−20.5%	−6.5%
	Q2	57,660	53,210	52,868	58,859
			4,450	4,791	−1,199
			8.4%	9.1%	−2.0%
	Q3	106,781	96,055	96,666	100,952
			10,726	10,115	5,829
			11.2%	10.5%	5.8%
France	Q4	1,820	3,776	3,008	3,964
			−1,956	−1,188	−2,144
			−51.8%	−39.5%	−54.1%
	Q1	2,098	3,069	2,608	3,522
			−971	−510	−1,424
			−31.6%	−19.6%	−40.4%
	Q2	6,002	6,747	1,768	7,366
			−745	4,233	−1,364
			−11.0%	239.4%	−18.5%
	Q3	18,159	17,623	11,700	18,121
			536	6,458	38
			3.0%	55.2%	0.2%
Germany	Q4	2,979	8,409	3,836	6,635
			−5,430	−857	−3,655
			−64.6%	−22.3%	−55.1%
	Q1	2,529	4,877	6,214	5,240
			−2,348	−3,685	−2,711
			−48.1%	−59.3%	−51.7%
	Q2	8,825	17,417	15,221	18,726
			−8,593	−6,397	−9,902
			−49.3%	−42.0%	−52.9%
	Q3	28,067	36,806	24,988	40,856
			−8,738	3,079	−12,788
			−23.7%	12.3%	−31.3%

crease in receipts is expected because income in the USA increased during the post-crisis period and Scotland became a cheaper relative to the other countries in the euro zone. Ignoring these factors would be misleading. In fact, once these factors are taken into account, receipts from American tourists show a decrease during the period of the crisis. In the case of France, both receipts relative to the average of the five previous years and the predicted values fell dramatically during the fourth quarter of 2001 and the first quarter of 2002, continued to fall during the second quarter, and only started to rise during the third quarter of 2002. Receipts from German tourists decreased even more dramatically than those for French tourists during all four quarters.

An overview of the effects of the crisis on arrivals and receipts from the different origin countries during the whole year is given in Tables 7 and 8. Comparison of the predicted figures for arrivals and receipts (the final columns of the tables) is particularly revealing. Clearly, considerable numbers of US tourists (a decrease of 21.2%) were deterred from visiting Scotland during the period following the crises. However, those who did arrive engaged in a high level of expenditure per capita, gen-

erating an increase in total receipts of 0.9%. In contrast, both the numbers of French tourists who arrived and the associated value of receipts decreased considerably, by 18.5% and 14.8% respectively. In the case of Germany, the falls in the numbers of arrivals and receipts were even greater, with decreases of 38.3% and 40.7% respectively.

CONCLUSIONS

Past research on tourism crises has highlighted the need for crisis management frameworks and, as an integral part of them, effective communications strategies directed towards both potential tourists and the mass media. However, the issue that has challenged policy makers is the content of the messages that should be communicated. Tourists from different countries respond differently to tourism crises and the messages that should be communicated to them should differ accordingly. More information about their responses to different types of crisis is required if crisis communications are to be formulated and targeted effectively. It is in this context that quantitative approaches, such as that provided in this paper, can complement past contributions to the literature and provide additional guidance for effective policy making.

This paper considered the responses of tourists to Scotland from the USA, France and Germany to two different types of crisis–foot and mouth disease and September 11. The results from the model showed that tourists from different countries do, indeed, respond differently to different types of events. In the case of FMD, the most severe effects on both arrivals and receipts related to tourists from the most geographically proximate country, France, followed by Germany and then the USA. However, in the case of September 11, both arrivals and receipts from Germany were the most adversely affected, followed by the USA and then France in the case of arrivals, and by France and then the USA in the case of receipts. One of the most striking results was that receipts from the USA were virtually unaffected by either crisis.

The information about the different degrees of responses by the different nationalities to

TABLE 7. September 11 Effect on the Number of Arrivals in Scotland (Totals)

Country	Year after Sept. 11	Average 5 previous years	Previous year	Prediction year after Sept. 11
USA	395,181	439,023	433,627	501,471
		−43,843	−38,447	−106,290
		−10.0%	−8.9%	−21.2%
France	110,352	114,340	60,617	135,396
		−3,988	49,735	−25,044
		−3.5%	82.0%	−18.5%
Germany	130,501	198,935	161,095	211,419
		−68,433	−30,593	−80,917
		−34.4%	−19.0%	−38.3%

TABLE 8. September 11 Effect on Receipts in Scotland (Totals)

Country	Year after Sept. 11	Average 5 previous years	Previous year	Prediction year after Sept. 11
USA	212,860	193,882	201,820	210,960
		18,978	11,041	1,901
		9.8%	5.5%	0.9%
France	28,078	31,215	19,085	32,972
		−3,137	8,993	−4,894
		−10.0%	47.1%	−14.8%
Germany	42,400	67,510	50,259	71,456
		−25,109	−7,859	−29,056
		−37.2%	−15.6%	−40.7%

the crises is particularly useful for communications and marketing policy. In Scotland, this is mainly the responsibility of the national tourism organisation, VisitScotland. In the case of France, tourists responded particularly adversely to the FMD crisis that affected rural areas and activities, both in terms of the numbers who arrived and the associated receipts. Policy makers could, as an immediate response to crises that affect rural areas, place even greater emphasis on providing information about the rural areas and activities that are unaffected. A longer term strategy could aim to attract more tourists from France to urban areas, emphasizing the range of activities and attractions within them.

German tourists were also affected significantly by both the FMD and the September 11 crises but differ from French tourists in that many travel longer distances to arrive and may place greater reliance on air travel. In this respect, VisitScotland's policy of publicising the availability of cheap airfares is appropriate and could be targeted more strongly towards the German market. In addition to communicating the message that many rural areas and activities are unaffected by the crisis, over the long run greater attempts could be made to decrease the sensitivity of German tourists to adverse events by strengthening their friendship and business ties with Scotland.

The results for the USA indicate that VisitScotland's strategies of emphasizing the cultural ties between Scotland and the USA were successful in maintaining the values of receipts from the USA during the crises. Such strategies included not only the obvious ones of increasing the level of advertising of Scotland within the USA but also the less obvious one of contacting clan societies in the USA and encouraging their members to visit Scotland. Hence, although the numbers of tourist arrivals fell, many of those who did arrive stayed for a significant period of time and engaged in a relatively high level of expenditure. Clearly, both the US visits to friends and relatives and business tourism markets are important for Scotland in times of crises and should be maintained. Strategies for strengthening these markets in France and Germany could be considered. Other strategies that have been put in place include those of planning for multiple events by means of scenario planning and forecasting (Prideaux et al., 2003; Blake et al., forthcoming; Yeoman et al., forthcoming).

The quantitative approach that has been developed and applied to the case of Scotland complements the approaches that have been provided by recent research on tourism crises. The latter has demonstrated the beneficial role that crisis management frameworks can play (Faulkner, 2001; Prideaux, 2004). This paper has indicated the ways in which a modelling approach can provide useful information to underpin and assist policy formulation within such frameworks. In particular, the modelling provides information about the differences in the responses to crises between tourists of different nationalities, thereby assisting policy makers to tailor their marketing and related communications strategies specifically towards the different origin markets. The approach is of general applicability and can be applied to other sets of origin and destination countries, as well as to a wide range of market segments within them. In this respect, it provides considerable scope for further research.

REFERENCES

Alderighi, M., & Cento, A. (2004). European airlines conduct after September 11. *Journal of Air Transport Management, 10,* 97-107.

Argenti, P. (2002). Crisis communication–lesson from 9/11. *Harvard Business Review,* p. 12.

Augustine, N.R. (1995). Managing the crisis you tried to prevent. *Harvard Business Review* on Crisis Management. Harvard: Harvard Business School Press.

Barton, L. (1993). *Crisis in organizations: Managing and communicating in the heat of chaos.* Cincinnati, Ohio: South-Western.

Beirman, D. (2003). *Restoring tourism destinations in crisis: A strategic marketing approach.* Wallingford: CAB International.

Blake, A., & Sinclair, M.T. (2003). Tourism crisis management: Response to September 11. *Annals of Tourism Research, 30*(4), 813-832.

Blake, A., Sinclair, M.T., & Sugiyarto, G. (2003). Quantifying the impact of foot and mouth disease on tourism and the UK economy. *Tourism Economics,* 9(4), 449-465.

Blake, A., Durbarry, R., Eugenio-Martin, J.L., Gooroochurn, N., Hay, B., Lennon, J., Sinclair, M.T., Sugiyarto, G., & Yeoman, I. (forthcoming). Integrating forecasting and CGE models: A case study of tourism in Scotland. *Tourism Management,* forthcoming.

Booth, S. (1993). *Crisis management strategy, competition and changes in modern enterprises.* London: Routledge.

Cassedy, K. (1991). *Crisis management planning in the travel and tourism industry: A study of three destinations and a crisis planning manual.* San Francisco: PATA.

Coles, T. (2003). A local reading of a global disaster: Some lessons on tourism management from an *Annus Horribilis* in South West England. *Journal of Travel and Tourism Marketing, 15*(1), 173-216.

Coombes, W.T. (1995). The development of guidelines for the selection of the "appropriate" crisis response strategies. *Management Communication Quarterly, 4,* 447-476.

Cushnahan, G. (2004). Crisis management in small-scale tourism. *Journal of Travel and Tourism Marketing, 15*(4), 323-338.

Datastream. (2004). *Datastream advanced software.* Datastream International Limited.

Drabek, T.E. (1995). Disaster responses within the tourism industry. *International Journal of Mass Emergencies and Disasters, 13*(1), 7-23.

Fallon, F. (2004). After the Lombok riots, is sustainable tourism achievable? *Journal of Travel and Tourism Marketing, 15*(2/3), 139-158.

Faulkner, B. (2001). Towards a framework for tourism disaster management. *Tourism Management, 22*(2), 135-147.

Fearn-Banks, K. (1996). *Crisis communications: A casebook approach.* N.J.: Lawrence Erlbaum.

Floyd, M.F., Gibson, H., Pennington-Gray, L., & Thapa, B. (2004). The effect of risk perceptions on intentions to travel in the aftermath of September 11, 2001. *Journal of Travel and Tourism Marketing, 15*(2/3), 19-38.

Gillen, D., & Lall, A. (2003). International transmission of shocks in the airline industry. *Journal of Air Transport Management, 9,* 37-49.

Glaesser, D. (2004). *Crisis management in the tourism industry.* Oxford: Butterworth-Heinemann.

González, P., & Moral, P. (1995). An analysis of the international tourism demand in Spain. *International Journal of Forecasting, 11,* 233-251.

González, P., & Moral, P. (1996). Analysis of tourism trends in Spain. *Annals of Tourism Research, 23*(4), 739-754.

Goodrich, J.N. (2002). September 11, 2001 attack on America: A record of the immediate impacts and reactions in the USA travel and tourism industry. *Tourism Management, 23,* 573-580.

Green, P.S. (1992). *Reputation Risk Management.* London: Pitman/Financial Times.

Green, C.G., Bartholomew, P., & Murmann, S. (2004). New York restaurant industry: Strategic responses to September 11, 2001. *Journal of Travel and Tourism Marketing, 15*(2/3), 63-80.

Greenidge, K. (2001). Forecasting tourism demand. An STM approach. *Annals of Tourism Research, 28*(1), 98-112.

Hall, G.M. (2002). Travel safety, terrorism and the media: The significance of the issue-attention cycle. *Current Issues in Tourism, 5*(5), 458-66.

Harvey, A.C. (1989). *Forecasting, structural time series models and the Kalman filter.* Cambridge: Cambridge University Press.

Heath, R. (1994). Dealing with the complete crisis–the crisis management shell structure. *Safety Science, 30,* 139-150.

Heath, R. (1998). *Crisis management for managers and executives.* London: Pitman Publishing/Financial Times.

Henderson, J.C. (2003). Terrorism and tourism: Managing the consequences of the Bali bombings. *Journal of Travel and Tourism Marketing, 15*(1), 41-58.

Hill, L., & Wetlaufer, S. (1998). Leadership when there is no one to ask–An interview with Eni's Franco Bernabe. *Harvard Business Review* on Crisis Management. Harvard: Harvard Business School Press.

Hitchcock, M. (2001). Tourism and total crisis in Indonesia: the case of Bali. *Asia Pacific Business Review, 8*(2), 101-120.

Hitchcock, M., & Darma Putra, N. (forthcoming). The Bali bombings: Tourism crisis management and conflict avoidance. *Current Issues in Tourism,* forthcoming.

International Monetary Fund. (2003). *International Financial Statistics.* Washington, D.C.: IMF.

Israeli, A.A., & Reichal, A. (2003). Hospitality crisis management practices: the Israeli case. *International Journal of Hospitality Management, 22,* 353-372.

Lim, C. (1997). The functional specification of international tourism demand models. *Mathematics and Computers in Simulation, 43,* 535-543.

Lovelock, B. (2003). New Zealand travel agent practice in the provision of advice for travel to risky destinations. *Journal of Travel and Tourism Marketing, 15*(4), 259-280.

McKercher, B., & Hui, E.L.L. (2004). Terrorism, economic uncertainty and outbound travel from Hong Kong. *Journal of Travel and Tourism Marketing, 15*(2/3), 99-116.

Meyers, G.C. (1986). *When it hits the fan: Managing the nine crises of business.* New York: Mentor.

Mitroff, I.I., & Pearson, C.M. (1993). *Crisis management: A diagnostic guide for improving your organization's crisis-preparedness.* San Francisco: Jossey-Bass.

Office for National Statistics. (2003). *International Passenger Survey, 1979-2003.* London: Office for National Statistics, Social Survey Division.

Organisation for Economic Co-operation and Development (OECD). (2003). *National Accounts of OECD Countries–Vol. 1.* Parts II to IV. Paris: OECD.

Papatheodorou, A., & Song, H. (forthcoming). International tourism forecasts: Time series analysis of world and regional data. *Tourism Economics,* forthcoming.

Pender, L., & Sharpley, R. (2004). International tourism: the management of crisis. In L. Pender & R. Sharpley (Eds.), *The Management of Tourism*. London: Sage.

Prideaux, B. (2004). The need to use disaster planning frameworks to respond to major tourism disasters: Analysis of Australia's response to tourism disasters in 2001. *Journal of Travel and Tourism Marketing*, *15*(4), 281-298.

Prideaux, B., Laws, E., & Faulkner, B. (2003). Events in Indonesia: Exploring the limits to formal tourism trends forecasting methods in complex crisis situations. *Tourism Management*, *24*, 475-487.

Ray, S.J. (1999). *Strategic communication in crisis management: Lessons from the airline industry*. Westport CT: Quorum Books.

Regester, M., & Larkin, J. (2002). *Risk issues and crisis management: A casebook of best practice*. (2nd ed.). London: Kogan Page.

Ritchie, B.W., Dorrell, H., Miller, D., & Miller, G.A. (2004). Crisis communication and recovery for the tourism industry: Lessons from the 2001 Foot and Mouth Disease outbreak in the United Kingdom. *Journal of Travel and Tourism Marketing*, *15*(4), 199-216.

Rosenthal, U., & Pijnenburg, B. (1991). *Crisis management and decision making: Simulation oriented scenarios*. Dordrecht: Kluwer.

de Sausmarez, N. (2004). Implications for tourism and sectoral crisis management. *Journal of Travel and Tourism Marketing*, *15*(4), 217-232.

Seddighi, H., Nuttall, M., & Theocharous, A. (2001). Does cultural background of tourists influence the destination choice? An empirical study with special reference to political instability. *Tourism Management*, *22*(2), 181-191.

Seymour, M., & Moore, S. (2000). *Effective crisis management: Worldwide principles and practice*. London: Cassell.

Slatter, S. (1984). *Corporate recovery*. Harmondsworth: Penguin.

Smith, D. (1990). Beyond contingency planning: towards a model of crisis management. *Industrial Crisis Quarterly*, *4*, 263-275.

Smith, D., & Spipika, C. (1993). Back from the brink– post crisis management. *Long Range Planning*, *26*(1), 28-38.

Soemodinoto, A., Wong, P.P., & Saleh, M. (2001). Effect of prolonged political unrest on tourism. *Annals of Tourism Research*, *28*(4), 1056-1060.

Song, H., & Witt, S.F. (2000). *Tourism demand modelling and forecasting: Modern econometric approaches*. Oxford: Pergamon.

Song, H., Witt, S.F., & Li, G. (2003). Modelling and forecasting the demand for Thai tourism. *Tourism Economics*, *9*, 363-387.

Sönmez, S., & Graefe, A. (1998). Influence of terrorism risk on foreign tourism decisions. *Annals of Tourism Research*, *25*(1), 112-144.

Sonnenfeld, S. (1994). Media policy–What media policy? *Harvard Business Review* on Crisis Management. Harvard: Harvard Business School Press.

Tate, P. (2002). The impact of 9/11: Caribbean, London and NYC case studies. *Travel and Tourism Analyst*, *5*(October), 1-25.

Thapa, B. (2004). Tourism in Nepal: Shangri-La's troubled times. *Journal of Travel and Tourism Marketing*, *15*(2/3), 117-139.

Witt, S.F., & Martin, C.A. (1989). Demand forecasting in tourism and recreation. In C.P. Cooper (Ed.), *Progress in tourism, recreation and hospitality management*. London & New York: Belhaven, 4-32.

Yeoman, I., Lennon, J., & Black, L. (forthcoming). Foot and mouth disease–A scenario of reoccurrence for Scotland's tourism industry. *Journal of Vacation Marketing*, forthcoming.

Young, W.B., & Montgomery, R.J. (1998). Crisis management and its impact on destination marketing: A guide to convention and visitors bureaus. *Journal of Convention and Exhibition Management*, *1*(1), 3-18.

Tourism and the Impact
of the Foot and Mouth Epidemic in the UK:
Reactions, Responses and Realities
with Particular Reference to Scotland

David Leslie
Lynn Black

SUMMARY. This article aims first to establish an overview of the reactions to the impact on tourism of the Foot and Mouth disease [FMD] and ensuing crisis in the UK leading on to consider the reaction and responses of the Government and leading players. The focus then turns to Scotland to explore and develop the theme of the impact of FMD on rural tourism and the responses of key public sector organisations involved. In furthering the analysis, the author draws on the findings of empirical research undertaken to investigate the actual impact of FMD on tourism enterprises in a rural area of Scotland. The outcomes of this study not only bring into question the impact portrayed through the media but more significantly, raise issues as to the way government agencies and professional organisations involved in tourism responded to the crisis engendered by FMD. In concluding, a number of key lessons are identified. *[Article copies available for a fee from The Haworth Document Delivery Service: 1-800-HAWORTH. E-mail address: <docdelivery@haworthpress.com> Website: <http://www.HaworthPress.com> © 2005 by The Haworth Press, Inc. All rights reserved.]*

KEYWORDS. Crisis management, government policy, rural tourism, tourism enterprises, media, marketing

INTRODUCTION

The availability of food, as opposed to food services, for tourists is perhaps one of the least considered aspects of tourism development. It has generally received little attention in tourism literature and research, perhaps because it is axiomatic that food needs to be available; notable exceptions are Hudman (1986) and Hughes (1995). Yet, food ". . . has a claim to be the world's most important subject. It is what matters to most people most of the time" (Fernandez-Armesto, 2001, p. xiii). Perhaps belatedly in the light of this, there has been a relative flood of publications which attest to current interest in what is termed "Food Tourism" (Hjalager & Richards, 2002; Boniface, 2003; Hall, Sharples, Mitchell, Macionis &

David Leslie is affiliated with the Reader in Tourism, Glasgow Caledonian University, Cowcaddens Road, Glasgow G4 0BA (E-mail: D.Leslie@gcal.ac.uk). Lynn Black is a Freelance Researcher, Sandend Place, Ardgowan View, Iverkip, PA16 0HU.

[Haworth co-indexing entry note]: "Tourism and the Impact of the Foot and Mouth Epidemic in the UK: Reactions, Reponses and Realities with Particular Reference to Scotland." Leslie, David, and Lynn Black. Co-published simultaneously in *Journal of Travel & Tourism Marketing* (The Haworth Hospitality Press, an imprint of The Haworth Press, Inc.) Vol. 19, No. 2/3, 2005, pp. 35-46; and: *Tourism Crises: Management Responses and Theoretical Insight* (ed: Eric Laws, and Bruce Prideaux) The Haworth Hospitality Press, an imprint of The Haworth Press, Inc., 2005, pp. 35-46. Single or multiple copies of this article are available for a fee from The Haworth Document Delivery Service [1-800-HAWORTH, 9:00 a.m. - 5:00 p.m. (EST). E-mail address: docdelivery@haworthpress.com].

Cambourne, 2003; Quan & Wang, 2004). Collectively these encompass much that is to be said about food and tourism but, and perhaps surprisingly, little attention is given to the effect of "food scares" on demand. Possibly this is because such scares tend to be localised, of short-term duration and gained limited media coverage. However, the latter is arguably changing as we all become more and more a part of a global community. There is growing widespread interest in health and food production issues, for example, organic farming, genetically modified crops.

The increase in interest can be illustrated by reference to two particularly notable events in the U.K. First, the radioactive fallout from the Chernobyl disaster of 1986 was particularly evident in the western upland regions of the U.K. and caused high levels of radioactivity in sheep in Wales and Cumbria leading initially to a ban on their movement (Hinchliffe & Blowers, 2003). This incident was given limited media attention. However, the next food scare, Mad Cow disease (Bovine Spongiform Encephalopathy (BSE)), received substantial media attention. Considerable concern arose over the potential of dangers of developing CJD, a human form of BSE, through eating beef. The level of coverage was such that actual and potential visitors from America and Germany became concerned over the possibility of consuming beef during a trip to the U.K. This concern over food safety, notably in the context of air travel, has gained some academic attention (McLaurin, 2001), but is very limited in other discourses on food and tourism, as noted above, or to the influence on the tourist's experience (Quan & Wang, 2004). Hitherto, it has been media commentators who have made the connections, albeit sensationalist.

However, the influence of major food scares on tourism demand is an area that merits wider attention and research. Not only because of the influence on demand and that food is of such importance but also because of the increasing development and promotion of food-related tourism initiatives, often based on local produce (Leslie, 2001; Boyne, Hall & Williams, 2003). It is therefore apposite that this article presents the main findings of research into the impact on tourism of the "Foot and Mouth" epidemic of 2001 in the U.K. First, we establish,

by way of background, the initial response to the outbreak of the disease. Subsequently, and in order to place the outbreak in context, the attention turns to rural tourism before focusing on the impacts on tourism. Given the significance of the part played by government and public sector related tourism organisations, there follows an analysis of the roles of these key players and their actions. The empirical research, involving interviews with major role players and a survey of tourism businesses in an appropriate rural location in Scotland, is then presented and discussed. In concluding we draw out the lessons to be learnt from this study.

BACKGROUND

The Foot and Mouth Disease (FMD) of 2001, first reported in England in February quickly spread to Scotland being particularly widespread in the southwest border region. In response the Government quickly put measures in place to contain the spread of disease (McConnell & Stark, 2002). In addition to most pathways being closed throughout the country, many tourist attractions closed and land belonging to organisations such as the Forestry Commission and the National Trust became out of bounds to visitors. These measures effectively put the whole of the countryside in the UK under quarantine with access to many areas greatly reduced. The media chose to depict large areas of rural Scotland as "out of bounds" to visitors. The overriding impression given by the media was that the whole of the United Kingdom (UK) countryside was "closed for business." Such misleading reports had the effect of potentially changing the travel decisions of both domestic and international visitors to the UK (DCMS, 2001a). This had the effect of engendering in the public eye a perception that tourism was in an "unexpected crisis" (Booth, 1993). Moreover, the fact that the Prime Minister took personal charge of the situation and even postponed the General Election scheduled for May–a factor which clearly emphasises the significant influence of politics on the Government's action–further exacerbated the situation. Overall, there was an estimated loss in revenues attributed to FMD from the international and domestic tourism markets of £1.5bn and £2.7bn respectively, in rural areas (Morris, 2002). In effect, this action by the Government is said to have sent out signals to the wider world that the UK was in the midst of chaos (McConnell & Stark, 2002). The UK Government was also criticised for focusing only on agricultural problems caused by the FMD outbreak and issues regarding safety and access to the countryside while neglecting the difficulties faced by non-agricultural businesses (Committee of Public Accounts, 2003). The Government belatedly became aware of the impact of the reduction in visitors in rural areas and undoubtedly this contributed to visitor uncertainty and ultimately to further loss of revenue by rural enterprises. This reflects McConnell and Stark's point that ". . . bureaucratic conflicts and operational fragmentation . . ." act against forming a ". . . focused and coherent . . ." response in a crisis ". . . FMD is no exception to this rule" (2002, p. 672).

RURAL TOURISM

The UK's countryside has been shaped and managed by agricultural practices for centuries. But agriculture as the main bulwark of rural economies has been in decline throughout the UK (total income from farming in Scotland fell from £690m in 1995 to approximately £200m in 2000 (Royal Society of Edinburgh, 2002, p. 5)) for well over the past two decades whilst tourism activity has grown. For example, the proportion of the population who spend at least one day in the countryside each month rose from 25% in 1987 to 40% in 1998 (Hunt, 2001). Tourism generates substantial more income than agriculture and in 2000 the estimated total revenue generated by tourism amounted to £64bn compared with £16bn (DCMS, 2001b) for the agricultural sector.

In Scotland the numbers involved in outdoor recreation showed continuous growth throughout the 1990s further expanding the demand for rural tourism. For example, 60% of Scottish adults visited the countryside in 1998 (NCSR, 1999) with walking the most popular growing sector growing by 8% annually (Warren, 2002, p. 225). Walking together with cycling in the countryside contributes £438m in expenditure

(Scottish Parliament, 2002a). Tourism is now the biggest sector of the economy in many rural areas of Scotland, having overtaken the established land uses of farming, forestry, fishing and field sports both in terms of employment (around 8% of all employment in Scotland) and GDP (accounting for 8% as opposed to agriculture at 1.4% (SE, 2002)). The entrepreneurship opportunities and the associated low costs in starting up tourism businesses make this a popular choice for residents and "incomers" within rural areas (Wilson, Fesenmaier & van Es, 2001; Leslie, 2001). These factors all have a bearing on the diversification of rural businesses into tourism. Such is the significance and pervasiveness of tourism activity in many rural areas that a downturn in demand for any one area, or more widely, has potentially serious implications. Thus, the Government's primary strategy for, and the media coverage of, the FMD suggesting that "the countryside is closed" had potentially substantial domino effects on rural economies and tourism enterprises.

IMPACTS ON TOURISM

Research has found that in the UK as a whole, 5.43 million consumers changed travel plans due to the FMD outbreak, 2.9 million called off trips and 120,000 travelled abroad (ETC, 2001). As regards employment, the English Tourism Council (ETC) stated that in the same month: ". . . 14% of tourism enterprises paid off staff as a consequence of the FMD outbreak" (ETC, 2001). In terms of earnings from tourism it is hard to quantify the impact of FMD on domestic tourism; however, the UK tourist sector was estimated to have lost between £2.7 and £3.2 billion in 2001 (Blake & Sinclair, 2003). However, in contrast, some commentators have argued that losses in rural tourism, at least in part, were compensated by increased visits/visitor expenditure to urban destinations (see McDonald, Roberts and Kay, 2003 in the case of Scotland; and more generally Turner, 2001; Sloyan, 2002). In Scotland, overall visitor numbers to rural visitor attractions for July (the high season) were 914,300 compared with 991,800 in July, 2000 (Moffat Centre for Travel and Tourism, 2001). Conversely, the same survey found that city based attractions experienced an increase of 5% in visitors for July, 2001; more specifically Greater Glasgow and Clyde Valley experienced a 14% increase in visitors. In contrast, for example, Dumfries and Galloway evidenced a decrease of 24% in visitors to their attractions whilst Ayrshire and Arran's visitor figures decreased between 2000 and 2001 by 102,000 (Ayrshire and Arran Tourist Board, 2003). Yet, Fife enjoyed a particularly successful year (Fife Tourist Board, 2002). Taken together, these findings further affirm that there was some displacement of visitors during this period. Indeed, one commentator argued that London would gain visitors at Scotland's expense due to the problems (Turner, 2001). Overall the effects of the FMD are well summed up as follows:

> Although, losses to sectors directly affected by the disease were, from a macroeconomic perspective, largely off set by increased spending elsewhere, the impact on tourism in affected areas was devastating. Some of that activity was diverted to other UK locations and to consumer spending on unrelated items. This reduced the effect on total output. (Sportscotland, VisitScotland & SNH, 2001, p. 132)

Further, "Foot and mouth may be a disaster for Britian's agriculture industry. For rural tourism it is a full-blown crisis. . ." (Crace, 2001, p. 1). As the ETC is reported to have warned ". . . 3,000 small businesses and 250,000 jobs could go to the wall as a result of foot and mouth, and that without extra government aid the tourist industry would lose £5bn this year" (Crace, 2001, p. 1).

KEY PLAYERS AND THEIR ACTIONS

Our concern here is to concentrate on the response of the key agencies in the tourism sector rather than Government's response per se which is well discussed elsewhere (McConnell & Stark, 2002). However, the tourism agencies took their lead from the Government's response, which in concert with both professional bodies and representatives of the tourism industry they were arguably instrumental in forming. The Government eventually established measures to: address access to the countryside; provide advice on financial aid and assistance packages for tourism enterprises; and, through the National Tourist Organisations, assist with promotional campaigns to redress the negative publicity.

A Rural Task Force was set up towards the end of March, which contributed to reducing the existing confusion (McConnell & Stark, 2002). Their brief was to improve information as regards access to the countryside, rebuild confidence, both in the UK and overseas in the tourism sector, and to implement a series of measures to assist rural communities (DCMS, 2001a). Specific measures for rural tourism enterprises included the possiblity of: rates relief; suspension of tax and national insurance payments; extended overdrafts and delayed capital repayment; and support for applications to the Small Firms Loan Guarantee Funds. Similar measures were introduced in Scotland including workshops and counselling (SE, 2002). However, the recovery scheme for small businesses, supported by £50m in funds, was fraught with difficulties not the least of which was the burdensome administration and influence of EU regulations on state aid (McConnell & Stark 2002; Muckspreader, 2001). In Scotland, an additional £5m was granted to the Enterprise Network to provide emergency assistance and guidance to tourism enterprises affected by the outbreak. In May, the Department for Culture, Media and Sport (DCMS) issued a strategy to provide a: "Consistent and comprehensive picture of what is open as well as a clear list of do's and don'ts for visitors" and embraced:

- opening up attractions and footpaths without spreading FMD;
- assistance to businesses affected by the disease;
- establishing a clear message to people abroad and at home of the true situation of FMD in the UK. (DCMS, 2001a)

Also, all parties involved were asked to cooperate to make the most of all resources to hand in order to resurrect the tourism sector. The main thrust of this strategy was to emphasise the problems caused in the tourism sector, rather than focus on the Government's strategy for the recovery of the agriculture industry or the eradication of FMD. VisitScotland was the agency that led the management of the response to the FMD outbreak, together with local area tourist boards, local authorities and enterprise companies. Various support was offered, including, general advice, counselling, workshops and seminars. The Small Business Gateway, established by Enterprise Councils in their areas, was considered to be the focal point for advice and information to businesses and individuals suffering the consequential impact of the FMD outbreak. The support available included business information, one-to-one sessions with a business advisor and specialist workshops involving contributions from banks, accountants and government agencies such as the Inland Revenue and Customs and Excise. Effective communication during such times is recognised as very important (Phillipson, Bennett, Lowe & Raley, 2003) and thus it is notable that the communication of the guidelines and level of support from the Scottish Executive was considered "good if a bit general" (SportsScotland et al., 2001).

Promotion of inward and domestic tourism was undertaken by the British Tourism Authority (BTA), now VisitBritain, with additional funding from Government and also an extra £5m for VisitScotland (SE, 2002). The campaign included offering advice and reassurance to visitors and involving national and regional/area Tourist Boards and overseas offices of the BTA. British Embassies and the British Council were also involved in giving assurances regarding the safety of visiting the British countryside. However, the success of these initiatives and promotional campaigns, such as the BTA's "Open for Business" and Scotland's "Comeback Code," was variable. For example, the results of a survey in June 2001 found that 97% of respondents from the 11 overseas markets surveyed were aware of the UK's Foot and Mouth outbreak, and significantly, 29% of those surveyed still thought the countryside was closed (ETC, 2001). This reflects the potency of the negative images portrayed and press coverage.

Similar actions were taken in Scotland, with the launch in March, of the "Come Back Code" led by Scottish National Heritage (SNH) with the cooperation of major agencies involved in tourism and notably in liaison with the State Veterinary Service and the Scottish Executive Rural Affairs Department. This constituted an effort to attract people back into the countryside. The promotion of the "Code" was countrywide, involving media advertising, and leaflets and posters throughout Scotland which also served to publicise tourist attractions and rural destinations. This was a particularly important action designed to give timely and accurate information to counteract media hype. Despite these efforts it took some time for many parts of the countryside to be re-opened, prompting the Chairman of SNH (2001) to call for a " 'Keep Out' Clearout" in mid-May. It was observed by delegates at a major "tourism" conference in November, 2001 that: "Land should be closed for the minimum period necessary. The countryside is relatively easy to close down but much more difficult to reopen" (SportScotland et al., 2001, p. 3).

THE STUDY

The spread of FMD was quickly recognised and, as noted above, led to restrictions on access to the countryside. This, coupled with the extensive media coverage, had the effect of promoting the "closure of the countryside." The impact of this gave rise to many comments on the effect of the loss of visitors and claims of substantial impacts on rural tourism enterprises and consequential losses. However, such claims may have been overstated and rather sweeping; for example, hotels in the Lake District National Park reported substantial variances in the early impact on occupancy, much of which could be attributed to their specific locations in terms of access and rurality whilst farm based tourism enterprises were all substantially affected (Franks, Lowe, Phillipson & Scott, 2003). The question therefore arises as to the extent of the impact of FMD in popular rural tourist destinations and whether impacts were variable within the area. To explore these questions a study was undertaken to investigate the effects of FMD in the rural region of Ayrshire and Arran in the west of Scotland, north of Dumfries and Galloway and southwest of the conurbation, and adjacent areas, of Greater Glasgow. The specific focus was to establish the impact of FMD on tourism enterprises, particularly on their performance, and influencing factors, over the period of the FMD outbreak. The primary approach involved a postal survey of a representative sample of 80 tourism enterprises within the study area based on local authority and Tourist Board publications, together with structured interviews with relevant agencies involved in the events surrounding the FMD outbreak. These included Enterprise Ayrshire, North Ayrshire, Inverclyde and Renfrew Councils, Ayrshire and Arran Tourist Board and Clyde Muirshiel Regional Country Park (CMRCP), SNH, VisitScotland and the Scottish Tourism Forum. Regrettably the Ayrshire and Arran Tourist Board, VisitScotland and the Scottish Tourism Forum were uncooperative.

The design of the survey questionnaire was given much consideration to avoid leading responses by respondents on FMD. Secondly, the design needed to be succinct because of the plethora of bureaucratic demands placed on small owner/managed enterprises. Further, to promote participation we opted for pre-coded broad responses (with opportunities for open comment) to questions rather than requesting detailed recollections or referral to specific records. This approach contributed to achieving a response rate of 34%.

KEY PLAYERS AND THEIR ACTIONS

The Councils involved in the FMD crisis were comparatively quick in establishing a Local Authority Emergency Planning Team, comprising Renfrew, North Ayrshire and Inverclyde Councils. The Planning team prepared guidelines, undertook an information campaign, and provided advice to enterprises. Further, Ayrshire Enterprise implemented a "Foot and Mouth Revival" project and various other initiatives, including: Ayrshire Pathways, Girvan Valley Countryside Ranger Initiative and The Ayrshire Food Festival. The objectives of the local revival project included securing assistance for businesses affected by FMD and the stimulation of the local economy through reduction of restrictions of access to the countryside. The project was seen as crucial in rebuilding the confidence of the public and thus visitor demand. These initiatives generated positive publicity and had a number of secondary benefits including improved relationships with the

landowners and tenant (CMPA, 2002). This view reflects more generally the very positive coordination of all parties during the FMD outbreak. Clyde Muirshiel Regional Park, SNH and North Ayrshire all stated that the communication by the SE had been clear, although SNH did voice concerns on the haste with which footpaths and countryside access had been closed.

Aryshire and Arran can be considered as comprising three general categories of destination: inland, coastal and island. It was found from the agencies involved that requests for support from "inland" North Ayrshire were minimal and that FMD was not considered to restrict many visitors to the area. Also all the golf courses remained open during the outbreak suggesting that as golf is one of the major tourism assets in the area, this served to buffer the effects of FMD. The effects of the promotional campaigns may also be considered a factor in CMRCP's visitor numbers recovering steadily with July 2001 showing an increase over July, 2000. The coastal locations were also considered to have avoided much of the effects of FMD and may well have gained from the restrictions on countryside access. However, the island locations were more seriously affected. For example, many enterprises on the Isles of Arran and Cumbrae did take up the offer of advice with workshops, particularly for tourism enterprises, being generally well attended.

Overall, the area most affected was Arran because sheep and deer roam the island freely. Arran was a "powder keg" as far as access was concerned and this issue has always been a contentious issue with tourism enterprises, farmers and other landowners. As soon as the crisis broke, Arran "shut down" and there was considerable opposition from island residents and businesses. Restrictions on movement on the island was an understandable reaction to FMD because of concerns that the disease would spread rapidly. The main body involved with SNH in actions during this time was the "Arran Access Trust," a body representing members of the local community, and which had been established few years previously to deal with access issues. The Trust set up weekly meetings to discuss the up-to-date situation and prepare and distribute "position statements." By early April, as FMD became better understood, the Trust realised that most restrictions could be removed, access improved and signage revised to advise which areas were open. For these efforts SNH were acknowledged by local tourism enterprises. Notably visitor numbers for April were almost double that of April 2000 which, in part, is arguably due to the promotional campaigns aimed at "bring back visitors."

It is against this background, that we can now consider the findings of the survey of tourism enterprises, the data for which has been presented in percentage terms to facilitate comparative analyses.

FINDINGS FROM THE SURVEY OF TOURISM BUSINESSES

A profile of the participating enterprises is presented in Table 1 which shows a cross section of categories of tourism enterprises, not surprisingly dominated by hospitality operations, and one which over the three factors covered bears comparison with other rural areas (Leslie, 2001). Though overall relatively small, the sample is

TABLE 1. Profile of the Enterprises

Factor	Response (%)
Category	
Bed & Breakfast/Guesthouse	22
Hotel	15
Public House/Restaurant	19
Caravan Camping Site	7
Self Catering	15
Visitor Attraction	11
Other (Marina, Sports Centre, Riding Centre)	11
Type of Ownership	
Sole Trader	60
Public Ltd Co.	19
Partnership	7
Public Sector	11
Other (Private Ltd Co)	4
Length of time in operation	
3-5 years	30
6-10 years	7
> 10 years	63

N = 28

similar to that in Phillipson et al.'s study (2003) which allows for meaningful comparisons, as appropriate, to be drawn.

Business Performance–1999/2001

First, it should be noted that there had been a decline in overall tourism expenditure between 1997 to 2000 (VisitScotland, 2002). The main factors which have been attributed to this are the strength of the pound, the weather and poor value for money in terms of standards of service and quality of food available (Scottish Parliament, 2002b).

The participants were invited, in general terms, to indicate if the operations turnover had varied during the three year period (see Table 2). For 1999 and 2000, 11% of the enterprises reported decreases in turnover (two enterprises for both years), which was attributed to 'poor weather' [8%] and the 'strength of sterling' (4% case); reasons also cited, though noted elsewhere in the questionnaire, e.g., "Whilst terrorism did deter visitors, weather and sterling always do".

However, for 2001 a different pattern emerges, 44% of the enterprises reported a decrease in turnover. According to 7% of respondents, turnover was adversely influenced by poor weather with another 26% citing the threat of terrorism as the factor directly responsible for the decrease; though no one cited "strength of sterling." A minority of enterprises (15%), each a different category, stated that "foot and mouth disease" had depressed turnover which partly reflects the more general findings for Scotland for the period (Scottish Parliament, 2002b). This reinforces Phillipson et al.'s research that "Although hospitality was the most extensively affected sector, the largest grouping of hospitality businesses fell into the low impact category" (2003, p. 6).

TABLE 2. Variances in Turnover: 1999 to 2001

Response of the Enterprise (%)

Variance	1999	2000	2001
Increased	41	26	26
About the Same	48	63	30
Decreased	11	11	44

N = 28

Overall, the findings on turnover indicate that enterprises considered that the repercussions of "September 11th" were primarily the cause of any reduced tournover. But as one respondent noted: "Turnover is always affected by weather. Terrorism and sterling have had little impact." When one considers that tourism in Scotland is over 90% domestic, it is easy to understand how the weather affects visitor numbers and trips; well demonstrated by the very good summer weather of 2003 (Guy, 2003). In other words the perennial influence of the weather on demand at the local level was more of a factor on reflection than FMD. Indeed, the weather was generally poor in February and March in Scotland and northern England of 2001.

Employment

A key indicator of variance in business performance is change in the numbers of employees. Evidently in 1999 and 2000 these remained relatively stable with 8% of the enterprises reporting decreases in 1999 and 2000 which correlates with those enterprises indicating downturns in turnover over this period and vice-versa with 11% reporting increases in full-time staff (see Table 3). For 2001, a different picture emerges with 19% to 22% indicating increases in full-time and part-time staff respectively. This appears to conflict with Fawcett and Head's (2001) reporting on FMD, that enterprises stopped recruiting or postponed taking on staff as a result of the FMD outbreak. However, there is a marked decrease in part-time staffing levels over this period

with 33% reporting a reduction which, as noted above, is attributed more to "September 11" than FMD.

Seasonality

Rural tourism across the UK is highly seasonal, generally peaking in July/August and low in January/February. The FMD outbreak commencing in February, the media reporting and restrictions on access thus coincided with a comparatively quiet period of tourism activity. However, for these small enterprises–predominantly micro-businesses–a small downshift in demand can have potentially substantial effects. Thus, it might be expected that any significant variances to the seasonal pattern of demand would be noted (see Figure 1). However, January to March is consistent over the three years, April/May shows a slight decline for 2001 though June to August was better than the previous years. The comparatively slight decline in September/October supports the perception of the impact of "September 11." The key market segment in decline was identified as visitors from North America, substantially so for 2001. This substantial difference for 2001 is undoubtedly an outcome of FMD and "September 11"; though one respondent noted: "Americans stopped touring this part of Scotland when flights were changed to Glasgow instead of Prestwick." But, the noticeably lower mean for April/May correlates with those enterprises who did indicate FMD as a factor.

TABLE 3. Variances in Full and Part-Time Employees 1999-2001

Response (%)						
Variance	1999		2000		2001	
	F/T	P/T	F/T	P/T	F/T	P/T
Increased	15	15	11	15	19	22
About the Same	85	81	85	81	74	44
Decreased	-	4	4	4	7	33

F/T = full time; P/T = part time.
N = 28

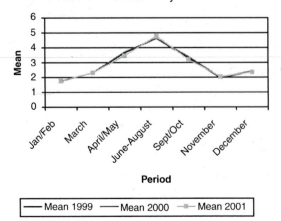

FIGURE 1. Seasonality 1999-2001

Requests for Assistance

In recognition of both media reporting and agency assistance, the survey investigated whether these enterprises had sought assistance (see Table 4), the reasons for such enquiries and whether they felt the responses to be helpful. Whilst 55% indicated they sought assistance during 2001 (compared with 37% for 1999 and 41% for 2000), none made any reference to the FMD situation as the reason for this. Reasons that were given for these requests mainly related to financial support, financial advice or training assistance (accounting for 50%) whilst other advice sought related to staff training assistance, web site design, marketing advice and so forth. Of those enterprises seeking assistance in some way, 50% reported downturns in business activity for 2001, the majority of whom gave the cause for the downturn as poor weather, just one enterprise cited FMD and one cited stated the threat of terrorism. The inference is that the effects of FMD were not as significant as purported to be by the Area Tourist Boards and government agencies at the time of the FMD outbreak.

On a wider note, of those enterprises which did obtain advice or support, 30% of the respondents felt that this was either "not useful" or "slightly useful." Several other concerns, unrelated to any "crisis" noted by respondents related to their negative views of the role of the Tourist Board, as opposed to any other agency.

CONCLUSIONS AND LESSONS

The foregoing discussion and empirical research into FMD and its effects on tourism

TABLE 4. Agencies Approached for Support/Advice: 1999 to 2001

Agency	Response (%)		
	1999	2000	2001
Local Enterprise Agency	19	22	37
Local Tourist Board	7	4	7
Local Authority	11	15	11
Other	0	0	0
Not applicable	63	60	44

N = 28

within the rural area of Ayrshire and Arran, in particular on tourism enterprises, has established that:

- FMD was initially treated as just an agricultural problem, without the realisation that the domino effects, particularly the actions taken to control and contain FMD, would have potentially substantial effects on rural economies and tourism especially;
- Once this had been realised, more often first at local level, the main public sector agencies and tourism organisations formulated appropriate local area action plans and initiatives which generally were coordinated and clear advice provided for tourism enterprises in the area.
- As regards tourism enterprises, whilst it is accurate to say that FMD did have some effects these were variable within rural areas and some tourism enterprises in urban/semi-urban areas undoubtedly gained.

Though it emerges that 44% of the tourism enterprises in the study did experience a downturn in business in the year 2001, the majority were of the opinion that the threat of terrorism, i.e., "September 11th," was the major cause of reduced turnover rather than FMD, which is affirmed by the 33% of respondents who referred to FMD as the cause. However, partly favouring the FMD factor is the variance in seasonality for April/May; greater than September/October but conversely to this is the consistency of the seasonality over the period for January to March. These findings, as regards the effects of FMD, appear to conflict with Fawcett and Head's study (2001) in which over half of the tourism enterprises surveyed reported that FMD had a negative impact on their business. This latter finding is perhaps not surprising given the timing of the survey, i.e., pre-September 11th, and its leading nature. This brings into question the likelihood of over reporting of effects of the outbreak at the time. Certainly, in terms of the retrospective responses of the participants, the effects of FMD on performance are not for the most part considered significant and certainly less significant than September 11th or more generally cited influences on demand, e.g., the weather and strength of the pound. This confirms the view that while some rural businesses were seriously affected in the aftermath of the outbreak many of the owners regarded a down turn in business as a "blip"–as an additional problem, rather than the sole cause of their difficulties (BBC, 2002) and reinforces the findings of Phillipson et al. (2003) that these enterprises are often found to be very resilient to external events with good coping strategies to deal with such occurrences.

In total, the evidence both empirical and drawn from other independent studies, indicates that the overall impact of FMD was overstated (for example, Hannah, 2002; McDonald et al., 2003). Even so, a downturn in the business performance of these rural tourism enterprises (more often micro-businesses (Leslie, 2001), comparative to many general businesses, has potentially significantly greater impacts on the financial standing of the business given their limited margins and flexibility.

Lessons

First, the key issues that needed to be addressed in the first instance by government are whether FMD was going to be short or long term, what are the secondary impacts, i.e., domino effects, and what are their options. Essentially, the Government primarily failed to recognise these aspects in that it initially appeared to consider FMD as being short in duration and quickly contained; a response arguably more to do with the Government of the day's politics. They clearly failed to consider the secondary impacts and were slow to recognise that the real crisis was in rural tourism. Indeed, the failure to realise the consequences of the strategy to contain and stop FMD on tourism was, ". . . more damaging that the success of the primary strategy" (McConnell, 2003, p. 408). In other words, the crisis in tourism was to an extent self-made by the Goverment.

Second, there was a degree of confusion arising from what can only be described, initially at least, as a rather ad hoc response, with too many agencies, different levels of government and players further complicated by devolution, resulting in: "A vacuum of central direction and that the Scottish Executive was slow to take the initiative . . ." (Sportscotland et al., 2001, p. 11). In effect, what was needed was a coherent and strategic response for the UK as a whole which empowered regional/local agencies to take responsive action in addressing regional/local needs.

Third, the early failure to recognise the consequences for tourism is arguably partly due to the lack of effective communication and the ineffectiveness of the DCMS in representing tourism interests in the Government (Sloyan, 2002)–a situation which was even weaker in Scotland. This, coupled with the multiplicity of agencies involved, undoubtedly influenced the development of an effective, coherent and comprehensive management strategy to redress the problems.

Fourth, the FMD outbreak highlighted the weaknesses in the measurement of the impact of tourism and this was brought into sharp focus for the Government. As Middleton (2002) observed, there are indications that Government representatives were taken aback by the paucity of data and the limitations of the methods used to quantify the impact of FMD on tourism.

Fifth, those agencies charged with addressing the effects on tourism enterprises must have their respect and support if they are to be effective. Therefore, it is important that due consideration is given to the agencies empowered to take responsive action and that they are close to the "coal face"; exemplified by Arran Access Trust which, as the key player in the area, helped smooth out a very difficult situation with decision-making based on consensus of opinion from an elected representative body drawn from the island's community.

Finally, the national tourism organisations were slow to recognise the potency of media reporting and misunderstandings that arose, e.g., humans could potentially catch FMD–particularly at the international level. Thus, great effort and thought should have been put into international promotional campaigns to address such factors; such promotion could potentially have benefits in the longer term if suitably presented and should thus be designed with that in mind.

REFERENCES

Aryshire and Arran Tourist Board. (2003). *Annual Report*. Ayr: Author.

BBC. (2002). *Farm disease a 'blip' for businesses*. Retrieved March 9, 2003, from *http://www.news.bbc.co.uk/1/low/scotland/2176262.stm*.

Blake, A., & Sinclair, M.T. (2003). Tourism crisis management: US response to September 11. *Annals of Tourism Research, 30*(4), 813-832.

Boniface, P. (2003). *Tasting tourism: Travelling for food and drink*. Aldershot: Ashgate Publishing.

Booth, S.A. (1993). *Crisis management strategy*. London: Routledge.

Boyne, S., Hall, D., & Williams, F. (2003). Policy, support and promotion for food-related tourism initiatives: A marketing approach to regional development. *Journal of Travel & Tourism Marketing, 14*(3/4), 131-154.

CMPA. (2002). *Annual report of Clyde Muirshiel Regional Park, 2000/2001*. Lochwinnoch: Clyde Muirshiel Park Authority.

Committee of Public Accounts. (2003). *The 2001 outbreak of Foot and Mouth Disease*. London: United Kingdom Parliament.

Crace, J. (2001, May 15) Know your stuff. *The Guardian*, p. 3

DCMS. (2001a). *National tourism recovery strategy–A strategy to tackle the effects of the foot and mouth outbreak on the tourism industry across England, and on incoming tourism to Britain*. London: The Stationery Office.

DCMS. (2001b). *Tourism–the hidden giant–and foot and mouth. Culture, Media and Sport Committee, Fourth Report, Vol. 1*. London: The Stationary Office.

ETC. (2001). *Foot and mouth: Special report. NewsET Cetera*, June (Issue 10). London: English Tourism Council.

Fawcett, J., & Head, R. (2001). *Foot and Mouth Disease: Business impact tracking survey Scotland. (September 2001) Third Wave*. Edinburgh: Scottish Executive Central Research Unit.

Fernandez-Armesto, F. (2001). *Food: A history*. London: Macmillan.

Fife 'Tourist Board. (2002). *Growth in tourism confirmed*. Retrieved August 7, from the Fife Exchange, official tourism trade website.

Franks, J., Lowe, P., Phillipson, J., & Scott, C. (2003). The impact of foot and mouth disease on farm business in Cumbria. *Land Use Policy, 20*, 159-168.

Guy, A. (2003 July/August) Investing in Britain. *Leisure Opportunities*, p. 9.

Hall, M., Sharples, L., Mitchell, R., Macionis, N., & Cambourne, B. (Eds). (2003). *Food tourism around the world: Development, management and markets*. Oxford: Butterworth-Heinemann.

Hannah, V. (2001, April 3). Crisis to cost tourism industry £400m. *The Herald*, p. 3.

Hinchliffe, S., & Blowers, A. (2003). Environmental responses: Radioactive risks and uncertainty. In S. Blowers & S. Hinchliffe (Eds.), *Environmental responses* (pp. 7-49). Milton Keynes: Wiley.

Hjalager, A.M., & Richards, G. (Eds.). (2002). *Tourism and gastronomy*. London: Routledge.

Hudman, L.E. (1986). The travelers perception of the role of food and eating in the tourist industry. In *The impact of catering and cuisine upon tourism*. Proceedings of the 36th AIEST Congress, August/September, Montreux, AIEST.

Hughes, G. (1995). Food, tourism and Scottish heritage. In D. Leslie (Ed.), *Tourism and leisure: Towards the millennium. Volume 1: Tourism and leisure: Culture, heritage and participation* (pp. 109-120). Eastbourne: Leisure Studies Association.

Hunt, J. (2001). How do people enjoy their natural heritage? Patterns, trends and predictions of recreation in the Scottish countryside. In M.B. Usher (Ed.), *Enjoyment and understanding of the natural heritage* (pp. 17-25). Edinburgh: The Stationery Office.

Leslie, D. (2001). *An environmental audit of the tourism industry in the Lake District National Park*. Murley Moss, Kendal: Friends of the Earth.

McConnell, A. (2003). Overview: Crisis management, influences, responses and evaluation. Parliamentary affairs. *Hansard Society for Parliamentary Government, 56*, 393-409.

McConnell, A., & Stark, A. (2002). Foot and mouth 2001. The politics of crisis management. *Parliamentary Affairs, 55*, 664-681.

McDonald, S., Roberts, D., & Kay, A. (2003). *The economy-wide impacts of the foot and mouth disease outbreak in Scotland: A computable general equilibrium analysis*. Scottish Economic Policy Network, Universities of Stirling and Strathclyde.

McLaurin, T.L. (2001). Food safety in travel and tourism. *Journal of Travel Research, 39*(3), 332-333.

Middleton, V.T.C. (2002). *Measuring the local impact of tourism: A review for the British Resorts Association and Local Government Association*. Report prepared for British Resorts Association and Local Government Association and the National Tourism Best Value Management Group. London: BRA.

Moffat Centre for Travel and Tourism. (2001). *2001 Scottish visitor attraction barometer–July 2001 report*. Edinburgh: VisitScotland.

Morris, H. (2002). Rural tourism: Post FMD, will they come flooding back? *Insights*, January, D21-D26. London: English Tourism Council.

Muckspreader. (2001, November). *Not the Foot and Mouth report: A special investigation*. London: Private Eye.

NCSR. (1999). *Leisure days visits: Report of the 1998 UK day visits survey*. London: National Centre for Social Research.

Phillipson, J., Bennett, K., Lowe, P., & Raley, M. (2003). Adaptive responses and asset strategies: The experience of rural micro-firms and Foot and Mouth Disease. *Journal of Rural Studies, 20*(2), 227-243.

Quan, S., & Wang, N. (2004). Towards a structural model of the tourist experience: An illustration from food experiences in tourism. *Tourism Management, 25,* 297-305.

Royal Society of Edinburgh. (2002). *Inquiry into Foot and Mouth Disease in Scotland.* Edinburgh: The Royal Society of Edinburgh.

Scottish Parliament. (2002a). *Rural Tourism. SPICe Briefing 02/92.* Edinburgh: The Information Centre, Scottish Parliament.

Scottish Parliament. (2002b). *The Economics of Tourism. SPICe Briefing 02/97.* Edinburgh: The Information Centre, Scottish Parliament.

SE. (2002). *Response to lessons to be learned; Royal Society; and Royal Society of Edinburgh inquiries into Foot and Mouth Disease.* Edinburgh: Scottish Executive, Scottish Parliament.

Sloyan, P. (2002). Tourism from the flames. *Leisure Manager, August,* 12-13.

SNH. (2001). *SNH calls for 'keep out' clear-up.* Edinburgh: Scottish Natural Heritage, Secretariat.

Sportscotland, VisitScotland & SNH. (2001). *The experience for outdoor recreation of Foot and Mouth Disease (FMD)–Lessons, legacy and legislation.* Report from the Foot and Mouth Conference held September 11, Edinburgh.

Turner, D. (2001, April 11). Scotland worst hit as tourists look to London. *Financial Times,* p. 7.

VisitScotland. (2002). *Tourism in Scotland–2000.* Edinburgh: Author.

Warren, C. (2002). *Managing Scotland's environment.* Edinburgh: Edinburgh University Press.

Wilson, S., Fesenmaier, D.R.J., & van Es, J.C. (2001). Factors for success in rural tourism development. *Journal of Travel Research, 40,* 123-138.

The Impacts of Foot and Mouth Disease on a Peripheral Tourism Area: The Role and Effect of Crisis Management

Wilson Irvine
Alistair R. Anderson

SUMMARY. This study reports on the consequences of endemic cattle and sheep disease (2001) on two separate areas on the tourist industry; (a) the Grampian Region of Scotland (indirectly affected) and (b) Cumbria in England (directly affected), and secondly on the effects of various crisis management strategies to alleviate the ensuing problems in both areas. Data were collected by a survey of a sample of 200 tourism orientated SME operators in Grampian and 170 businesses in Cumbria.

The results show two forms of impact caused by the disease, direct and those less obvious or tangible. Direct impact was the dramatic loss of trade, most dramatically experienced by the lack of tourists visiting the areas. Indirect effects included loss of supply, change to the product offered and cuts in future investment. In the combination of these impacts, it was clear that the effects would have longevity far beyond the period of the actual crisis. Although the actual presence of the disease was geographically limited in Grampian, the consequences rippled out to affect areas that had no direct connection. In Cumbria, the effects were only slightly more severe but the response more direct and initially effective. Significantly the data also demonstrated a perception of minimal effort by the government to limit the consequences to the farming industry especially in Grampian. We conclude that the tourist industry in peripheral regions is fragile and highly vulnerable to any external shocks. However, we also note the ability of small rural firms to respond to such catastrophes and to avert the worst impacts of crisis. *[Article copies available for a fee from The Haworth Document Delivery Service: 1-800-HAWORTH. E-mail address: <docdelivery@haworthpress.com> Website: <http://www.HaworthPress.com> © 2005 by The Haworth Press, Inc. All rights reserved.]*

KEYWORDS. Foot and Mouth disease, small to medium enterprises, peripheral areas, crisis

INTRODUCTION

This paper examines the impact of the outbreak of Foot and Mouth disease in sheep and cattle on peripheral British tourism areas. The study considers two tourism areas, Grampian in the north of Scotland and Cumbria in the north of England. Whilst both can be conventionally described as peripheral, the Cumbria area was directly affected in the outbreak, with

Wilson Irvine, Senior Lecturer, (E-mail: w.irvine@rgu.ac.uk) and Alistair R. Anderson are affiliated with the Aberdeen Business School, The Robert Gordon University, Garthdee Road, Aberdeen, U.K. AB10 9NU.

[Haworth co-indexing entry note]: "The Impacts of Foot and Mouth Disease on a Peripheral Tourism Area: The Role and Effect of Crisis Management." Irvine, Wilson, and Alistair R. Anderson. Co-published simultaneously in *Journal of Travel & Tourism Marketing* (The Haworth Hospitality Press, an imprint of The Haworth Press, Inc.) Vol. 19, No. 2/3, 2005, pp. 47-60; and: *Tourism Crises: Management Responses and Theoretical Insight* (ed: Eric Laws, and Bruce Prideaux) The Haworth Hospitality Press, an imprint of The Haworth Press, Inc., 2005, pp. 47-60. Single or multiple copies of this article are available for a fee from The Haworth Document Delivery Service [1-800-HAWORTH, 9:00 a.m. - 5:00 p.m. (EST). E-mail address: docdelivery@haworthpress.com].

Available online at http://www.haworthpress.com/web/JTTM
© 2005 by The Haworth Press, Inc. All rights reserved.
doi:10.1300/J073v19n02_05

a high number of reported or suspected cases of the disease. In contrast, Grampian had no incidence of the disease, but was nonetheless sorely affected by the adverse publicity. Our study suggests that we can make some general and some specific conclusions about this crisis. We find, for example, that tourism businesses in peripheral areas are particularly vulnerable to crisis. We note how government communication, directed to stopping the outbreak, resulted in a very high profile media presentation which, in possibly exaggerating the effect, actually amplified the impact. In specific terms, we note how some small businesses reacted quickly to the disaster by taking action to minimise the effects of the dramatic loss of business. In particular we observe how the presence of a "plan" seemed to avert the worst effects of catastrophe.

The first section briefly explores the nature of crisis to argue that disasters on the scale of the foot and mouth outbreak will inevitably become a crisis for tourist firms. We explain this point by demonstrating that the demand for tourism is uniquely sensitive to the hedonistic and eudemonistic perceptions of pleasure seeking or happiness generation. Because these aspects are highly subjective perceptions of tourist destinations, any negativity impacts disproportionately. Moreover, the attraction of peripheral places appears to depend upon images. These images, the manifestations of what Lash and Urry (1994) call the economies' Signs and Space seem to create the very attraction of tourist destinations. However, in the case of foot and mouth disease, the dramatic media images amplified the negativity. This section completes our theoretical overview and is followed by a brief account of the foot and mouth epidemic. We then present our survey data, which consists of three surveys. Two surveys took place in Grampian; survey A was conducted at the height of the disaster and reports on the anticipated crisis, whilst survey B reports on the actual effects taking account of the management of the crisis. The third survey was conducted in Cumbria and reports on the impact on business. We discuss the data in the light of perceptions and actions. The contribution of the paper is first to address the need identified by Okumus, Alintay and Arasli (2005) on the limitations of the existing literature on the impact of crisis on a tourist destination. More abstractly, we hope to contribute to a fuller understanding of the links between communication and crisis and to the role of planning in avoiding the worst impacts for rural small firms.

THE NATURE OF CRISIS AND DISASTER

Faulkner (2001) comments that the casual observer, exposed to the plethora of media that informs us, may believe that we live in an increasingly disaster prone world. Gonzalez-Herrero and Pratt (1998, p. 85) note how the business environment is becoming more complex and unstable, hence signalling "an era of crises," whilst Richardson (1994) suggest that the world is more turbulent and crisis prone. Many attribute the apparent increase in disaster to the increasing complexity of the modern world, as for example, in Ulrich Beck's idea of Risk Society (1992). Others propose that the incidence of disaster may not be increasing in absolute terms, but merely that our heightened awareness of and on the global scale, the space-time compression, of Harvey (1989) simply make it appear so. Whichever may be the case, the role of media in transmitting signals, messages in McLuhan's (1967) sense, seems to play a pivotal role in our perception of disaster. Baudrillard (1998) suggests that the raw event (of disaster, in this case) becomes consumable when filtered, fragmented and reworked by the mass media into a finished product. This causes it to be conjured up, as Baudrillard describes it (1998, p. 330), and captured for consumption. Disaster makes news. However, as Ritchie (2004) comments, tourism, although increasingly economically important, is highly susceptible to external factors.

Most poignant of disaster is the "natural" disaster, the earthquake, the flood or famine. Somehow man's puny efforts in the grim face of mother nature remind us of our limitations. But increasingly we have come to interpret, even understand, disaster as rather more than natural, and understand that it is the interface of man and nature which creates disaster. The impact of floods in Bangladesh are magnified by the limited resources available to mitigate. Nature is more contained in wealthy societies. Perhaps never entirely tamed, but sufficiently domesticated so that "natural" disaster only rarely manifests itself as widespread crisis to the extent of Selbst's (1978, cited in Faulkner, 2001) definition of crisis, "Any action or failure to act that interferes with (an organisation's) on-going functions, the acceptable attainment of its objectives, its viability or survival, or that has a detrimental personal effect as perceived by the majority." Yet this interface of man and nature helped to provide some understanding of the distinctions of and between disaster and crisis. Faulkner (2001) explains how Selbst's definition attributes crisis to the organisation, whilst disaster is used to refer to situations where the enterprise, or collection of enterprises in the case of tourist destinations, is confronted with sudden and unpredictable catastrophic changes over which it has no control. Stafford, Yu and Armoo (2002) focus on the nature of business crisis. Such crises are defined by Lerbinger (1997) as an event that is severely detrimental to profitability or even survival. Stafford et al. (2002) note that all such crisis share three common characteristics; suddenness, uncertainty and time compression. So a disaster becomes a crisis when the organisation(s) believe they cannot cope. Similarly, Kash and Darling (1988) define crisis as an event which threatens customers or employees and endangers financial status and future viability, Indeed, Carter (1991, p. 23) defines disaster as an event, natural or man-made, sudden or progressive, which impacts with such severity that the affected community has to respond by taking exceptional measures. Interestingly, Ritchie (2004), discussing Selbst's focus on perceptions of crisis, argues that if a "crisis" is perceived by stakeholders, a real crisis may emerge. Thus he highlights the role of perception management. Similarly, marketing and communications are crucial in what Gonzalez-Herrero and Pratt (1998) define as business crisis. This distinction, or continuum between crisis and disaster, as Faulkner suggests, is useful because it highlights the human role, the agency, in mitigating, or not, the impact of disaster. Thus, as Fink (1986) argues, if crisis planning and ac-

tivities are effective the impact of the crisis can be limited.

The very notion of crisis, however, is not quite as cut and dried as the above suggests. Fink (1986), for example, notes how, in business, managers are either in crisis, or in a state of pre-crisis. Others (including Okumus et al., 2005; Mitroff & Anagnos, 2002) emphasise the stages of crisis. These are broadly speaking, prodromal, acute, chronic and crisis resolution. Our primary interest lies at the first stage, the prodromal, which Fink (1986) describes as the stage when it becomes evident that the crisis is inevitable. It is at this stage that agency is most likely to be most influential in shaping the outcomes of the crisis. Thus this interplay between disaster, action and crisis forms the basis of our research question. Drawing on the literature described above we propose that disaster and crisis and its impact can be modelled as a linear progression with two possible outcomes of catastrophe or control of the effects. Seen this way the role of agency in crisis, in terms of preparedness and appropriate responses to disaster, determines the impact of the disaster.

Catastrophe

Disaster > Crisis >   < Agency

Controlled Effects

Thus our questions surrounding the foot and mouth outbreak centre on what and how agencies, in the form of the small business owners, professional bodies and state and local authorities, responded to the disaster. As Bennett, Phillipson, Lowe and Ward (2002b) argued, because of their resilience and flexibility, small businesses should be encouraged and supported in the business environment. However, to complete our theoretical framework to approach this question we require to have an appreciation of the forces of attraction or repulsion applied to tourist destination.

THE BRITTLENESS OF TOURIST PERIPHERAL DESTINATION IMAGE

Brown and Hall (1999) describe a peripheral area as one which suffers geographic isolation, distant from core spheres of activity, poor access to and from markets. Such areas, they claim, are characterised as economically marginalised with much of the business activity confined to micro-business. Peripherality has been viewed as the biggest problems for tourism, being held responsible for the increasing amount of difficulties being experienced within the industry (Baum, 1996) and is most often viewed as the most consistent policy issue within cold-climate areas. A peripheral area is seen as an area of remote geographical isolation that is far away from central areas of activity, with poor infrastructure meaning access is difficult (Brown & Hall, 2000). But as Wanhill (1997) notes, the European Union's Maastricht Treaty acknowledged that tourism could reduce regional disparities. Taken together we see the importance of tourism for the peripheral place, highly dependent on the "difference" of image from the core, but equally we see how it appears to depend on a positive image. Tourism image is defined by many authors as an individual's overall perception or total set of impressions about a place (Fakeye & Crompton, 1991; Hunt, 1998; Phelps, 1999), or as the mental portrayal of a destination (Alhemoud & Armstrong, 1996; Crompton, 1979a, 1979b). Such images are the manifestations of the social construction of a place. In other words, as Carter (1998) puts it, the symbolic contributes to the sense of place. The image of a destination consists, therefore, of the subjective interpretation of reality made by the tourist. There is now considerable evidence (Crompton & Ankomah, 1993; Gartner, 2000; Kent, 1996) of the influence of tourism image on the choice of holiday destination. Places with stronger positive images will have a higher probability of being included and chosen in the process of decision making. Gonzalez-Herrero and Pratt (1998) even suggest that people must be informed about a travel destination, and be interested in going there, before a tourist market can be created. Schutz (1972) talks about the stocks of knowledge of a phenomenon acquired inter-subjectively by individuals; formed through organic representations produced by media, education, government and other institutions. Tiefenbacher, Day and Walton (2000) argue that such perceptions are generated by advertisement, movies and word of mouth. Places

are transformed into a tourist site through the system of symbolic and structural processes. As Harvey (1989, p. 293) put it so well, "Mass television ownership coupled with satellite communication make it possible to experience a rush of images almost simultaneously, collapsing the world's spaces into a series of images on a television screen . . . mass tourism."

Rurality, and its attraction as a destination, is also a matter of perception. Brown and Hall (1999) identified that a place that is remote and difficult to reach may be perceived by tourists to have certain qualities symptomatic of its situation, such as natural beauty, quaintness and otherness. Such places are seen as authentics (Urry, 1990), rich in symbolic representations of the unspoilt, the pristine and the traditional. Urry (1995) also makes a powerful case to show that it is this otherness which creates attraction. Thus, as Blomgren and Sorensen (1998) propose, the attractiveness of rurality relies on the subjective interpretation of such symbols. Anderson (2000) argues that peripheral spaces have moved from outlying production zones to become areas which are consumed in their own right. He argues that it is their very "otherness," non-industrial, distance and an absence of core activities, which creates value in the consumer's eye. One problem with image and motivation to visit is the fragility of symbolic otherness. Pearce (1982) considers appropriate images as transitory, but ones insulated from danger. Meethan (2001) talks of trust in a destination; trust in it measuring up to its image. He makes the salient point that the elimination of risk and issues of safety appear as prime factors in choice of destination. Cavlek (2002) points out that peace, safety and security are the primary conditions for the tourism development of a destination. He also notes (2002, p. 479) how "nothing can force them to spend a holiday in a place they perceive as insecure." Indeed, Sonmez and Graefe (1998, p. 120) argue that if the destination choice is narrowed down to two alternatives which promise similar benefits, the "one that is safe from threat–is likely to be chosen." Pearce (1988) suggests that concern with personal security is a major factor in the decision-making process through which individuals make their travel choices. Drabek (2000) notes how the effects of crisis ripples out to areas where no such problem exists (Cavlek, 2002). Cavlek (2002) suggests that government warnings to potential tourists always have strong psychological effects, thus creating a major impediment to selling holidays, even to parts of the country still entirely safe. After the Foot and Mouth epidemic started the media contributed to the overall gloom with reports and graphical representations of burning pyres and closures; "national and international images of foot and mouth crisis did most to deter tourists" (Ireland & Vetier, 2002, p. 16). Many Americans were convinced that foot and mouth was contagious BSE, the degenerative human disease (Hotel News, 2002). Moreover, the portrayal of the Prime Minister in a yellow boiler suit apparently fighting the disaster was not helpful, "the images ensured that FMD was rarely absent from the public gaze" (Scott, Christie & Midmore, 2004, p. 3).

Yet crises have become integral to business activity, but tourism, in particular, suffers more than any other. Faulkner and Vikulov (2001) propose that all destinations face the prospect of either a natural or a human-induced disaster. In particular, Cavlek (2002) suggests that government warnings to potential tourists always have strong psychological effects, thus creating a major impediment to selling holidays, even to parts of the country still entirely safe. Arguing that the market for tourism is fragile, Gonzalez-Herrero and Pratt (1998) see tourist travel as a dispensable luxury. Blake and Sinclair (2003) similarly argue that tourism demand is particularly sensitive to security and health concerns. Thus the marketing of tourism products and services depends largely on the degree of perceived risk that potential tourists are willing to bear. Tourism demand presents a higher elasticity index per level of perceived risk than any other industry because of the benefits consumers ascribe to its products. Thus far we have explored the importance of image in motivating tourism. We have demonstrated that the "otherness" of rurality is a key mechanism for attracting tourists. This otherness, we have argued, is an incomplete social construction, driven by globalisation but dependent upon a positive impression of local place. We have also noted how perceptions of risk, real or imagined, like the images themselves, can act to reverse the attraction and

turn it into a repelling force. Moreover, as Cole (1995) points out, disasters have their most severe impacts on isolated localities and small or marginal communities.

RURAL SMALL BUSINESS PLANNING

In peripheral rural areas, small business is the norm. Indeed, the important business sectors consist of small organisations. In tourism, more than three quarters of Britain's tourism organisations have a turnover of less than £250,000 a year (Frisby, 2002). Of these businesses, approximately half are situated in remote locations. North and Smallbone (1996) note how the relentless decline of rural traditional industries has created a need for the new jobs arising from new and existing small firms in the service sectors, such as tourism, as well as in manufacturing. Morrison (1998, p. 192) points out that in the tourist accommodation sector, owner operators account for some 85% of establishments but she also notes the typical weakness of such small firms. When combined with the characteristics of peripheral destinations, such as seasonality, low occupancy rates, "the challenges to successful business development are accentuated." Nonetheless, tourism, especially small firm tourism, remains central to rural development (Briedenhann & Wickens, 2003)

Small businesses in rural places are part of the community (Spillan & Hough, 2003) and "often strive to put something back into this community" (Barringer & Greening, 1999, p. 12). Although crucial to the rural community, small businesses are much more fragile than large businesses. They may lack expertise and management skills and require more extensive advice because of the very nature of their smallness. Because of their heterogeneous nature they require a large amount of different types of support agencies. The main business support is provided by Phillipson, Bennett, Lowe and Raley (2002): public agencies 53%, and collective agencies (includes trade and professional organisations) 34%. Interestingly, Bennett et al. (2002b) note that only 24% of non-farm businesses generally require any information on planning support. Support and advice are normally available to large organisations in the shape of a board of directors, experienced managers and a hierarchy. Outside day-to-day management, rural small firms may lack the knowledge to deal with change. Many small businesses do not have the time or resources to implement plans and follow and live very much hand to mouth; "too much month left at the end of the money" (Brown & Hall, 2000, p. 26). The viability of small businesses may depend on their ability to identify and respond to trends and opportunities (North & Smallbone, 1996: Smallbone, North & Kalantaridis, 1999) presented and threatened by their external environment, yet smaller firms have little ability to shape their macro-environment (Smallbone et al., 1999). Moreover, in times of crisis, there may be a lack of some sort of planning or "due process" to cope with a turbulent environment where crisis and disaster lurk around every corner. Vaessen and Keeble (1995) argue that many owner managers have to develop strategies to overcome the constraints presented by the environment. "Successful firms may be those that recognise potential threats and through adjustment convert them into opportunities" (North & Smallbone, 1996, p. 157). Owner managers in small resilient enterprises will show characteristics of cost minimisation, adaptability and resilience through reduced management and personnel. Indeed the small micro business "often forms part of a composite pluriactive household" (Phillipson et al., 2002, p. 67) that gives it a certain resilience through a recourse to multiple incomes.

Rural small businesses require flexibility, self sufficiency and less reliance on outside contractors (North & Smallbone, 1996). They cannot externalise their various functions due to their size and remoteness. Planning and strategy are often more implicit than explicit, so that leadership and management skills become extra important. Although the benefits of planning in small firms is contentious (Anderson & Atkins, 2002), Barringer and Greening (1999) identified that successful firms engaged in formal planning and that those that failed, did not. Significantly, they also recognised that successful firms also required outside sources of assistance to help facilitate the planning process. A number of studies have established a relationship between planning and small firm performance. Schwenk and Schrader (1993), Boag and Rinholm (1989), and Roure and Maidique (1988) found that planning is an important factor in small business performance. Duchesneau and Gartner (1990) identified effective small business firms as those that planned, were flexible, participative and adaptive. Barringer and Greening (1999) found that flexibility was found to have a positive influence on managing growth and performance relationship, whereas environmental turbulence was found to have a negative effect on small businesses achievement.

Crisis management receives little attention in the small business and a crisis event may have to occur before crisis planning becomes a real concern (Spillan & Hough, 2003). The liability of newness and the fragility of smallness are at their greatest in times of crisis and disaster. Yet, crisis, broadly defined, is highly probable, so that all small businesses will eventually be confronted with some type of crisis or disaster. The relevant question seems to be not whether a crisis/disaster will occur, but what kind and when (Copanigro, 2000; Kruse, 1993). The ability of the business to manage the crisis successfully can mean the difference between survival and disaster and even life and death (Fink, 1986; Offer, 1998). The case for having a disaster plan is strong; 50% of all businesses who do not have one, either explicit or implicit, do not survive and 90% will fail within two years of the disaster (Pedone, 1997, in Spillan & Hough, 2003).

TOURISM IN PERIPHERAL AREAS AND FOOT AND MOUTH: THE EFFECTS

Tourism in Peripheral Grampian

We studied two peripheral areas, Grampian and Cumbria. Cumbria was affected directly with a large number of affected cases but Grampian only indirectly, as it did not have one case during the outbreak and was more than 150 miles from the nearest case in the southwest of Scotland. Grampian is an integral part of the Scottish tourism industry. Tourism is Scotland's most important industry, injecting £2.5 billion into the economy annually (Scotexchange, 2003). It is the fourth biggest employer, employing 193,000, some 8% of the workforce. In 1995 the UK ranked fourth in the top 10 tourist destinations in Europe, with 23.7 million arrivals (De Vaal, 1997). The year 2002, did however, experience increased visits to Scotland by UK residents, with visits being up by 10% on 2001 (McKay, 2003). Grampian is the northeast shoulder of Scotland with a tourist product primarily focused on scenery and castles. Heritage and history play a major part in tourist attraction; seeing historic houses and castles is important for 8 out of 10 visitors. Grampian's attractions currently range from outdoor activities, natural and built heritage to adventure and theme parks (www. ElectricScotland.com, 2002). It is an area with a mainly peripheral structure with poor roads and a large rural community not dissimilar to Cumbria.

Tourism in Peripheral Cumbria

Cumbria is devoted to tourism and includes the Lake District National Park and the Hadrian's Wall World Heritage Site and has recently been awarded, after a rigorous assessment, Green Globe Destination Status (Cumbrian Tourist Board, 2003). It is a relatively remote area composed of sparsely populated rural sectors with some minor concentrations of populations and many small businesses. The Lake District itself offers a wonderful rural experience with a plethora of cultural events, museums and galleries. It is dominated by small owner managed businesses and the wealth is retained in the local economy and thus supports other industries. However, it has been directly affected by Foot and Mouth and other threats since before 2001 and there was a marked decrease in visitor numbers.

Foot and Mouth Disease in Peripheral Areas

Foot and Mouth disease is one of the most contagious animal diseases; although most affected adult animals will recover within two weeks, the drop in yields could have enormous economic impact. It has few effects on humans. Nonetheless, the UK government policy of slaughtering affected or at risk herds had an enormous impact on Britain's countryside. The first cases of Foot and Mouth disease (since 1967) were confirmed on the 10th of February 2001. Within 2 weeks the disease had spread to a large number of cases. After peaking in April/May numbers tailed off to October 2001. As Anderson (2002) noted, a total of 2,026 cases of the disease were identified but a total of over 4 million animals were culled during the crisis. Media attention during the crisis focussed dramatically on the agricultural community, showing the destruction of livestock and the closure of farms across the county, but the impact was experienced by the tourist industry. Some support was provided in both areas both by the Scottish Executive, Government and other Agencies, but the usefulness (Bennett et al., 2002b) and the limited uptake through the myriad of requirements to qualify (BBC News, 2001) has been seriously questioned.

FOOT AND MOUTH IN GRAMPIAN AND CUMBRIA

Grampian had no recorded incidents of the disease. According to MAFF (2001), only one sheep has been slaughtered in Aberdeenshire because of "dangerous contacts." Aid was offered to organisations in a number of Scottish regions apart from those directly affected including Aberdeenshire. There was a broadbrush approach to closing footpaths in the region. Inbound tourist statistics show that only 1.9 million of United Kingdom visitors came to Scotland in 1998 (Scotexchange, 1999), with that figure dropping to 1.5 million in 2001 (Star UK, 2003). This decrease is blamed on the effects of the September 11th terrorist attack and Foot and Mouth disease. It also contains some unique tourist attractions and wonderful scenic beauty comparable to the northwest of England. However, Aberdeen and Grampian visitor numbers fell by 13.1% from 140,743 in 2001 to 122,255 during the same period in 2002 (Scotexchange, 2003). This drop was confirmed by the local tourist board; at −12.8%, it was the second lowest level in the country. Most of these effects may be directly attributed to the effects of Foot and Mouth.

Cumbria was directly affected by Foot and Mouth as 44% of all confirmed cases happened in this county (Ward, Donaldson & Lowe, 2002). Cumbria's main industries are agriculture and tourism, and tourism was affected just as badly as agriculture. As Ireland and Vetier (2002, p. 6) put it: "it is . . . evident that demand failure among tourists has a severe impact on the British tourism industry." The BBC News website (April 2001) dramatically described the devastation and fear of the unknown future for the farmers of Cumbria saying; "Cumbria is holding its breath, not just in dread of future outbreaks, but also because of the smell of the burial sites." Television dramatised the extreme actions taken by the government and the effect on peoples' lives. Television coverage of the Foot and Mouth epidemic detailed every case and scare within Cumbria. This television coverage scared many potential tourists away from the countryside; many areas that had no contact with the outbreak suffered because of the media messages given. Ireland and Vetier (2002, p. 1) argued that: "Exaggerated media reporting of a crisis can be as damaging as inept Government policy." Many of the tourism businesses within Cumbria closed because of the dramatic reduction of visitors within the area. Although there were considerable efforts to try and rebuild the businesses by extra advertising and property upgrading, tourist numbers are still poor.

Table 1 shows the drop in numbers experienced by tourism businesses due to the Foot and Mouth epidemic. The trips refer to the summer months of June to September 2000-2002. The table demonstrates that, of the four representative locations, Cumbria was the worst affected with the largest drop in visitor numbers.

Phillipson et al. (2002) identified that the disease control strategy and discouragement of countryside visits triggered a major shock within the wider rural economy. However, only 20 cases of business failure in the northeast of England could be directly attributed to F&M. Phillipson et al. (2002) also argue that the impacts were absorbed by rural firms and households. Foot and Mouth caused a decrease in tourists so great, that all tourism businesses within the area were affected. A large number of the Cumbria attractions were shut down for

TABLE 1. Tourism Trips in England

Summer trips	All tourism trips 2000	All tourism trips 2001	All tourism trips 2002
	Million	Million	Million
England	64.9	55.5	63.0
Cumbria	2.3	1.8	1.8
Yorkshire	6.0	4.4	5.8
London	9.1	7.7	8.0

(Adapted from Star UK, 2003)

at least three months. Many of these never re-opened. As well as the closure of businesses, the loss in tourism numbers reduced turnover within the area; many people lost their jobs because businesses couldn't afford to support themselves, let alone pay wages, nearly all business investment stopped. The effects were also felt for more than a season by the majority of the tourism businesses (Ward et al., 2002).

Table 2 shows the drop in employment numbers in Cumbria between 2000-2001. The businesses include hotels, restaurants, tour operators and cultural activities, all of which rely greatly on tourism within small rural areas. Job losses of more than 25% were experienced. Lee and Harrald (1999) identified that incidents can also disrupt the supply and distribution chain for service.

Tourism businesses in Cumbria were offered direct support from the Government through government aid schemes but often felt caught up "in a confusing myriad of help lines" (Bennett et al., 2002a, p. 6). Scott et al. (2004) pointed out how the Countryside Agency reported on the imbalance between compensation paid to farmers for culled livestock and the much smaller sums devoted to the mitigation of the far more serious impact on the non-farm rural economy.

From the above it is clear that Foot and Mouth had a major impact on rural tourist industry. However, it is not yet clear what role planning had, if any, in ameliorating these impacts. Our research questions therefore focus on this aspect.

METHODOLOGY

Our sample frames were drawn from tourist businesses in Grampian and Cumbria. The Grampian sample of 180 businesses was drawn

TABLE 2. Employment in Cumbria

	2000 Jobs	2001 Jobs
Tour operator	655	549
Hotel	9,633	6,843
Restaurant	5,816	4,409
Cultural activity	850	720

(Adapted from Star UK, 2003).

from a sample frame provided by Dunn and Bradstreet. The Cumbrian sample, 170 businesses, was selected by choosing one in five from a list taken from the official Cumbria Tourist Board Guide (2002). The Grampian sample, the main locus of our study, was surveyed twice. The first survey, Survey A, was carried out in April 2001 at the height of the outbreak and had 85 responses (47%). The second survey, Survey B was carried out in March 2003 and had 60 responses; (33%) 18 others were returned uncompleted. The Grampian surveys were intended to provide data to allow us to compare the anticipated with the real effects. The Cumbrian survey, Survey C was carried out in February 2003 and contained a number of identical or similar questions to the Grampian survey. We had a response of 70, giving a 39% response rate. In the surveys many of the questions were open ended to allow respondents to enlarge on the data.

DATA AND DISCUSSION

The data were analysed using descriptive statistics to analyse single variables and simple non-parametric tests were used to compare variables and significance of normally distributed results. The tests included frequency analysis and cross tabs analysis. The cross tabs analysis (Pearson chi-square test) was used to check significance within the normally distributed results. Significance was tested at a 90% confidence level. (The majority of tests proved significant and are all represented.) All of the tests were carried out after the variables were coded onto SPSS (Statistical Package for Social Sciences). A large number of the variables had open-ended responses, which were grouped using a Pragmatic Content Analysis in order to collate the similar responses and include them

as part of the descriptive analysis. A number of tables were constructed at appropriate stages to describe the results. Data has been presented on the effects on different businesses by size, different number of employees.

The characteristics of our samples are shown in Table 3. Small firms, reflecting the rural structure, were predominant. Interestingly, a greater percentage of larger businesses responded in the second survey in Grampian which may mean that more survived or had grown in the intervening period.

Survey A and B took place in Grampian at the height of the disease and could be expected to reflect the worst expectations of the impact. We also expected these prognoses to reflect the general gloom created by the vivid and dramatic media portrayal (Ireland & Vetier, 2002), which may suggest that even the tourism suppliers were overly influenced by the negative perspective. The results shown in Table 4 below confirm our expectations and show the extent of business reduction and other effects anticipated and experienced in Grampian and that experienced in Cumbria.

In Survey A the view was very pessimistic; more than half our Grampian respondents anticipated cancellations and large decreases in the business and profits. Some 25% expected to have to lose staff and a significant number anticipated closure of their business. Most expected the impact to last for some considerable time. Taken by size, the smaller micro businesses, representing 78% of the population, anticipated

TABLE 3. Characteristics of the Samples

Survey	Business Type by Size	N	% of Total	Professional Body Membership %	Customer Type: Tourist %
A, Grampian, Apr 01	Micro < 6	66	78	57	36
(total n = 180)	Larger > 5	19	22	67 (.066)	39 (.065)
B, Grampian Apr 03	Micro < 6	39	65	62	26
(Total n = 180)	Larger > 5	21	35	86 (.3)	50 (.042)
C, Cumbria Feb,03	Micro < 5	50	71	66	93
(total n =170)	Larger > 4	20	29	58 (.031)	75 (.1)

Notes:
Survey A, B and C Business Types are by size: number of F/T staff.
Figures in parentheses are the significance confidence levels.
Customer Types are Leisure Tourists; other types are Business Tourist.

TABLE 4. The General Effects of the Disease in Grampian: 2001, 2003 and Differences (All %)

Type (Size)	Cancella-tions An-ticipated > 10	Busi-ness De-crease	Re-duced Profit	Staff Cuts	Clo-sure	Extent of Im-pact > year	Supply Yes (Y)	Prod-uct (Y)
Survey A: Grampian 2001								
< 6	60 (12)	69 (14)	70	42	21	52	36	23
> 5	48 (.13)	50 (.003)	49 (.1)	11 (.01)	5 (.002)	38 (.14)	41 (.1)	14 (.003)
Survey B: Grampian 2003								
< 6	71 (10)	46 (10)	38	7	8	24	8	18
> 5	60 (.1)	43 (.3)	42 (.1)	19 (.2)	0 (.2)	24 (.07)	9 (.06)	9 (.1)
Difference between the two Surveys								
< 6	+ 11	23	32	35	13	28	28	5
> 5	+ 12	07	07	+08	05	14	32	5

Notes: All %
Cancellations are those:
- Anticipated over the immediate tourism season, Survey A and actually experienced, Survey B.
- Supply (Y) indicates that the business supply was affected.
- Product (Y) indicates that the product to customers was affected.
- Figures in Brackets are the significance confidence levels.

Figures in brackets for cancellations and business decrease are for the smaller businesses.

suffering more in all areas apart from supply, where they may have had more flexibility.

Survey B measured the real impact in Grampian and shows that, whilst the impact was greater on the micro businesses, the picture was not as clear as in Survey A. It is worth noting that 10% of our original sample had gone away. This could be partially attributed to the impact or simply business churn. Overall cancellations at 64% of bookings reflect a major loss of business. Nonetheless, we note that actual business volume decrease was "only" 44%, suggesting that some replacement visitors were found. This view corresponds to the study by Phillipson et al. (2002). Taken by size, the results demonstrate that the major impacts of decrease in cancellations, business volume and effect on product offered were clearly worse for the smaller businesses with some 8% experiencing closure. The other effects were only marginally different with 24% of both types experiencing effects for more than one year. The results shown in Survey B are not as bad as were anticipated in Survey A and reflect an overly pessimistic anticipation of effects in 2001.

THE CUMBRIA SURVEY

The Cumbrian survey (Table 5) is a snapshot of data collected two years after the epidemic. The data show a dramatic reduction in visitor numbers with a 96% and 93% in each size category indicating a decrease in visitor numbers. Some 98% and 88% respectively experienced a "loss of business" of more than 25%. When asked about specific percentages of "loss of business," about 20% in both sizes of business identified an actual loss of business of "more than 50%." Staff cuts were highest in the larger types of business. A very large percentage in both types experienced the effects for more than a year, whilst a large number, especially in the larger businesses were still experiencing the effects at the present time (Ward et al., 2002). A greater number of small businesses owners suffered from depression during the outbreak; this may be because of the responsibility carried. Interestingly, nearly all the businesses situated in Cumbria, on reflection, considered that the F&M epidemic had the worst effect on their organisation when compared to BSE and 9/11.

Table 6a, b and c shows how the businesses were prepared and acted to mitigate against the effects by size in the three surveys. In Survey A, Table 6a, a greater number of the larger businesses had a plan but very few considered it to be effective, with none considering the Government supported them; this may be because the majority were located in the core city where there was no support and limited effects. The smaller businesses in Survey A had less plans but more that considered them to be effective, and a greater percent considered that

TABLE 5. The General Effects of the Disease in Cumbria 2003 (All%)

Type (Size)	Visitor Number Decrease	Loss of Busi-ness (> 25%)	Staff Cuts	Extent of Impact > year	Extent of im-pact (still feeling)	De-pres-sion	Worst Effect: F&M
Survey C: Cumbria 2003							
< 5	96	98	20	46	28	14	94
> 4	93 (.09)	88 (.1)	40 (.2)	53 (.2)	40 (.4)	0 (.21)	100 (.6)

Notes: All %
The F and M Epidemic was compared to the Effects of BSE and 9/11.

TABLE 6a. Responses, Survey A

Size Employees'	Contingency Plan	Effective	Government Supported	Membership
< 6	25	18	25	57
> 5	52 (.1)	07 (.12)	0 (.02)	66 (.03)

TABLE 6b. Responses, Survey B

Size Employees'	Contingency Plan	Effective	Government Supported	Membership	Alter/ Changes
< 6	17	13	21	58	26
> 5	10 (.1)	0 (.23)	19 (.1)	86 (.12)	18 (.07)

TABLE 6c. Responses, Survey C (All in %)

Size Employees	Personal Plan	How plan Effective	Government Suppor/ effective	Membership	Accept Help	Help effective
0-4	58	60	88/15	66	72	70
> 4	34 (.2)	24 (.1)	100/0 (.2) (.4)	44 (.1)	75 (.12)	45 (.003)

Notes: All %
Government Support is % felt supported.
Effective is % felt effective.

the Government supported them as they may all have been located in urban areas, however a large number of all businesses had potential support from membership.

In Table 6b, the later Grampian Survey B, a greater number of smaller businesses had plans and considered them to be effective. Government support was given to a similar number of businesses and the smaller businesses had a substantial but less potential for support than larger businesses. They (the smaller businesses) did, however, make more changes and alterations to their processes than the larger businesses. This is reflected in the effects being similar and less severe in both types of business in Survey B. (See Table 4, Effects in Grampian, Survey B.) Also the results of Survey B were real and not anticipated.

In Table 6c (Cumbria), the smaller businesses were generally much better prepared with a personal plan that a much greater number considered effective than larger businesses, although the effects were similar in both sizes of business (see Table 5), although smaller businesses recovered more quickly. A large number in both types of business considered

that the Government offered support, although very few considered it to be effective.

Overall especially when the impacts were actually experienced as in Survey B, and direct and actually experienced as in Cumbria, smaller businesses seemed to have more effective internal support mechanisms, were more flexible and responded better to support when provided, resulting in a quicker recovery time.

CONCLUSIONS

From these data, we conclude that the effects of foot and mouth disease on peripheral tourism business was considerable, this confirmed the view of Phillipson et al. (2002). The Grampian longitudinal studies indicate that although bad, these effects were not quite as bad as anticipated. In both areas the impact was both immediate, manifest in dramatic drops in volume of business, profitability and reductions of staff numbers. It was also long term, a large number of businesses taking almost a year to recover. However, the most significant result in our data is the demonstration that firms who planned appeared to weather the crisis better.

In comparing the larger and smaller firms we note that small firms anticipated a much worse effect than actually experienced. Given that the larger firm group did experience worse effects, it seems reasonable to conclude that small firms, in the prodromal stage of crisis (Fink, 1986) were quickest to recognise the impending crisis and best at reacting. We can conclude that they responded more effectively. It is not clear exactly how planning operated. It may have been that the smaller scale of operations made planning easier, both to formulate and to implement. It may also have been that the inherent flexibility of smaller firms allowed them to change direction more rapidly. However, our data does support the argument that if the prodromal stage of crisis is attended it may not become catastrophe. From a theoretical perspective, we note the crucial role of communication. In this instance, the impact of the media presentations of Foot and Mouth exacerbated a bad situation into a national crisis. Globalisation through media exposure may have conspired to produce the foot and mouth crises for the tourism industry. The portrayal of "otherness" is symbolically dependent upon an arcadian image. The confrontation to this imagery with media pictures of smoking cattle funeral pyres resulted in repelling visitors to places where no such pyres existed (Scott et al., 2004). This seems to confirm that perceptions, rather than facts or real circumstances, create the disastrous effects of catastrophe. It is very difficult to image what sort of planning, at the macro level, could alleviate the impact of sensationalism.

In terms of the implication arising from our survey, there seems no doubt that there were real problems with planning and environmental shocks at national level as all the reports (Anderson, 2000; DEFRA, 2002; CIEH, 2002) articulated. However, although the effects were felt both directly and indirectly, peripheral businesses seemed to be prepared and coped effectively using their own or the support provided. However, the evidence suggests that organisations in peripheral areas seemed to cope better with plans and support in place. Turning to the practical aspects of the impact on small business, it is notable that the impact in Grampian was less severe than anticipated. This difference between potential havoc, anticipated effect and the real total effect can probably best be explained by the agility of small firms to cope with crisis. Supply and distribution channels were markedly affected in both small and larger businesses, especially the product in smaller organisations (Lee & Harrald, 1999), who generally required and had a more flexible approach.

REFERENCES

Alhemoud, A.M., & Armstrong, E.G. (1996). Image of tourism attractions in Kuwait. *Journal of Travel Research*, *34*(4), 76-80.

Anderson, A.R. (2000). Paradox in the periphery; and entrepreneurial reconstruction? *Entrepreneurship and Regional Development*, *12*, 91-109.

Anderson, A.R., & Atkins, M. (2002). Configuration and reconfiguration–Planning for uncertainty. *Journal of Entrepreneurship and Innovation Management*, *2*(4/5), 406-423.

Anderson, I. (2002). *Foot and mouth disease 2001: Lessons to be learned inquiry report, HC888*. London: The Stationery Office.

Barringer, B.R., & Greening, D.W. (1999). Small business growth through geographic expansion. *Journal of Business Venturing*, *13*(6), 467-492.

Baudrillard, J. (1998). *The consumer society*. London: Sage.

Baum, T. (1996). Images of tourism past and present. *International Journal of Contemporary Hospitality Management*, *8*(4), 25-30.

BBC News. (2001, May 20). *Firms "ignoring" farm disease aid*. [Online]. Available from the BBC News site, http://news.bbc.co.uk/. Retrieved Accessed May 17, 2001.

Beck, U. (1992). *Risk society: Towards a new modernity*. London: Sage.

Bennett, K., Carroll, T., Lowe, P., & Phillipson, J. (Eds.). (2002a). *Coping with crisis in Cumbria: The consequences of foot and mouth disease*. Centre for Rural Economy Research Report, University of Newcastle upon Tyne.

Bennett, K., Phillipson, J., Lowe, J., & Ward, N. (2002b). *The impact of the foot and mouth crisis on rural firms: A survey of micro-businesses in the north east of England*. Centre for Rural Economy, University of Newcastle.

Blake, A., & Sinclair, T. (2003). Tourism crisis management, US response to September 11. *Annals of Tourist Research*, *309*(4), 813-832.

Blomgren, K.B., & Sorensen, A. (1998). Peripherality–factor or feature? Reflections on peripherality in tourist regions. *Progress in Tourism and Hospitality Research*, *4*, 319-336.

Boag, D., & Rinholm, B. (1989). New product management practices of small high technology firms. *Journal of Product Innovation Management*, *6*, 109-112.

Briedenhann, J., & Wickens, E., (2003) Tourism routes as a tool for the economic development of rural areas–vibrant hope or impossible dream? *Tourism Management*, in press.

Brown, F., & Hall, D. (2000). *Tourism in peripheral areas*. Great Britain: Channel View Publications.

Brown, F., & Hall, D. (Eds.). (1999). *The paradox of periphery, introduction to paradox of periphery, Report 15*. Denmark: Research Centre of Bornholm.

Carter, S. (1998). Tourists' and travellers' social construction of Africa and Asia as risky locations. *Tourism Management*, *19*(4), 349-358.

Carter, W.N. (1991). *Disaster management: A disaster manager's handbook*. Manila: Asian Development Bank.

Cavlek, N. (2002). Tour operators and destination safety. *Annals of Tourism Research*, *29*(2), 478-496.

CIEH (2002). *Foot and Mouth Disease: The lessons learned enquiry, Consultation Response*. C1294. London: Author.

Cole, S. (1995). Lifelines and livelihood; A social accounting matrix approach to calamity preparedness. *Journal of Contingencies and Crisis Management*, *3*(4), 228-240.

Copanigro, J. (2000). *The crisis counselor: A step to step guide to managing a business crisis.* Chicago: Contemporary Books.

Crompton, J.L., & Ankomah, P.K. (1993). Choice set propositions in destination decisions. *Annals of Tourism Research, 20*, 461-476.

Crompton, J.L. (1979a). An assessment of the image of Mexico as a vacation destination and the influence of geographical location upon that image. *Journal of Travel Research, 14*, 4, 18-23.

Crompton, J.L. (1979b). Motivations for pleasure vacations. *Annals of Tourism Research, 6*, 408-424.

Cumbrian Tourist Board. (2003). *Facts about Cumbria.* [Online]. Available from the Cumbrian Tourist Board site, http://www.golakes.co.uk. Retrieved July 23, 2003.

De Vaal, D. (1997). *A survey of continental European visitor attractions.* Delotte and Touche Consulting Group, UK, pp. 12-40.

DEFRA. (2002). *The 2001 outbreak of the Foot and Mouth Disease.* (No. 2121). London: Author.

Drabek, T. (2000). *Emergency management, principles and applications for tourism, hospitality and travel management.* [Data file]. Available from the Federal Emergency Management Agency site, http://www.fema.gov/emi/edu/higher.htm.

Duchesneau, D., & Gartner, W. (1990). A profile of new venture success and failure in an emerging industry. *Journal of Business Venturing, 5*(5), 297-312.

Fakeye, P.C., & Crompton, J.L. (1991). Images differences between prospective, first-time and repeat visitors to the Lower Rio Grande Valley. *Journal of Travel Research, 30*(2), 10-16.

Faulkner, B. (2001). Towards a framework for tourism disaster management. *Tourism Management, 22*, 135-147.

Faulkner, B., & Vikulov, S. (2001). Katherine, washed out one day, back on track the next: A post-mortem of a tourist disaster. *Tourism Management, 22*, 331-344.

Fink, S. (1986). *Crisis Management.* New York: American Management Association.

Frisby, E. (2002). Communicating in a crisis. The British Tourist Authority's response to the Foot and Mouth outbreak and 11th September, 2001. *Journal of Vacation Marketing, 191*, 89-100.

Gartner, W.B., 1990, A profile of new venture success and failure in an emerging industry, Journal of Business Venturing, 5, 5, pp. 297-312.

Gonzalez-Herrero, A., & Pratt, C.B. (1998). Marketing crises in tourism: Communication strategies in the United States and Spain. *Public Relations Review, 24*(1), 83-97.

Harvey, D. (1989). *The condition of postmodernity.* Blackwell: Oxford.

Hotel News. (2002). *Perceptions of Foot and Mouth in the U.K.* Available from Hotel News site, http://www.hotelnewsresource.com/studies global. Retrieved May 16, 2003.

Hunt, J.D. (1998). Image as a factor in tourism development. *Journal of Travel Research, 13*(3), 1-7.

Ireland, M., & Vetier, L. (2002). *The reality and mythology of the Foot and Mouth Disease crisis in Britain: Factors influencing tourist destination choice.* Working Paper.

Kash, T., & Darling, J. (1988). Crisis management: Prevention, diagnosis and intervention. *Leadership and Organizational Development Journal, 19*(4), 179-186.

Kent, P. (1996). People, places and priorities: Opportunity sets and consumers holiday choice. In G. Ashworth & B. Goodall (Eds.), *Marketing tourism places* (pp. 42-62). London: Routledge.

Kruse, C. (1993). Disaster plans stand the test of hurricane. *Personnel Journal, 72*(6), 36-43.

Lash, S., & Urry, J. (1994). *Economies of signs and space.* London: Sage.

Lee, Y., & Harrald, J. (1999). Critical issue for business impact area analysis in business crisis management: Analytical capability. *Disaster Prevention and Management, 8*(3), 184-189.

Lerbinger, O. (1997). *The crisis manager: Facing risk and responsibility.* New Jersey: Erlbaum Associates.

McKay, D. (2003). *Future of tourism to be debated at Abertay,* The Press and Journal, 13 January, Aberdeen.

McLuhan, M. (1967). *The medium is the message.* New York: Random House Inc.

Meethan, K. (2001). *Tourism in global society: Place, culture, consumption.* Basingstoke: Palgrave.

Mitroff, I., & Anagnos, G. (2002). Managing crises before they happen: What every executive needs to know about crisis management. *Journal of Product Innovation Management, 19*(1), 103-105.

Morrison. A. (1998). The tourist accommodation sector in Scotland. In R. Mclellan & R. Smith (Eds.), *The Scottish tourism industry.* London: International Business Press.

North, D., & Smallbone, D. (1996). Small business development in remote rural areas: The example of mature manufacturing firms in northern England. *Journal of Rural Studies, 12*(2), 151-167.

Offer, J. (1998). Pessimists charter. *Accountancy, 121*(4), 50-51.

Okumus, F., Alintay, M., & Arasli, H. (2005). The impact of Turkey's economic crisis of February 2001 on the tourism industry in Northern Cyprus. *Tourism Management, 26*(1), 95-104.

Pearce, P.L. (1982). *The social psychology of tourist behaviour.* Oxford: Pergamon.

Pearce, P.L. (1988). *The Ulysses factor: Evaluating visitors in tourist settings.* New York: Springer-Verlag.

Phelps, A. (1999). Holiday destination image–the problem of assessment: An example developed in Menorca. *Tourism Management, 7*(3), 168-180.

Phillipson, J., Bennett, K., Lowe, P., & Raley, M. (2002). Adaptive responses and asset strategies: The experience of rural micro-firms and Foot and Mouth Disease. *Journal of Rural Studies, 20*(2), 227-243.

Richardson, B. (1994). Crisis management and the management strategy: Time to loop the loop. *Disaster Prevention and Management, 6*(5), 59-80.

Ritchie, B.W. (2004). Chaos, crises and disasters: A strategic approach to crisis management in the tourism industry. *Tourism Management, 25*(6), 669-683.

Roure, J., & Maidique, M. (1988). Linking prefunding factors and high technology venture success: An exploratory study. In R.A. Burgelman & M. Maidique (Eds.), *Strategic management of technology and innovation* (pp. 414-423). Homewood, IL: Irwin.

Scotexchange. (1999). *Know your market: Tourism attitudes survey 1999.* [Data File]. Available from Scotexchange.net site, http://www.scotexchange.net. Retrieved January 12, 2003.

Scotexchange. (2003). *Scotland's most important industry.* [Online]. Available from Scotexchange.net site, http://www.scotexchange.net. Retrieved January 14, 2003.

Scott, A., Christie, M., & Midmore, P. (2004). Impact of the 2001 foot-and-mouth disease outbreak in Britain: Implications for rural studies. *Journal of Rural Studies, 20*(1), 1-14.

Schutz, A. (1972). *The phenomenology of the social world.* London: Heinemann.

Schwenk, C., & Shrader, C. (1993). Effects of formal strategic planning on financial performance of small firms. *Entrepreneurship Theory and Practice, 17*(3), 53-64.

Smallbone, D., North, D., & Kalantaridis, C. (1999). Adapting to peripherality; A study of small rural manufacturing firms in Northern England. *Entrepreneurship and Regional Development, 11*, 109-127.

Sonmez, S., & Graefe, A.R. (1998). Influence of terrorism risk on foreign tourism decisions. *Annals of Tourism Research, 25*(1), 112-144.

Spillan, J., & Hough, M. (2003), Crisis planning in small businesses: Importance, impetus and indifference. *European Management Journal, 21*(3), 398-407.

Stafford, G., Yu, L., & Armoo, A.K. (2002). Crisis management and recovery. *Cornell Hotel and Restaurant Administration Quarterly, 43*(5), 27-40.

Star UK. (2003). *Key facts of tourism for Cumbria 2000-2002.* [Online]. Available from the Star UK site, http://www.staruk.org.uk. Retrieved July 20, 2003.

Tiefenbacher, J.P., Day, F.A., & Walton, J.A. (2000). Attributes of repeat visitors to small tourist-orientated communities. *Social Science Journal, 37*(2), 299-308.

Urry, J. (1990). *The tourist gaze.* London: Sage.

Urry, J. (1995). *Consuming places.* London: Routledge.

Vaessen, P., & Keeble, D. (1995). *Growth oriented SME's in unfavourable regional environments.* Working Paper 6. University of Cambridge: ESRC, Centre for Business Research.

Wanhill, S. (1997). Peripheral area tourism–A European perspective. *Progress in Tourism and Hospitality Research, 3*, 47-70.

Ward, W., Donaldson, A., & Lowe, P. (2002). *The Foot and Mouth crisis and the management of lesson learning.* Working Paper 67. Centre for Rural Economy.

Canadian Seasonality and Domestic Travel Patterns: Regularities and Dislocations as a Result of the Events of 9/11

Wayne W. Smith

Barbara A. Carmichael

SUMMARY. On September 11th, 2001 the North American tourism environment changed dramatically as a result of the terrorist events that occurred in New York and Washington D.C. As Canadians watched the events of 9/11 unfold south of the border, the shift in their travel patterns was almost immediate. Using secondary data analysis from the Canadian domestic travel survey, this study reveals the changes in travel behavior that occurred in overall trip characteristics and for different demographic market segments post-September 11. Comparisons are made between actual and expected travel patterns. These findings have implications for disaster recovery marketing strategies in general. *[Article copies available for a fee from The Haworth Document Delivery Service: 1-800-HAWORTH. E-mail address: <docdelivery@haworthpress.com> Website: <http://www.HaworthPress. com> © 2005 by The Haworth Press, Inc. All rights reserved.]*

KEYWORDS. 9/11, Canada, seasonality, domestic travel patterns, disaster recovery, marketing strategies

INTRODUCTION

On September 11th, 2001 the North American tourism environment changed dramatically as a result of the terrorist events that occurred in New York and Washington D.C. The travel implications of the political and social landscapes created as a result of the events of that day are being felt worldwide. Canada for instance, lost an estimated $815 million in tourism revenues from September 11th to December 31st 2001 alone (Canadian Tourism Commission, 2002a). As Canadians watched the events unfold south of the border, the shift in travel patterns was almost immediate. Air travel decreased in demand, not just because of perceived safety but also because of tighter border security, aircraft groundings and cuts in flight availability. Urban tourism experienced a dip in demand, as any North American city

Wayne W. Smith (E-mail: smit3246@wlu.ca) is a PhD Candidate, and Barbara A. Carmichael (E-mail: bcarmich@wlu.ca) is Associate Professor, both at the Department of Geography and Environmental Studies, Wilfrid Laurier University, Waterloo, Ontario, N2L 3C5.Canada.

[Haworth co-indexing entry note]: "Canadian Seasonality and Domestic Travel Patterns: Regularities and Dislocations as a Result of the Events of 9/11." Smith, Wayne W., and Barbara A. Carmichael. Co-published simultaneously in *Journal of Travel & Tourism Marketing* (The Haworth Hospitality Press, an imprint of The Haworth Press, Inc.) Vol. 19, No. 2/3, 2005, pp. 61-76; and: *Tourism Crises: Management Responses and Theoretical Insight* (ed: Eric Laws, and Bruce Prideaux) The Haworth Hospitality Press, an imprint of The Haworth Press, Inc., 2005, pp. 61-76. Single or multiple copies of this article are available for a fee from The Haworth Document Delivery Service [1-800-HAWORTH, 9:00 a.m. - 5:00 p.m. (EST). E-mail address: docdelivery@haworthpress.com].

Available online at http://www.haworthpress.com/web/JTTM
© 2005 by The Haworth Press, Inc. All rights reserved.
doi:10.1300/J073v19n02_06

that had skyscraper buildings, Canadian and American alike, could be perceived as a potential target for a similar terrorist attack.

After September 11th, 2001, the Canadian Tourism Commission (CTC, 2002a) undertook a study to examine the effect the events had on the Canadian travel psyche. The intention to travel was basically the same as before the events of 9/11; however, Canadians were altering travel plans in order to accommodate their desire to travel with a need to feel safe (CTC, 2002a). As a result of this shift in travel patterns, Canada's travel account deficit fell to its lowest level since 1986 ($1.3 billion) (CTC, 2002b). The shift towards staying close to home was displayed but little research was conducted into understanding where the shifts occurred. This study is undertaken to examine if domestic travel patterns continued to follow traditional seasonal patterns after the events of 9/11. Further, this study examines whether travelers with different demographic and trip characteristics displayed different travel dislocations as a result of the tragedy. The basic premise behind this study is that safety is a destination and travel attribute that tourists consider when making their travel plans. When a disaster occurs it alters the relative importance of safety in the potential traveler's mind and disrupts, at least temporarily, the normal pattern of behavior for travel choice, for example in terms of type of travel, destination choice, length of trip and mode of transportation. Such changes in the dynamics of the tourism system have marketing and management implications for the tourism industry, both within Canada and also for other destinations recovering from crisis.

THEORETICAL BASE

Safety is always a factor that tourists consider when making destination choices (Shaw & Williams, 2002; Faulkner, 2001; Sonmez, 1998). Cases from around the world show that in places where tourists perceive danger from crime, terrorism or political instability, those destinations experience large decreases in overall visitation (Seddighi & Theicharous, 2002; Pizam, 1999; Sonmez, 1998; Bar-On, 1996;

Hall & O'Sullivan, 1996; O'Neil & Fritz, 1996; Schwartz, 1991). How much the destinations experience change is based on a variety of factors: (a) who are the victims (Seddighi & Theicharous, 2002; Pizam, 1999; Mansfeld, 1999); (b) the location of the disturbance (Mansfeld; 1999; Pizam, 1999; Bar-On, 1996; O'Neil & Fritz, 1996); (c) the severity of the disturbance (Mansfeld, 1999; Pizam, 1999); (d) the frequency of the disturbance (Mansfeld, 1999; Pizam, 1999; Sonmez, 1998); (e) the type of disturbance (Mansfeld, 1999; Pizam 1999); and (f) the volume of press coverage the disturbance entails (Sonmez, 1998; Sonmez, Apostolopoulos & Tarlow, 1999; Bar-On, 1996; Quarantelli, 1996). All of these factors contribute to how tourists and the tourism industry react. For instance, in Spain, in 1996, the Basque Fatherland and Liberty Organization (ETA) sent over 200 letters to foreign embassies, travel agents and foreign media threatening the safety of tourists going to Spain. They followed up this threat with six bomb attacks, which affected Spain's image and resulted in a significant decrease in international arrivals to Spain (Bar-On, 1996).

Previous studies on tourism and crisis events have focused on the countries where such events occurred (Seddighi & Theicharous, 2002; Pizam, 1999; Sonmez, 1998; Bar-On, 1996; Hall & O'Sullivan, 1996; O'Neil & Fritz, 1996; Schwartz, 1991; Sonmez, Apostolopoulos & Tarlow, 1999; Quarantelli, 1996). Despite these recent studies, little systematic research addresses fully the link between the disaster or crisis phenomenon and tourism; the wider impacts on the tourism industry and government agencies; and their coping strategies (Faulkner, 2001). Pizam and Smith (2000) identified the need for further research on the specific temporal effects on tourism demand of terrorism acts. Furthermore, there is a dearth of research on the spillover effects of disasters on neighboring countries and how the events in one country can change the tourism patterns of its neighbors.

Generally, in countries where there are attacks on tourists, there are higher declines in tourism arrivals than when the attacks occur against residents (Pizam, 1999). Nevertheless, the type of location of the disturbance is understudied. The focus of previous research is on whether disturbances occurred in traditional tourist spaces rather than on whether the spot had historical, cultural or economic significance (Pizam, 1999). In the case of the events of 9/11, an important iconic feature in the form of the Twin Towers of the World Trade Centre was destroyed in a city that is often regarded as the center of American culture. It is because the terror attacks focused on highly significant space in a highly significant place that the effects of the tragedy were that much greater. Furthermore, the destruction of this landmark resulted in the deaths of a number of non-Americans who both worked in and visited these icons.

The severity and frequency of disturbances are major factors in influencing the amount of tourism decline (Krakover, 2000; Mansfeld, 1999; Pizam 1999; O'Neil & Fritz, 1996). While evidence suggests that severity greatly affects visitation levels (Krakover, 2000), frequency can negatively brand a destination in that it may cause longer-term effects. This is the case in Northern Ireland where recovery has been slow due to the long-term and recurring nature of the political unrest (O'Neil & Fritz, 1996).

In addition, it can be argued that decline in demand is related to the amount of media attention that the event garners (Sonmez, Apostolopoulos & Tarlow, 1999; Bar-On, 1996; Quarantelli, 1996). With globalization, communication media play a larger role in shaping world perceptions regarding a specific event. For instance, after 9/11, news channels such as CNN, BBC World, CBC (Canada's News Agency) showed around the clock coverage of the events for nearly a month. These channels played a vital role in shaping world perception regarding the event and even of the possibility of further danger (Quarantelli, 1996). This perpetuation caused Canadians and Americans alike to become concerned about the safety of border crossings and airports in general (CTC, 2002a).

9/11 was one tragedy that had immediate and far-reaching measurable impacts on surrounding countries and arguably on the world. It was estimated, by the World Travel and Tourism Council (WTTC), that 9/11 created a decrease of 1.7 percent in the world's GDP and a loss of 8.8 million jobs outside of the United States (WTTC, 2001, cited in CTC, 2003). Canada alone lost 11,500 jobs as a re-sult of the events of 9/11 (CTC, 2002a). While the vast majority of research has focused on the wounded destination itself, there is a need to understand the spillover effect on travel patterns in neighboring countries and destinations.

While it is known that where tourists perceive danger from crime, terrorism, or political instability, affected destinations experience large decreases in overall visitation (Seddighi & Theicharous, 2002; Pizam, 1999; Sonmez, 1998; Bar-On, 1996; Hall & O'Sullivan, 1996; O'Neil & Fritz, 1996; Schwartz, 1991), little research has been conducted into what specific changes actually occur in tourist choice behavior. Such decision-making is complex and is affected by a variety of factors (Bargeman, Joh & Timmermans, 2002; King & Woodside, 2001). These factors include: (a) the individual's demographic and psychographic characteristics; (b) the influences of family, friends and reference groups; and (c) the effects of marketing and the media (King & Woodside, 2001; Morrison, 1996). Typically, a segmentation approach is taken to the study of travel choice. However, this does not address the role disaster plays in the decision-making process (Bargeman, Joh & Timmermans, 2002; King & Woodside, 2001; Seddighi & Theicharous, 2002; Sonmez, 1998).

Figure 1 provides a conceptual framework that suggests how the influence of a disaster may affect the tourism decision-making process. Potential travelers hold beliefs about possible destination attributes that form the tourist image of such destinations. As previously discussed, safety is one of these attributes. The relative importance of such attributes to an individual tourist varies according to the potential tourist's characteristics (location, demographics, psychographics, interpersonal and media influences and motivations). Tourists may evaluate potential destinations according to their beliefs that destinations possess particular attributes and their liking and the importance to them of such attributes. However, in the event of a disaster, depending on its location, type, severity, frequency and extent of media coverage, tourist destination images can be altered and the importance of safety and security may be increased. The tourist decision-making process may be disrupted in terms of destination

FIGURE 1. The Influence of Disaster on the Tourism Decision-Making Process

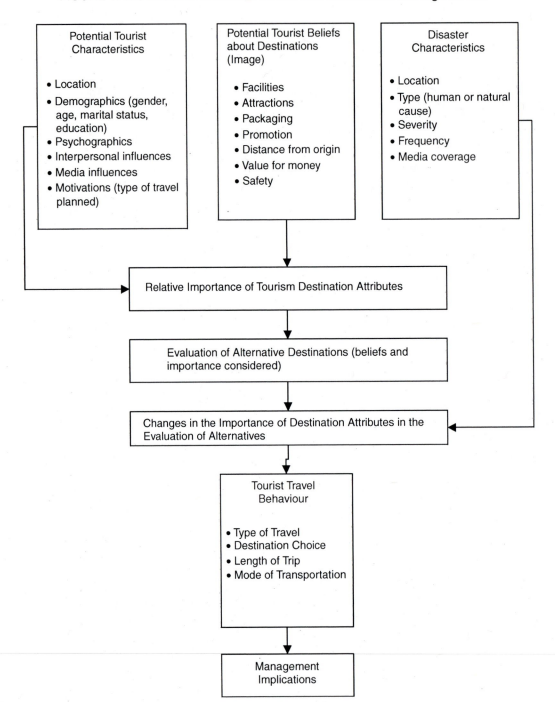

choice, mode of transportation, type of travel and length of trip. A disaster such as the events of September 11 is likely to create turbulence in the tourist market place, altering tourism decisions and causing ripple effects through many sectors in the tourism industry.

This conceptual framework raises a number of interesting questions. What changes do potential travelers make to their travel plans in a crisis situation? Who is most likely to modify their travel plans and if so what types of modifications are made? Furthermore, if modifications do occur, how long after a crisis do such modifications play a role in overall travel decision-making? While this paper cannot address all of the above questions, it will focus on the first two within a domestic travel situation.

The rationale for this domestic focus is that the major modification most residents of neighboring countries are likely to make is to favor domestic travel more than usual (Mansfeld, 1999; Burton, Kates & White, 1993). Marketing efforts after 9/11 centered heavily on promoting to the domestic market place (CTC, 2002a). Various marketing techniques were employed to entice the visitor to stay near home. These included reduced prices, special attractions and a focus on safety-based issues. With the TV and Internet media discussing the possibilities of further danger and the domestic tourism industry promoting itself heavily, this provided the potential tourist with enough information to make adjustments to their travel choices. Therefore, this study focuses on the Canadian domestic travel market and on what changes were made and by whom after 9/11.

METHODOLOGY

The data used in this study is derived from the Canadian Travel Survey (CTS) Person-Trip file (1998-2001). The methodology employed in gathering the CTS data is based on a panel design and employs a telephone survey based on monthly data gathering. The CTS is Canada's method for estimating domestic travel and its results are weighted to represent residents travel patterns as a whole.

The CTS is administered to sub-samples of households in the monthly Labour Force Survey (LFS) (Statistics Canada, 1998). Except for differences in sample size, the design features of the LFS sample are maintained in the CTS sample. The LFS is a household survey whose sample is representative of Canadian society over 15 years of age excluding those who are institutionalized, serving in the military, or living on First Nation's Reserves or in the territories. These exclusions represent about 2% of the Canadian population age 15 or older (Statistics Canada, 1998). The sample is drawn from an area frame and is based on a stratified, multistage design that uses probability sam-

pling (Statistics Canada, 1998). "The main advantage of using a stratified sample design is that when sampling is applied separately to many diverse strata, each stratum having a relatively homogeneous population, the efficiency of the sample is higher than that obtained from simple random sampling without stratification" (Statistics Canada, 1998, p. 65).

The LFS uses a panel design whereby the entire monthly sample of households consists of six panels or rotation groups of approximately equal size (Statistics Canada, 1998). Each of these panels alone could be considered to be representative of the entire Canadian population. All households remain on the panel for six months when a new panel is introduced. This is done to minimize respondent burden. This also has the advantage of providing a common sample base for short term, month-to-month comparisons. Because of this feature, supplementary surveys like the CTS using the LSF design can be employed using less than the full sample size. The 1996 CTS used two of the six rotation groups in the LFS in all provinces except for Newfoundland where three were used. One person per household was randomly chosen for the CTS.

Weights are provided in the CTS to permit the creation of estimates representative of the entire Canadian population. The weighting is used only when Statistics Canada guidelines for making inferences from a given sub-sample are met. Despite the large sample size of the CTS, disaggregating the data by selected variables, such as travel regions, can sometimes result in very small sub-samples. Caution needs to be exercised in dealing with small numbers for disaggregated components of the overall sample. Statistics Canada has produced a user's guide that outlines the minimum sizes of estimates for release of results (Statistics Canada, 1998, p. 91). Guidelines are based on the un-weighted data and the coefficient of variation (CV). The coefficient of variation is based on "using the variance formula for simple random sampling and incorporating a factor which reflects the multi-stage, clustered nature of the sample design" (Statistics Canada, 1998, p. 92). If any un-weighted count is under 30 for any cell, Statistics Canada advises that the findings should not be released regardless of the CV.

In this study, the person trip weight function was used in the calculation of an aggregate of visitation over the time series. 1998-2000 results were examined for significant differences in overall travel patterns. Generally, these years displayed a homogeneous pattern of travel with small travel variations. This is consistent with the findings of Wilton and Wirjanto (1998) who described a traditional "saw tooth" pattern in Canada's domestic seasonal travel choices. The three years were merged to estimate the expected pattern in 2001 if it followed usual variations. If it had a "saw tooth" pattern, the seasonal variation would have followed the pattern of a low in travel in January with a gradual slight rise until May, a sharp rise in June, a peak in August and a decrease in September flowed by another low in November and a slight rise in December. This assumption was employed in order to develop a baseline or "expected" line.

Using this assumption, an index was developed to compare the time periods. The baseline of three years was created by averaging 1998-2000 monthly visitation rates. Subtracting the overall percentage of travel for each month from the expected percentage of trips for each given month created the index used to compare travel patterns. An index score of "0" would indicate that there was no difference in the percentage of travel for the given month. The results of this index can be seen on Figures 2 through 9 with the percentage change displayed on the Y-axis on a monthly basis.

It must be noted, however, that 2001 was going to be a "down year" regardless of the events of September 11th, 2001. The June-August peak was weaker than previous years, even before the events of 9/11, and that factor alone affected the seasonal travel patterns. While these effects were important, the events and subsequent recovery period after 9/11 altered overall travel patterns significantly. While overall travel patterns were significantly different before 9/11, travel choice and demographic patterns remained consistent until after September 2001 (there was an overall lowering of visitation during that period rather than a shift in travel patterns). It was therefore decided to focus further on the travel choices and demographic factors and their deviations in travel.

The variables were analyzed using SPSS 11.0 and Excel 2000 and contained 2001's actual pattern versus 2001's expected pattern (developed using the method described above). The bi-variate analysis was conducted using contingency tables, χ^2 and Cramer's V. Cramer's V is a modification of χ^2 in which the value of χ^2 is divided by the sample size and square root of the result is taken. This has the effect of reducing the impact of the sample size on the significance level of the results. χ^2 tends to become more significant with larger sample sizes. Cramer's V ranges between ± 1.00. The closer to one of these extreme values, the stronger is the relationship. The following tables provide results for both χ^2 and Cramer's V. All the results were then put into graphic form through the use of bar and line graphs and determinations were made as to whether a pattern in 2001 deviated significantly from the expected pattern for that year.

RESULTS

The results are reported in three sections with comparisons made between actual and expected patterns for 2001. The first section provides an overview of the overall travel patterns changes. The second section examines the impact of 9/11 on the following travel characteristics: (a) destination choice, (b) modal choice and (c) primary purpose of travel. The final section investigates the post-September 11 responses by Canadians with different demographic characteristics: gender, age grouping and educational attainment.

Overall Patterns

The overall domestic travel patterns indicate that at the end of 2001, there was a significantly different travel pattern than in the three previous years (Figure 2). 1998-2000 displays the traditional "saw tooth" as Wilton and Wirjanto (1998) describe; however, 2001 follows this course until August 2001 but then deviates from the pattern culminating in a large increase in December travel over previous years.

FIGURE 2. Travel Distribution Change–Canadian Domestic Visitation–1998-2001

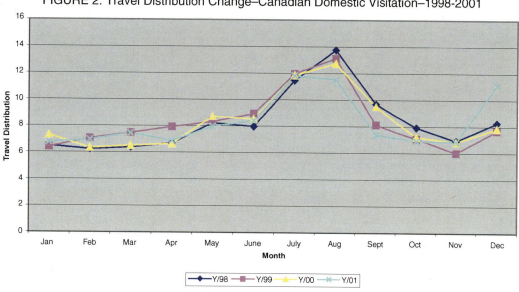

FIGURE 3. Travel Differential–Canadian Domestic Visitation 2001 Actual vs. 2001 Expected and 2001 Actual vs. 2000 Actual

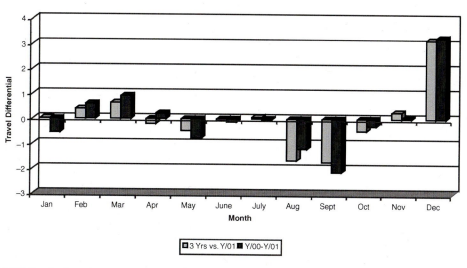

Source: 1998-2001 Canadian Travel Survey (CTS)

Figure 3 shows that higher than expected proportions of travelers were present in February, March and December and lower than expected proportions were present in May, August September and October. While all the months had statistically significant variations, January to March and October to December showed the strongest periods of change (Table 1). This is consistent with what was expected, whereby the first and second quarters were expected to have higher than regular proportions of travel given the especially weak fourth quarter. The December rise is a surprising result that shows a strong recovery after the events of 9/11.

Travel Characteristic Patterns

Destination choice displayed a wide variation from what was expected in 2001 (Figure 4).

FIGURE 4. Travel Differential–Destination Choice 2001 Actual Compared to 2001 Expected (3 Years Avg 1998-2000)

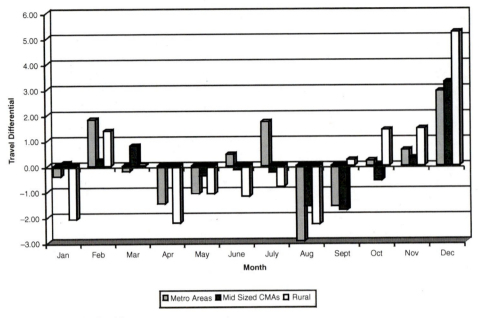

Source: 1998 through 2001 Canadian Travel Survey

FIGURE 5. Travel Differential–Modal Choice 2001 Actual Compared to 2001 Expected (3 Years Avg 1998-2000)

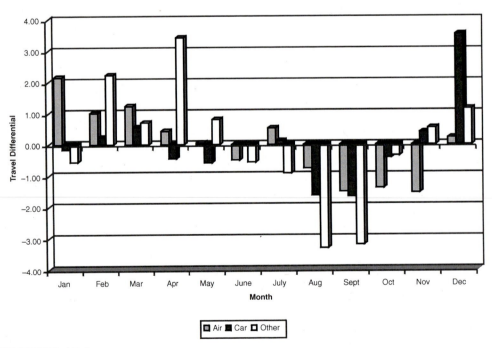

Source 1998-2001 CTS (weighted)

FIGURE 6. Travel Differential–Purpose of Travel 2001 Actual Compared to 2001 Expected (3 Years Avg 1998-2000)

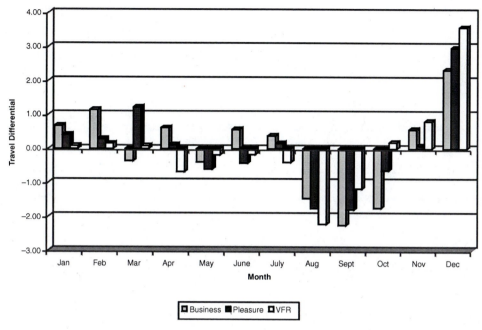

Source: 1998 through 2001 CTS (Weighted)

FIGURE 7. Travel Differential–Gender 2001 Actual Compared to 2001 Expected (3 Years Avg 1998-2000)

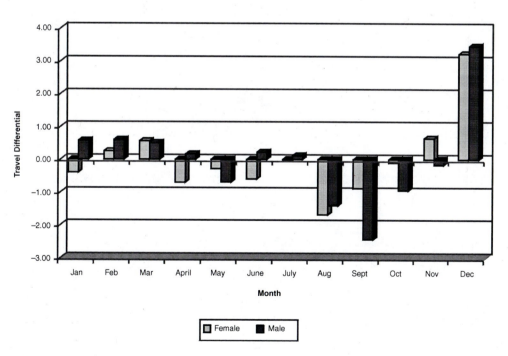

Source: 1998 through 2001 CTS (Weighted)

FIGURE 8. Travel Differential–Age 2001 Actual Compared to 2001 Expected (3 Years Avg 1998-2000)

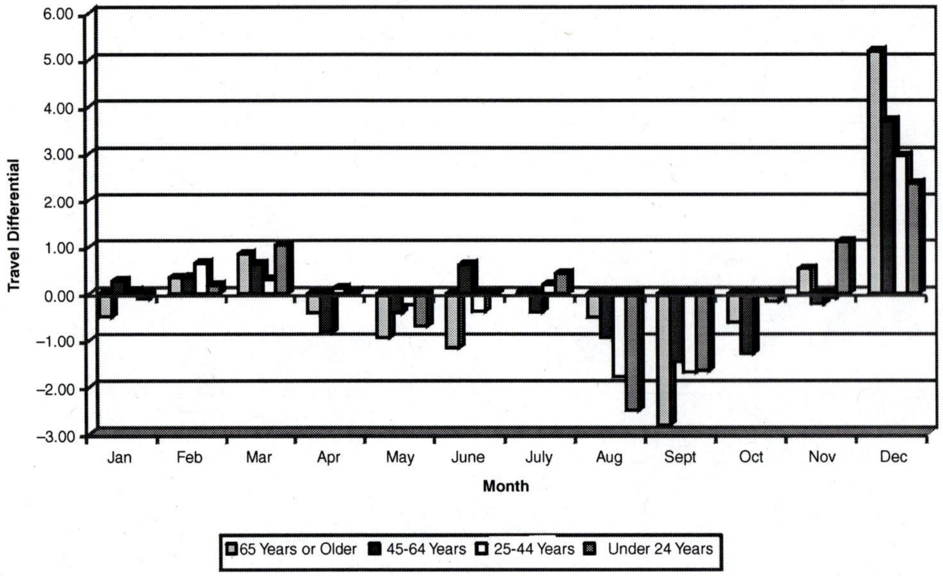

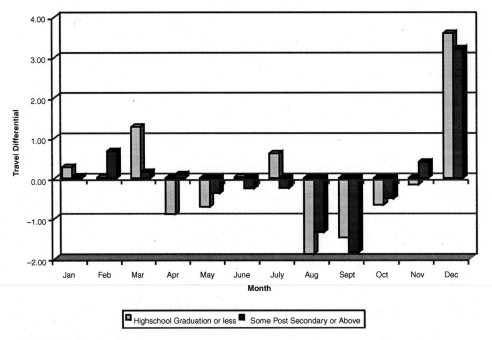

Source: 1998-2001 CTS (Weighted)

FIGURE 9. Travel Differential–Educational Attainment 2001 Actual Compared to 2001 Expected (3 Years Avg 1998-2000)

Source: 1998-2001 CTS (Weighted)

The proportion of travel to metropolitan areas was lower than expected in April, August and September. Rural areas actually benefited from the events of September 11th, with the proportion of travel to those areas significantly rising after September 2001. Mid-sized cities displayed the most consistent year of the three types with large decreases in August and September 2001 offset by a large increase in December. Again, all months showed significant

TABLE 1. Overall Variation in Visitation Rates 2001 Actual vs. 2001 Expected

Month	Difference in N	χ^2	df	Asymp. Sig. (2-sided)	Cramer's V	Sig.
Jan	36,985,312	443,967.54	9	0.000	0.110	0.000
Feb	36,537,652	433,939.47	9	0.000	0.109	0.000
Mar	38,680,112	390,787.2	10	0.000	0.101	0.000
Apr	39,878,909	592,977.95	12	0.000	0.122	0.000
May	46,953,149	333,293.44	9	0.000	0.084	0.000
June	47,807,009	274,588.15	10	0.000	0.076	0.000
July	63,388,767	3,154,461.5	9	0.000	0.071	0.000
Aug	69,249,915	681,334.78	9	0.000	0.099	0.000
Sept	49,677,796	285,523.01	11	0.000	0.076	0.000
Oct	42,019,338	358,200.16	8	0.000	0.092	0.000
Nov	38,209,044	358,200.16	11	0.000	0.097	0.000
Dec	46,898,543	318,157.48	9	0.000	0.082	0.000

Source: Data from 1998-2001 CTS (Weighted)

TABLE 2. Destination Choice Patterns 2001 Actual vs. 2001 Expected

Month	Difference in N	χ^2	df	Asymp. Sig. (2-sided)	Cramer's V	Sig.
Jan	52,034,003	142,409.8	2	0.000	0.052	0.000
Feb	50,980,054	13,842.8	2	0.000	0.016	0.000
Mar	53,328,802	213,345.6	2	0.000	0.063	0.000
Apr	53,972,851	262,316.5	2	0.000	0.070	0.000
May	63,986,729	179,038.9	2	0.000	0.053	0.000
June	65,002,730	64,559.81	2	0.000	0.032	0.000
July	90,447,703	18,300.95	2	0.000	0.014	0.000
Aug	98,152,807	326,341.1	2	0.000	0.058	0.000
Sept	66,840,601	110,445.6	2	0.000	0.041	0.000
Oct	55,941,953	55,500.47	2	0.000	0.031	0.000
Nov	51,267,482	110,824.2	2	0.000	0.046	0.000
Dec	66,890,437	294,153.5	2	0.000	0.066	0.000

Source: Data from 1998-2001 CTS (Weighted)

variation in the proportion of travel expected between the destination choices, however March, April and December show the greatest variation in travel rates (Table 2). March and April are attributable to the consistency show in travel proportions by the mid-sized cities. In December it is notable that the large proportion of travel to rural areas remained strong, despite the growing strength of travel to mid-sized and metropolitan areas.

Modal choice was strongly influenced by the events of September 11th as all modes of transportation showed sharp decreases over the patterns established in previous years (Figure 5). Air travel, as expected, displayed the largest overall decrease in fourth quarter; however, an indication of recovery for this modal choice was shown as a smaller than expected gain in December 2001 was seen. Auto travel performed as expected with a sharp recovery after September 2001. This sharp recovery for auto travel may be explained by the shifting in primary purpose of travel to visiting friends and relatives as explained below. Alternative forms of transportation were found to display the sharpest decrease after September 11th; however, this form recovers quickly with gains being shown in November and December. While all modes show significant differences, the strong shifting proportions of air travel pro-

vides a good summary of how deeply the travel industry was affected by the events of 9/11 (Table 3).

Primary purpose of travel was strongly affected by the events of September 11th, 2001. As Figure 6 indicates, business travel was down significantly in August, September and October. Pleasure travel had lower proportions of travel in August, September and October. However, it did rebound more strongly and faster than business travel. Visiting friends and relatives (VFR) was the strongest rationale given for travel after the events of 9/11. Its recovery period was very short and showed a significantly different travel pattern than the two other primary purposes (Table 4).

Demographic Patterns

Women recovered faster in their travel behavior after the events of 9/11 (Figure 7). Women displayed a slight decrease in September but quickly returned back to expectations in October and traveled at rates higher than expected in November and December. Men, on the other hand, displayed a more expected pattern with the exception of December which showed a much higher than expected travel increase. Overall, gender displayed significantly different travel patterns after 9/11. However,

TABLE 3. Modal Choice Patterns 2001 Actual vs. 2001 Expected

Month	Difference in N	χ^2	df	Asymp. Sig. (2-sided)	Cramer's V	Sig.
Jan	52,034,003	135,960	2	0.000	0.051	0.000
Feb	50,980,053	49,567.06	2	0.000	0.031	0.000
Mar	53,328,804	21,923.06	2	0.000	0.020	0.000
Apr	53,972,852	153,398.7	2	0.000	0.053	0.000
May	63,986,729	39,224.08	2	0.000	0.025	0.000
June	65,002,728	1,664.553	2	0.000	0.005	0.000
July	90,447,703	26,453.39	2	0.000	0.017	0.000
Aug	98,152,807	43,754.14	2	0.000	0.021	0.000
Sept	66,840,603	16,902.91	2	0.000	0.016	0.000
Oct	55,941,954	797.5256	2	0.000	0.004	0.000
Nov	51,267,483	20,102.14	2	0.000	0.020	0.000
Dec	66,890,436	65,143.54	2	0.000	0.031	0.000

Source: Data from 1998-2001 CTS (Weighted)

TABLE 5. Gender 2001 Actual vs. 2001 Expected

Month	Difference in N	χ^2	df	Asymp. Sig. (2-sided)	Cramer's V	Sig
Jan	44,821,335	71,616.31	1	0.000	0.040	0.000
Feb	44,027,962	17,992.99	1	0.000	0.020	0.000
Mar	45,606,517	1,928.452	1	0.000	0.007	0.000
Apr	46,999,514	57,307.66	1	0.000	0.035	0.000
May	55,192,963	170.9545	1	0.000	0.002	0.000
June	55,575,951	49,417.97	1	0.000	0.030	0.000
July	73,244,657	10,608.49	1	0.000	0.012	0.000
Aug	79,528,371	11,095.1	1	0.000	0.012	0.000
Sept	57,896,387	54,499.21	1	0.000	0.031	0.000
Oct	49,140,432	11,688.25	1	0.000	0.015	0.000
Nov	45,638,903	13,468.03	1	0.000	0.017	0.000
Dec	56,333,198	9,451.413	1	0.000	0.013	0.000

Source: Data from 1998-2001 CTS (Weighted)

TABLE 4. Primary Purpose of Travel 2001 Actual vs. 2001 Expected

Month	Difference in N	χ^2	df	Asymp. Sig. (2-sided)	Cramer's V	Sig.
Jan	52,034,002	203,451.8	5	0.000	0.063	0.000
Feb	50,980,052	243,011	5	0.000	0.069	0.000
Mar	53,328,802	143,310.3	5	0.000	0.052	0.000
Apr	53,972,849	78,059.11	5	0.000	0.038	0.000
May	63,986,730	44,342.02	5	0.000	0.026	0.000
June	65,002,730	65,431.64	5	0.000	0.032	0.000
July	90,447,703	100,346.9	5	0.000	0.033	0.000
Aug	98,152,808	99,642.54	5	0.000	0.032	0.000
Sept	66,840,604	54,371.39	5	0.000	0.029	0.000
Oct	55,941,954	93,334	5	0.000	0.041	0.000
Nov	51,267,483	42,893.93	5	0.000	0.029	0.000
Dec	66,890,436	83,635.54	5	0.000	0.035	0.000

Source: Data from 1998-2001 CTS (Weighted)

as Cramer's V indicates, these differences in patterns are not as strong as for some of the other variables (Table 5).

Those over the age 65 displayed the greatest decrease in expected travel in September 2001 (Figure 8). This group, however, had the largest increase in a December recovery of all age groupings. Those under 24 years, while showing a decrease in September 2001, displayed a larger than expected travel deficit in August. They also had a December increase as the only significant rise in travel beyond expected rates. Those with ages 25-44 showed a September decrease that was compensated for with a rise in December proportion of travel. The 45-64 age group visitors lost the second least amount of share (next to under 25 years) but overall remained on course with the exception of the December pick up. All of the months show significant variations in travel pattern but only December displayed a strong variation when considering Cramer's V score (see Table 6).

Those with higher levels of education recovered after the events of 9/11 more quickly than those whose education levels were lower. However, the December increase was stronger among those with lower levels of education (Figure 9). Once again, in examining the levels of the Cramer's V, the significance level is not as strong as some of the other variables examined in this study (Table 7).

IMPLICATIONS

Overall, domestic travel patterns in 2001 deviated significantly from 1998-2000 traditional travel patterns and demographics and trip characteristics proved to be useful seg-

TABLE 6. Age Group Patterns 2001 Actual vs. 2001 Expected

Month	Difference in N	χ^2	df	Asymp. Sig. (2-sided)	Cramer's V	Sig.
Jan	52,034,004	40,025.26	3	0.000	0.028	0.000
Feb	50,980,053	15,297.89	3	0.000	0.017	0.000
Mar	53,328,802	25,788.92	3	0.000	0.022	0.000
Apr	53,972,850	25,448.25	3	0.000	0.022	0.000
May	63,986,728	35,693.69	3	0.000	0.024	0.000
June	65,002,729	107,937.4	3	0.000	0.041	0.000
July	90,447,701	17,265.05	3	0.000	0.014	0.000
Aug	98,152,807	63,525.31	3	0.000	0.025	0.000
Sept	66,840,602	61,333.58	3	0.000	0.030	0.000
Oct	55,941,954	28,126.45	3	0.000	0.022	0.000
Nov	51,267,482	66,157	3	0.000	0.036	0.000
Dec	66,890,437	125,902.3	3	0.000	0.043	0.000

Source: Data from 1998-2001 CTS (Weighted)

TABLE 7. Educational Attainment 2001 Actual vs. 2001 Expected

Month	Difference in N	χ^2	df	Asymp. Sig. (2-sided)	Cramer's V	Sig.
Jan	44,821,334	2,187.34	1	0.000	0.007	0.000
Feb	44,027,962	48,960.1	1	0.000	0.033	0.000
Mar	45,606,517	12,988.77	1	0.000	0.017	0.000
Apr	46,999,514	85,989.65	1	0.000	0.043	0.000
May	55,192,962	24,514.55	1	0.000	0.021	0.000
June	55,575,950	3,876.034	1	0.000	0.008	0.000
July	73,244,657	18.84474	1	0.000	0.001	0.000
Aug	79,528,371	38,279.13	1	0.000	0.022	0.000
Sept	57,896,387	2,012.082	1	0.000	0.006	0.000
Oct	49,140,433	17,563.71	1	0.000	0.019	0.000
Nov	45,638,903	40,649.55	1	0.000	0.030	0.000
Dec	56,333,197	1,286.905	1	0.000	0.005	0.000

Source: Data from 1998-2001 CTS (Weighted)

mentation variables. The results suggest some interesting implications. The first is that demographic characteristics (age, gender, education) while statistically significant do not display an overwhelming differentiation between groups. This finding suggests that Bargeman, Joh and Timmermanns (2002) may be correct in their assertion that individual choice may play a larger role than demographic characteristics in determining travel choice. This implication is also supported by Burton, Kates and White (1993) who suggest choice made after hazards are based on factors of perceived safety. Based on this idea, tourists will not necessarily cancel their trips but rather alter them to meet safety needs. As suggested by Mansfeld (1999), an alteration in travel will mean a focus on domestic markets whereby visitors have safe, comfortable feelings. This is perhaps the strongest strategic marketing method for dealing with a crisis situation in a tourism context. When that trip is made, the alterations appear, as is shown in this study, to come in the form of trip characteristics.

As the trip characteristics changed (e.g., destination, modal and primary purpose choices) the shape of expected travel patterns also moved. The results of this study indicate that a shift towards visiting friends and relatives (VFR) travel during times of crisis is present. VFR travel is perceived as a safe and secure form of travel. This type of travel could also be conducive to modal change (i.e., auto trip rather than an air based trips) and is related to destination choice. As stated by Bargeman, Joh and Timmermans (2002), choice is based on perceived benefits of the destination. In times of crisis, there is a logical conclusion that those wishing to travel will revert back to safer, more secure destinations (home and or rural destinations). As the CTC (2002a) report noted, Canadians were looking for a back-to-basics vacations as a result of 9/11 and that is reflected in these results.

These findings raise some serious issues for the tourism industry. First, while the overall volume of travel remaining consistent is good, the shift towards VFR travel is difficult for the industry as a whole. VFR travelers tend to take shorter distance trips, mainly by car, and by definition do not usually use the accommodation sector. All told, this market does not represent a lucrative opportunity for the tourism industry. On the pleasure travel side, however, as shown by the large December resurgence, there was an indication that Canadians were altering travel plans with an emphasis on remaining within the country. With discounted hotel rooms and other marketing techniques being employed, Canadians were willing to alter their travel plans and stayed near home, over the short term at least. Marketing techniques that stimulate short-term demand include price discounts, special promotions (children stay free, two for one), package deals, blitz advertising are useful tools in crisis situations (Pizam, 2002). They were all used in this Canadian context. Tate (2002) identified five demand changes after 9/11 which included visitors seeking lower prices, shorter duration of visits, later booking habits, having different motivations for travel and seeking new approaches to product and service promotion.

This study shows that there is value in understanding the effects a crisis situation has on a neighboring country. This ripple effect on neighboring destinations from a crisis in another country is also reported in other recent work (Beirman, 2003, p. 3) The shifts in travel patterns in Canada have large marketing ramifications and show a focus on domestic markets in times of crisis is not unwarranted. Indeed, marketing strategies that target less sensitive markets first will more likely result in a quick recovery (Pizam, 2002). Concentration on the "driving" market since many potential tourists were afraid to fly and promoting the "friends and relatives" market that is less susceptible to the "fear" factor were both responses adopted by destination marketers in the US and Canada. Within the Canadian domestic travel market, recovery was varied for different types of travel markets and products, for example, rural areas suffered less than urban areas and specific products that focused on comfort and renewal may have even benefited (spa treatment centers).

As discussed above, some markets recovered more quickly than others but there is evidence that the "issue attention cycle of public attention" is relatively short even for the flying market. The overall volume of domestic travel did not seem to change based on the 9/11 crisis beyond that of a very short cycle. At the time of writing, even the air travel market is recovering. As reported by CTC (2003), the conference board of Canada's Travel Intentions Survey revealed that Canadians are feeling more confident about flying. Of Canadians polled in June, 2003, 21 percent indicated they plan on traveling by air for their domestic winter holiday, compared to only 10 percent that indi-

cated the same the previous year (CTC, 2003, p. 1). These results of a tourism short-term decline and recovery are consistent with the results of Pizam and Smith (2000) who tracked the effects of seventy terrorist acts reported in the news media. They found that a large proportion of these acts (76%) caused a significant decline in tourism demand that lasted from one to six months, with recovery in approximately 50% of the cases within three months or less.

MANAGEMENT RECOMMENDATIONS

Since September 11, "disaster crisis management has become a critical economic, political and social priority for many nations to which tourism forms a significant industry" (Beirman, 2003, p. 4). Knowledge, planning and co-operation are important in facilitating the destination recovery management process. Based on the results of this paper, three primary recommendations are made for tourism recovery in the event of a disaster. First, having a prepared emergency marketing plan that focuses on altering traditional markets for safer travel markets is imperative. While some have argued that government fiscal policy is a key component to tourism recovery (Blake & Sinclair, 2003), an effective marketing plan is needed to communicate the outcomes of the policy changes to the consumer. Second, there should be ongoing research into how travel markets react to differing disasters. For instance, since 9/11 Canada has faced the negative image effects of the wars in Iraq/Afghanistan, a Mad Cow scare, and major forest fires in the western portion of the country, as well as SARS. How did the travel market react to each of those types of disasters? Are the travel market responses similar to those experienced after 9/11? Large scale data sets like the CTS offer opportunities to track tourist behavior and travel patterns and indicate dislocations and trends. Finally, both government agencies and tourism industry managers need to set up a quick response mechanism for recovery after crisis. Ideally, effective partnerships and co-operation between the public and private sectors could facilitate rapid response and communication. As the world becomes increasingly turbulent the need to have systems in place to address crisis is imperative.

CONCLUSIONS

In conclusion, this empirical research contributes to applied knowledge on the impacts of disasters and crises on tourism patterns. Such research is a foundation to assist the tourism industry and relevant government agencies in learning from past experiences and in coping with similar disturbing events. Shortly after the 9/11 disasters, Canada had a number of crisis events to deal with of its own. In 2003, the tourist image of Canada became tarnished by SARS in Toronto, Mad Cow disease in Alberta and forest fires in BC. All required response strategies from the tourism industry that followed many of the marketing strategies adopted after 9/11 and focused on domestic travel.

Furthermore, while this empirical study shows some of the ways travel trips in Canada altered after the 9/11 crisis, it also raises a number of interesting questions. Unfortunately, this research is limited by the use of secondary data. Further study is needed to explore how travel choice and decision making in general is affected in times of crisis and what the relative importance of safety is in influencing choice behavior. Long-term research, not just in the destination directly affected, but in neighbouring geographic locations could reveal some of the stages that visitors may proceed through regarding travel choice after a crisis. Future research questions include how are travel choice alterations influenced by demographic characteristics and trip characteristics of different types of travelers. Key indicators in the form of altered behavior after a crisis need to be investigated; for example, how consistent is the switch to domestic travel, VFR, shorter trips, automobile travel in the event of an aircraft related disaster. Understanding how these characteristics of tourist choice behavior may change in the event of a disaster provides insights to tourism marketers who are able to monitor these switches in behavior and create response strategies and identify tourism products to satisfy these altered needs. Further, while some marketing techniques have been suggested as useful, measurement of their effectiveness needs more study in different crisis situations.

REFERENCES

Bargeman, B., Joh, C.H., & Timmermans, H. (2002). Vacation behaviour using a sequence alignment method. *Annals of Tourism Research*, 29(2), 320-337.

Bar-On, R. (1996). Measuring the effects on tourism of violence and of promotion following violent acts. In A. Pizam, & Y. Mansfeld (Eds.), *Tourism, crime and international security issues* (pp. 159-74). Chichester, UK: Wiley.

Beirman, D. (2003). *Restoring tourism destinations in crisis–A strategic marketing approach*. Wallingford, Oxon: CABI Publishing.

Blake, A., & Sinclair, M.T. (2003). Tourism crisis management–US response to September 11th. *Annals of Tourism Research*, 30(4), 813-832.

Burton, I., Kates, R.W., & White, G.F. (1993). *The environment as a hazard*. New York: Guilford.

Canadian Tourism Commission. (2003). Canadian Tourism Commission Tourism Intelligence Bulletin, September 2002. *Recovery Momentum Still Precarious*. Ottawa: Author, 19.

Canadian Tourism Commission. (2002a). Canadian Tourism Commission–Market Research–May, 2002. *Synopsis of Research Findings Post 9/11*. Ottawa: Author, 11.

Canadian Tourism Commission. (2002b). *Canadian Tourism Facts & Figures 2001*. Ottawa: Author, 2.

Faulkner, B. (2001). Towards a framework for tourism disaster management. *Tourism Management, 22*, 135-147.

Hall, C.M., & O'Sullivan, V. (1996). Tourism, political stability and violence. In A. Pizam, & Y. Mansfeld (Eds.), *Tourism, crime and international security issues* (pp. 105-121). New York: Wiley.

King, R.L., & Woodside, A.G. (2001). Qualitative comparative analysis of travel and tourism purchase-consumption systems. In G.I. Crouch, B. Ritchie, A.G. Woodside, & J.A. Mazanec (Eds.), *Consumer psychology of tourism, hospitality and leisure* (pp. 87-105). New York: CABI Publishing.

Krakover, S. (2000). Estimating the effects of atrocious events on the flow of tourism in Isreal. In G. Ashworth, & R. Hartmann. (Eds.), *Tourism, war and commemoration of atrocity*. New York: Cognizant Communication.

Mansfeld, Y. (1999). Cycles of war, terror and peace: Determinants and management of crisis and recovery of the Israeli tourism industry. *Journal of Travel Research, 38*(1), 30-36.

Morrison, A.M. (1996). *Hospitality and tourism marketing* (2nd ed.). Albany: Delmar.

O'Neil, M.A., & Fritz, F. (1996). Northern Ireland tourism: Any chance now? *Tourism Management, 17*, 161-163.

Pizam, A. (1999). A comprehensive approach to classifying acts of crime and violence at tourism destinations. *Journal of Travel Research, 38*(1), 5-12.

Pizam, A. (2002). Tourism and terrorism editorial. *Hospitality Management, 21,* 1-3.

Pizam, A., & Smith, G. (2000). Tourism and terrorism: A quantitative analysis of major terrorist acts and their impact on tourism destinations. *Tourism Economics, 6*(2), 123-138.

Quarantelli, E.L. (1996). Local mass media operations in disasters in the USA. *Disaster, Prevention and Management, 3*(2), 5-10.

Schwartz, R.D. (1991). Travelers under fire: Tourists in the Tibetian uprising. *Annals of Tourism Research, 18,* 588-604.

Seddighi, H.R., & Theicharous, A.L. (2002). A model of tourism destination choice: Theoretical and empirical analysis. *Tourism Management, 23,* 475-487.

Shaw, G., & Williams, A.M. (2002). *Critical issues in tourism: A geographic perspective.* Oxford: Blackwell.

Sonmez, S.F. (1998). Tourism, terrorism and political instability. *Annals of Tourism Research, 25*(2), 416-456.

Sonmez, S.F., Apostolopoulos, Y., & Tarlow, P. (1999). Tourism in crisis: Managing the effects of terrorism. *Journal of Travel Research, 38*(1), 13-18.

Statistics Canada. (1998). *Canadian travel survey microdata users guide.* Ottawa: Author.

Statistics Canada (1998). *Canadian travel survey: Review of 1996 results.* Ottawa: Author.

Tate, P. (2002). The impact of 9/11: Caribbean, London and New York case studies. *Travel and Tourism Analyst, 5,* 1.1-1.25.

Wilton, D. & Wirjanto, T. (1998). *An analysis of the seasonal variation in the national tourism indicators.* Ottawa: Canadian Tourism Commission.

The Significance of Crisis Communication in the Aftermath of 9/11: A National Investigation of How Tourism Managers Have Re-Tooled Their Promotional Campaigns

Lisa T. Fall

Joseph Eric Massey

SUMMARY. After September 11, 2001 (9/11), the United States immediately embarked upon a new way of life, or, as the media describes it, a "new normalcy" (Chura, 2002; Stark, 2002). Throughout Corporate America, managers had to instantaneously re-group, re-strategize, and re-tool their internal and external communication plans. The terrorist attacks on the United States created a crisis in the tourism industry, and have proved challenging even to experienced managers of corporate communication.

This investigation examines the post-crisis communication efforts among convention and visitors bureaus (CVB) managers responsible for promoting travel to their destinations. Two theoretical underpinnings serve as the framework for the study: crisis communication theory and strategic communication management. The study examined the tools tourism managers use to promote travel to their destination, how they have redesigned their promotional messages, and how they have redirected their target market focus in the wake of 9/11. Further, this research investigates how the tools used (advertising, tourism marketing, public relations, new media) serve as predictors for redesigning promotional messages and redirecting target markets. *[Article copies available for a fee from The Haworth Document Delivery Service: 1-800-HAWORTH. E-mail address: <docdelivery@ haworthpress.com> Website: <http://www.HaworthPress.com> © 2005 by The Haworth Press, Inc. All rights reserved.]*

KEYWORDS. Crisis management, crisis communication theory, public relations, tourism, travel, destination image, communication strategies

INTRODUCTION

It is difficult to overstate how dramatically the events of September, 11, 2001 (9/11) have impacted the global tourism industry. According to the International Air Transport Association (IATA), the global airline industry lost one-third its size–flights, fleets, crews, and passen-

Lisa T. Fall is Assistant Professor, School of Advertising and Public Relations, University of Tennessee, 476 Communications Bldg., Knoxville, TN 37996 (E-mail: lfall@utk.edu). Joseph Eric Massey is Assistant Professor, California State University, Fullerton, P.O. Box 6846, Fullerton, CA 92834-6846 (E-mail: jmassey@fullerton.edu).

[Haworth co-indexing entry note]: "The Significance of Crisis Communication in the Aftermath of 9/11: A National Investigation of How Tourism Managers Have Re-Tooled Their Promotional Campaigns." Fall, Lisa T., and Joseph Eric Massey. Co-published simultaneously in *Journal of Travel & Tourism Marketing* (The Haworth Hospitality Press, an imprint of The Haworth Press, Inc.) Vol. 19, No. 2/3, 2005, pp. 77-90; and: *Tourism Crises: Management Responses and Theoretical Insight* (ed: Eric Laws, and Bruce Prideaux) The Haworth Hospitality Press, an imprint of The Haworth Press, Inc., 2005, pp. 77-90. Single or multiple copies of this article are available for a fee from The Haworth Document Delivery Service [1-800-HAWORTH, 9:00 a.m. - 5:00 p.m. (EST). E-mail address: docdelivery@haworthpress.com].

gers–after 9/11. This crisis in the airline industry produced ripple-effects throughout the global tourism industry and the industry has still not recovered. According to the World Tourism Organization, the global tourism market has continued to decrease since 9/11 (*http://www.worldtourism.org*).

The crisis that was produced in the global tourism industry left managers searching for ways to strategically respond to a new kind of crisis. Regardless of how solid a communication plan may have been up until that point, managers were forced to react to a situation that had never been encountered before. Prior emergency preparedness and crisis management programs had not incorporated role-playing exercises depicting the enormity and intensity of this scenario. There were no handbooks, no blueprints, no "how to" manuals to refer to when dealing with a crisis of such magnitude and of such a type.

In the United States, where the effects of 9/11 on tourism are most pronounced, continued research on recovery efforts is of paramount importance to practitioners and theorists alike, as a new model of crisis management emerges in the 21st century. This investigation therefore examines the post-crisis communication efforts among domestic convention and visitor bureau (CVB) managers responsible for promoting travel to their destinations.

REVIEW OF THE LITERATURE

Strategic Communication Management

Travel, tourism, and hospitality researchers have examined the role of communication as it relates to the post-September 11 terrorist attacks. The results provide a common theme: strategic communication continues to play a dominant role in the revitalization process. The travel/tourism literature focusing on 9/11 represents a broad spectrum of subject matter. Analyses range from hotel operations revenue and performance studies (Enz & Canina, 2002; O'Neill & Lloyd-Jones, 2002) to employee-related issues such as job security and workplace security (Batterman & Fullerton, 2002; Cohen, 2002; Enz & Taylor, 2002), job sharing (Sherwyn & Sturman, 2002), workplace privacy (Sproule, 2002), and military service

and employee rights (Klein, Pappas & Herman, 2002).

Of special relevance to this study is research that investigates post-9/11 communication and promotional issues within the tourism industry. For example, Litvin and Alderson (2003) conducted a case study to find out how the Charleston Area Convention & Visitors Bureau (CACVB) responded. The CACVB employed several special strategies to meet the individual needs of this situation. First, managers immediately started focusing more communication efforts on attracting travelers from their "drive markets" and expanded the six-hour drive radius to a ten-hour radius. Second, advertising expenditures were reallocated from the international travel budget to the domestic drive market budget. Third, advertising copy messages were redesigned to stress the drive accessibility of the city. A new tag line was included: "A short drive down the road. A million miles away." A special holiday vacation advertising campaign was also launched. The CACVB also collaborated with other area organizations to create pre-packaged vacation opportunities for travelers.

In another study that focuses on promotional strategies, Frisby (2002) explored how the British Tourism Authority (BTA) responded to the terrorist attacks and the foot-and-mouth outbreaks. BTA managers first identified their most viable key travel markets, then they revamped their communication program accordingly. They redesigned their campaign strategies, objectives, tactics, evaluation and measurement procedures to meet the specific needs of these two crises. Enhanced media relations and publicity planning were included in the campaign updates. Disseminating accurate information on a consistent basis to key media served as the crux of the plan. The overarching message goals were three-fold: to stress the safety of the destination, to communicate that foot-and-mouth disease was not widespread in Britain, and to highlight the various special activities taking place for would-be travelers.

Hopper (2001) examined how London positioned and promoted itself in the wake of 9/11. The London Tourism Board (LTB) immediately developed the London Tourism Recovery Group, which was tasked with the duty of conducting research during a six-month period to measure the impact the 9/11 attacks were having on the local tourism economy. The research was conducted in phases. Continuous data were collected, leading to timely strategic action planning procedures that were methodically put into place. Marketing expenditures were diverted from the overseas budget to the United Kingdom budget. A special promotional campaign, "The Greatest Show on Earth," was launched to stimulate domestic business to London. Other special promotional campaigns followed (e.g., "Royal London" and "Only in Britain, Only in 2002").

From a hospitality crisis response perspective, Stafford, Yu and Armoo (2002) studied how Washington, DC hotels responded to the attacks. These organizations launched an aggressive public relations program that employed various media relations and publicity strategies. The hotels also worked closely with local, state, and federal government agencies to encourage people to travel–not just to the DC area–but also throughout America.

Among these studies, none of the organizations opted do nothing and follow a "business as usual" philosophy. Instead, immediate steps were taken to revamp their communication procedures and programs. The literature reinforces the point that immediate reactive, yet strategic, communication planning was apparent in the wake of the 9/11 attacks–especially among tourism organizations (Massey, 2002, in press). From the literature review, four overarching themes have evolved. Organizations are (1) restructuring messages (2) refocusing their target markets (3) readjusting communication channels for disseminating key messages and (4) revamping communication campaigns to include more public relations-oriented activities.

Crisis Communication Theory

Most researchers argue that modern crisis communication theory began in the early 1980s when Johnson & Johnson experienced the Tylenol crisis (Mitroff, 2004). A rich body of theory and research on crisis communication has ensued, with many empirical investigations producing prescriptions and "best practices" for crisis communication managers. However, many organizations, particularly in the immediacy created by 9/11, have implemented

crisis communication into their core business strategy with no clear understanding of organizational crisis or crisis communication. An organizational crisis is "an unpredictable though not completely unexpected event inducing a sense of urgency, resulting in serious threat and overwhelming loss" (Massey, Simonson, Ward & Campbell, 2004, p. 251). Because a crisis is an unexpected and untoward event, it creates the need to respond to stakeholders through communication–a practice that has come to be known as crisis communication. According to Seeger and Ulmer (2001), "crisis communication concerns the processes whereby organizations create and exchange meanings among stakeholders regarding the risk of crisis, cause, blame responsibility, precautionary norms and crisis-induced changes in the organization and its relationship to stakeholders" (p. 131).

Crisis communication is a three-stage model, including (1) Crisis Preparation, (2) Crisis Response, and (3) Crisis Recovery. In the Crisis Preparation stage, organizations must develop reservoirs of goodwill with internal and external stakeholders, and must maintain effective reputations with stakeholders if they wish to survive crisis. Also in the pre-crisis stage, the proactive efforts of crisis managers involve the development of strategic crisis communication plans (CCP) and the establishment of the CMT.

If an organization reaches the second stage of the model, Crisis Response, it has just experienced crisis. In the Crisis Response stage, the CCP is implemented by crisis communication managers, in coordination with members of the larger CMT (which has representatives from all appropriate organizational units, including, for example, operations, safety management, legal, advertising, and others). Key stakeholders are targeted in this stage of the model, and a dialogue with these stakeholders is developed. Note that this stage of the model will be more effective if the organization has created that dialogue with stakeholders prior to any crisis.

In the final stage of the model, the Crisis Recovery Phase, the organization focuses its efforts at reputation management and returning the organization to a sense of normalcy. Crisis communication allows the organization to strategically manage stakeholder perceptions. This is particularly true if a proactive approach to crisis communication has been taken, where a positive reputation has been developed and stakeholder relationships have been managed effectively. Figure 1 graphically represents our three-stage model of crisis communication.

Crisis has traditionally included the concept of threat–indeed our own definition of crisis includes this element. However, many cases demonstrate that a crisis may also be an opportunity for organizations (such as the Tylenol case referenced above, where Johnson & Johnson's reputation was better after the crisis than before it). Theorists who view crises more broadly oftentimes note that the Chinese symbol for crisis represents both opportunity and threat. Consistent with this mantra, crisis communication theory is increasingly viewing events like 9/11 as an opportunity as well as a threat to organizations. Ulmer and colleagues (Seeger & Ulmer, 2001; Ulmer & Sellnow, 2002) have argued that crisis communication is increasingly focused on a discourse of renewal, viewing crisis as an opportunity for the organization to rejuvenate itself through strategic communication behavior. And many industry experts argue that changes taking place in the tourism industry, particularly in the airline industry, are changes that needed to be made to make the industry more competitive. Therefore, the 9/11 crisis has been used as an opportunity to restructure administrative, technical and communication functions within the tourism industry.

Whether it is viewed as an opportunity or a threat, 9/11 certainly created a crisis for the tourism industry–a crisis that requires a strategic response. Fortunately for most organizations affected by 9/11, they had taken a proactive approach to crisis and had developed Crisis Management Plans (CMPs) and Crisis Communication Plans (CCPs) in antici-

pation of crisis events. Unfortunately for these organizations, none had anticipated a large-scale crisis such as that created on September 11, 2001.

CMPs and CCPs are tools of the trade for crisis managers, but crisis management and crisis communication are two distinct fields. Crisis management is the strategic management activity that directs all technical and administrative activities during crisis, while crisis communication is the strategic management activity that directs all communication with internal and external stakeholders during crisis.

One outgrowth of the work in crisis management is the development of a CMP, which "consists of a full range of thoughtful processes and steps that anticipate the complex nature of crises real and perceived" (Caywood & Stocker, 1993, p. 411). More organizations than ever have developed CMPs and the number continues to rise (Barton, 2001).

A key organizational initiative that is developed either as a separate plan or as a component of the CMP is the Crisis Communication Plan (CCP). A CCP outlines the steps to be taken to formalize a communication system to be put in place before any crisis occurs, in conjunction with the crisis management team (CMT). This aspect of the CCP is highly proactive, and it establishes protocols for stakeholder interaction both internally and externally, before, during, and after a crisis hits (Massey & Larsen, in press). The benefits of the CCP are enormous since organizational representatives, most notably those members of the CMT, know exactly who they should communicate with to send and receive valuable information. This is most critical during a crisis, since a crisis tends to create a chaotic environment, requiring the exchange of information between organizations and key stakeholders such as internal representatives including engineering, operations, manufacturing, public relations, and human resources, and external representatives such as regulatory agencies, the media, and the general public, among others. Finally, the CCP also develops plans for how to strategically respond, through communication, after a crisis has occurred, to restore consumer confidence

FIGURE 1. Crisis Communication Model

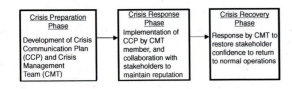

and help to ensure the well-being of the organization by protecting its reputation (Coombs, 1995, 1999, 2000).

CRISIS RESPONSE STRATEGIES

How an organization responds is dependent upon the type of crisis experienced (Coombs, 1995; Massey, 2002). Because of the large number of crises that any organization may experience, researchers have created typologies of organizational crises (Coombs, 1999; Meyers & Holusha, 1986; Mitroff & Anagnos, 2001; Pearson & Clair, 1998). Meyers and Holusha (1986) for example, argue that there are nine crisis types: crises in public perception, sudden market shifts, product failures, top management succession, cash crises, industrial relations crises, hostile takeovers, adverse international events, and governmental regulation/deregulation. Mitroff and Anagnos (2001) take a different approach to highlight the broad aspects of crisis. Their typologies include the following seven crises: economic, informational, physical, human resource crises, reputational crises, psychopathic acts, and natural disasters.

Although the efforts of these and other scholars to categorize crisis types have been heuristic, it must be noted that many of the different types of crisis have not yet been identified. Mitroff (2004) argues that this is because crisis managers are unable to think the unthinkable. For example, prior to 9/11, psychopathic acts such as terrorism were rarely addressed. Mitroff's (2004) data show that Fortune 500 CEOs' favorite size of a crisis is small, while terrorism is the crisis they least want to think about.

More important to the current investigation, little is known about how organizations should communicate following these kinds of crises. But there is literature that can serve as a blueprint. Much of the research in crisis communication suggests that a crisis has the potential to negatively impact an organization's image (Allen & Caillouet, 1994; Benoit, 1995; Coombs, 1995, 1999; Hearit, 1995; Fall, 1996; Massey, 2001; 2003). Coombs (1995) argues, for example, that crises threaten the image of organizations. Based upon this assumption, several

researchers have developed a rich tradition that examines the relationship between organizational image and strategic communication (Andriole, 1985; Benoit & Czerwinski, 1997; Fink, 1986). Coombs (1999), for example, has developed a typology of strategies that ranges from defensive to accommodative, including (1) attacking the accuser, (2) denial, (3) excuse, (4) justification, (5) ingratiation, (6) corrective action, and (7) full apologies. Coombs (1999) argues "organizations use impression management strategies . . . to repair the reputational damage from the crisis" (p. 122). This research tradition has provided sound guidelines for successful communication-based approaches to image restoration following an organizational crisis. Coombs (1995, 1999) refers to the systematic use of communication following events like 9/11 as "crisis response strategies." Crisis-response strategies have been demonstrated to mitigate the negative effects of crisis (Massey, 2001, 2002, 2003; Massey et al., 2004).

But the post 9/11 crisis that has impacted the tourism industry is unique, perhaps unthinkable as Mitroff (2004) argues, and therefore calls for a new model of crisis communication. Massey (2005) argues that the terrorism attacks of 9/11 represent a new form of organizational crisis, and because of this situation, extant theories of crisis management and crisis communication need to be re-evaluated and revised. He argues that three characteristics of the 9/11 crisis in particular are noteworthy and require immediate action. First, future crisis-response typologies must include acts of terrorism, such as those experienced on 9/11, to provide a more complete picture of the types of crises that can occur and how organizations should prepare for and respond to such crises. Second, definitions of crisis must now include a global component, since events like those experienced on 9/11 have clearly affected organizations around the world. And finally, a crisis must be treated as something that can harm entire industries and not just individual organizations. According to Massey (2005), "The 9/11 crisis provides a case of an entire industry in crisis and how a crisis of this magnitude can affect not only the organizations directly involved in the crisis, but the industry as a whole." When crisis management and crisis communication theories embrace this new concept of crisis, organizational communication approaches to crisis are improved.

RESEARCH QUESTIONS

A review of the public relations and crisis communication literature has led to one overarching question: how have managers restructured their crisis communication programs as a result of such an enormous and unprecedented crisis? To support this inquiry, the following research questions were addressed:

RQ1: In the aftermath of the September 11, 2001 terrorist attacks, what kinds of communication methods did tourism managers employ more and less frequently when marketing their destination?

RQ2: In the aftermath of the September 11, 2001 terrorist attacks, what kinds of message themes did tourism managers employ when marketing their destination?

RQ3: As a result of the September 11, 2001 terrorist attacks, how have tourism managers redirected their target market focus to promote travel to their destination?

RQ4: How is the choice to redesign promotional messages differentiated among the various types of communication techniques being employed (advertising, tourism marketing, public relations, new media)?

RQ5: How is the choice to redirect target market audiences differentiated among the various types of communication techniques being employed (advertising, tourism marketing, public relations, new media)?

METHOD

Selection of the Sample

Convention and visitors bureaus (CVB) were chosen for the study because these are the or-ganizations taxed with the primary duty of promoting their city/region as a destination location to external markets (leisure as well as business travelers). The initial sampling frame comprised organizations from three lists: CVBs that are members of the International Association of Convention & Visitors Bureaus, CVBs posted on the official Travel Industry Association of America web site and CVBs listed on each of the 50 state official tourism web sites. These lists were cross-referenced to eliminate replication.

A total of 800 respondents were randomly selected from the final list. During the pre-notification phase, a total of 195 surveys were returned as "undeliverable," diminishing the initial sampling frame to 605 potential respondents. A total of 184 industry professionals completed the survey, representing a 30% response rate.

Respondent Profile

Half the respondents have bachelors degrees and another 15% have masters degrees. Educational backgrounds range from communications (21%) and business, marketing, and management (21%) to nearly a third of the respondents who report "other" degrees in English, Journalism, Human Resources, Political Science and Hospitality Management. Approximately 75% of the respondents are female, which is indicative of the tourism profession in general. Geographically, the sample represents various sectors from across the United States, including the west (21%), midwest (33%), northeast (14%), and south (32%).

Administration Procedures

This study employs a web-based survey distributed via the Internet to e-mail addresses of CVB communication managers across the United States during June and July, 2002. Prior to launching the study, tourism managers were sent a pre-notification e-mail message to let them know the on-line survey was forthcoming. One week later they were sent another e-mail message that included a brief explanation of the study and the link to the on-line questionnaire. In the letter, it was clearly specified that the study was being conducted within the framework of the post-September

11 terrorist attacks and that all answers should be based on such activity.

Respondents were instructed to click on the link to be immediately directed to the questionnaire. A week before the assigned deadline, the researchers sent a follow-up e-mail message to remind respondents to complete the survey by the designated deadline. Again, the link to the on-line questionnaire was included in the e-mail correspondence.

Instrumentation/Operationalization of the Variables

The instrument consists of an on-line questionnaire that takes about 15 minutes to complete. As a validity check, the instrument was pre-tested among various CVB managers who were not part of the final sample. Revisions, based on their expertise, were made before the study was launched.

The primary variables under investigation are marketing messages, target market audiences, and communication techniques (channels). To address the refocusing of target markets, respondents were asked if they changed their primary target markets as a result of the September 11 attacks. If they did shift their focus, they were instructed to indicate who these new audiences were. To address the redesigned campaign message, respondents were asked to indicate how they revamped their messages. Questions addressing both of these variables were open-ended, allowing respondents to type in their answers.

The tourism literature defines channels of communication in a variety of ways, including information sources, communication tactics/techniques/methods, and channels. These terms are used interchangeably throughout this study (see Table 1). The communication techniques under investigation are based on a thorough review of the tourism literature (Fall, 2000a, 2000b, 2004; Fodness & Murrray, 1998, 1999; Andereck & Caldwell, 1993; Snepenger & Snepenger, 1993; Fesenmaier & Vogt, 1992; Rao, Thomas & Javalgi, 1992).

For each communication tactic, respondents were instructed to rate the *present* frequency of use compared to frequency of use before the September 11, 2001 terrorist attacks. A Likert-type 1-5 point scale was used: 1 = do not use it

at all now, 2 = use it slightly less now, 3 = use it the same, 4 = use it slightly more now and 5 = use it much more now. Respondents were also provided with an example for clarity: "If you use magazine media releases much more frequently now than you did before the September 11 attacks, you would choose use it much more now." Additional blanks were included for respondents to type in and rate any communication techniques not listed in the questionnaire.

Analyses

To address RQ1, frequency of use and mean scores were calculated and analyzed. For RQ2 and RQ3, the data were coded thematically for analysis. For the remaining two questions, the 14 communication variables were first collapsed into information source factors developed and validated in previous studies (Fall, 2000a, 2000b, 2004; Kinser & Fall, 2005). Alpha coefficient scores were determined to assure that the factors were reliable. Then the messages, target markets, and information source factors were submitted to discriminate analyses.

RESULTS

Addressing RQ1

Results in Table 1 reveal that public relations techniques are being used more frequently now than before the September 11, 2001 attacks. The data indicate that Internet web sites (18.6%), direct mail correspondence (10.6%), newspaper media releases (8.0%), newspaper ads (7.4%), auto club materials (6.9%), and magazine media releases (6.4%) represent the most increased use. Data also illustrate that paid advertisements (billboard ads 35.9%; radio ads 23.4%) are being the least used now, compared to before, September 11, as defined by "do not use it at all now." Overall mean scores among public relations/media relations tactics (newspaper, magazine and TV media releases) and the more traditional tourism marketing tactics (e.g., highway welcome center and auto club materials) demonstrate higher increased use scores than do the traditional advertising

TABLE 1. Frequency Scores of Communication Tactic Use: Use Now Compared to Before September 11 Terrorist Attacks

Communication Tactics Employed at USA CVBs	Use Much More Now (%)	Use Slightly More Now (%)	Use Same Now (%)	Use Slightly Less Now (%)	Do Not Use At All Now (%)
Billboard Ads	3.2	4.8	48.4	2.7	**35.9**
Magazine Ads	2.1	17.0	59.6	**17.0**	1.1
Newspaper Ads	**7.4**	**24.5**	46.8	**10.1**	6.5
Radio Ads	2.7	15.4	47.9	**5.3**	23.4
TV Ads	5.3	11.2	41.5	1.6	**35.0**
Internet Web Site	**18.6**	**38.3**	39.4	0	0
Industry Trade Show	1.6	11.7	**66.0**	13.8	2.2
Travel Agent	1.1	5.9	59.0	**8.5**	19.6
Highway Welcome Center	4.3	18.1	**72.3**	.5	1.1
Magazine Media Release	6.4	**21.3**	**64.4**	1.1	3.8
Newspaper Media Release	**8.0**	**23.9**	62.8	.5	1.6
TV Media Release	2.7	17.0	61.2	.5	10.3
Auto Club Materials	**6.9**	15.4	56.9	2.1	**12.0**
Direct Mail Appeal	**10.6**	**24.5**	48.4	1.1	8.5

Note: Bold-face figures indicate the highest scores for each category of use

tactics, as illustrated in Table 2. Overall, Internet web site has the highest mean score.

Addressing RQ2

A total of 43% of the tourism managers have re-designed their promotional message as a result of the September 11 attacks while the 48% kept the same message; 9% did not respond to this question. A thematic analysis of the message changes reported by respondents illustrates 13 overarching themes, as depicted in Table 3. The most frequently reoccurring themes reported focus on drivable destination/accessible location, safety, relaxation/getaway, destination branding, freedom/patriotism, and family.

Addressing RQ3

Findings demonstrate that 63% of the managers have not redirected their target markets while 33% have opted to do so; 4% did not respond to this question. A thematic analysis of the primary market shift changes reported in Table 4 reveals that managers' re-focusing of target markets fall into four categories. "Life-cycle/lifestyle" market segments include se-

TABLE 2. Overall Mean Scores, Standard Deviation Scores, and Ranking of Communication Tactic Use: Use Now Compared to Before September 11 Terrorist Attacks

Communication Tactics Employed at USA CVBs	Mean	Standard Deviations	Mean Rankings (1 = highest mean score; 13 = lowest mean score)
Billboard Ads	2.33	1.13	13
Magazine Ads	3.02	.69	8
Newspaper Ads	3.17	.95	6
Radio Ads	2.67	1.09	10
TV Ads	2.48	1.25	12
Internet Web Site	**3.78**	.74	1
Industry Trade Show	2.96	.65	9
Travel Agent	2.58	.92	11
Highway Welcome Center	**3.24**	1.00	4
Magazine Media Release	**3.26**	.76	3
Newspaper Media Release	**3.37**	.71	2
TV Media Release	3.04	.88	7
Auto Club Materials	3.04	.99	7
Direct Mail Correspondence	2.58	1.00	11

Note: bold-face figures indicate highest mean scores.

TABLE 3. Message Change Themes Resulting from the September 11, 2001 Terrorist Attacks

Message Change Focus	Frequency of Times Reported
Driveable/Accessible location	18
Safety	10
Relaxation/Getaway	10
Destination Branding	9
Family	7
Freedom/Patriotism	7
Cost (value for price paid)	5
Home away from Home	5
Recreation/Outdoors	4
Meeting Destination	3
State Message	3
Nostalgia/Sameness	3
Special post-9/11 message	2

Note: some respondents provided messages with multiple themes, so their message themes were coded in more than one category.

TABLE 4. Re-Targeted Markets Resulting from the September 11, 2001 Terrorist Attacks

New Primary Public Focus	Frequency of Times Reported
Life Cycle/Lifestyle	
Senior	2
Singles	1
Families	10
Couples	1
Geography	
Regional	15
In-state	9
Drive Market	22
Duration of Stay	
Day-Trippers	2
Weekend Travelers	1
Type of Traveler	
~ Business	
SMERF segments (social, military, educational, religious, fraternal)	2
Meeting Planners	3
Associations	2
~ Vacation/Leisure	
Leisure	8
Sports Enthusiasts/Golfers	2
~ Miscellaneous	
Domestic	2
Patriotic	2

Note: some respondents provided primary target markets with multiple categories, so their answers were coded in more than one category.

niors, families, singles and couples. "Geography" markets range from regional and state to drive markets while "Duration of Stay" markets are represented by day-trippers and weekend travelers. The fourth category, "Type of Traveler," is further sub-divided into three segments: business, vacation (leisure), and miscellaneous markets. Business markets entail meeting planners, associations, and SMERFs (social, military, educational, religious, fraternal); vacation markets are represented by golfers/sports enthusiasts, and general leisure. The last sub-category, miscellaneous, is represented by domestic and patriotic travelers. As shown, the most frequently reoccurring shift of target markets focuses on drive markets, regional markets, and families.

Addressing RQ4 and RQ5

To address the last two research questions, the 14 communication variables were first collapsed into information source factors developed and validated in previous studies (Fall, 2000a, 2000b, 2004; Kinser & Fall, 2005). Reliability scores indicate acceptable alpha coefficients: advertising, $\alpha = .77$; public relations, $\alpha = .72$; and tourism marketing, $\alpha = .77$. Internet web sites, as in the previous studies, represents its own factor. (See Table 5.)

The information source factors and the message and target marketing variables were then submitted to discriminant analyses. Message and target market shift variables were coded dichotomously as "yes, we made a change" or "no, we did not make a change." The source factors were entered as the predictors. Results indicate that there is a statistically significant difference among the four factors, explaining 63% of the variance: Wilk's Lambda = .941, $\chi (4, 184) = 9.932$, $p = .042$. In particular, the public relations/media relations factor is the largest predictor with a discriminant coefficient of .707, followed by tourism marketing with a score of .575. In other words, increased levels of public relations and tourism marketing tactic use predict the re-designing of promotional messages. Said another way, those managers who have opted to redesign their promotional messages are significantly more likely to increase public relations and tourism mar-

TABLE 5. Alpha Reliability Scores for Information Source Factors

INFORMATION SOURCE FACTORS		
Advertising	Tourism Marketing	Public Relations/ Media Relations
Billboard Ads	Industry Trade Show	Magazine Media Release
Magazine Ads	Travel Agent	Newspaper Media Release
Newspaper Ads	Highway Welcome Center Information	TV Media Release
Radio Ads	Auto Club Materials	
TV Ads	Direct Mail Appeal	
$\alpha = .72$	$\alpha = .77$	$\alpha = .77$

TABLE 6. Standardized Canonical Discriminant Function Coefficients

	Function
	1
Advertisements	−.353
Public Relations/Media Relations	.707
Tourism Marketing	.575
Internet Web Site	.211

TABLE 7. Structure Matrix

	Function
	1
Public Relations/Media Relations	.890
Tourism Marketing	.865
Advertisements	.648
Internet Web Site	.487

Pooled within-groups correlations between discriminating variables and standardized canonical discriminant functions. Variables ordered by absolute size of correlation within function.

TABLE 8. Functions at Group Centroids

	Function
	1
Message	
1.00	−.265
2.00	.235

Unstandardized canonical discriminant functions evaluated at group means.

keting technique use as well. Note: none of the information source factors serves as predictors of the CVB managers' choice to redirect their target markets. (See Tables 6-8.)

DISCUSSION

Two primary ramifications stem from this study. First, the results demonstrate the value of public relations as a management function for carrying out crisis communication strategies in the tourism industry. Results demonstrate that public relations techniques continue to serve as key components for communicating before, during, and after a crisis of such magnitude as the September 11, 2001 attacks. Second, the results illustrate that proactive managers who are restructuring their promotional messages to encourage travel to their destinations are also more significantly increasing their tourism marketing and public relations methods for disseminating such key messages. This result suggests that managers who tend to be more strategic in their planning also tend to be more assertive in employing marketing and public relations strategies.

Public Relations as a Strategic Crisis Communication Function

No "cookie cutter" formulas or "how to" crisis manuals were available to managers confronted with a crisis of such magnitude and intensity as 9/11. The theoretical underpinnings of public relations management are substanti-

ated among the details of these findings. The skepticism of the day-old question, "it sounds good in theory, but what about in practice?" is addressed as well. In short, two dominant mass media theories help us to better understand these results. First, according to the media systems dependency theory (DeFleur & Ball-Rokeach, 1975), during particular situations, such as crises, people tend become more dependent on the media for information. Hence, it makes sense that the CVB managers should be increasing their use of the media to disseminate post-9/11 messages. Second, the agenda setting theory (McCombs & Shaw, 1972) posits that the media sets the agenda (e.g., the topic) for what we think about–but not how we think about it. In the case of the September 11 attacks, any information related to this situation *was* the agenda. Therefore, the results suggest that the CVB managers are making decisions that are compatible with their information seekers. People are both tuned in (to the agenda) and tuning in (to the media). From a cost-benefit standpoint, these managers are spending money on communication channels that provide the most utility benefit to their target markets.

Results from this study also demonstrate that tourism managers are actively engaging in media relations as a primary function in the aftermath of the attacks. Since the "traveling public" encompasses a wide variety of people, the media serves as a beneficial vehicle to reach such broad audiences. In this case, managers are seeking to earn exposure in key newspapers, magazines and on specific television stations to effectively reach them. On the other hand, advertisements, which supply us with controlled information, may not seem as sincere in their attempts to communicate messages.

This study reinforces the shift toward increased use of public relations tactics to communicate messages to key publics among the tourism industry. In particular, the tourism managers in this sample are utilizing more public relations information channels when communicating with their target publics. More frequent use of print media relations tactics activities solidifies the point that managers continue to identify the critical need for disseminating messages via uncontrolled methods. These techniques tend to be viewed as more credible because they are filtered via gatekeepers (e.g., editors, producers, etc.) before they are actually published. In short, the sender has no control over the final content, style, placement and timing of the original message. Therefore, receivers may perceive this information as more genuine (Ries & Ries, 2002).

One must not forget, however, that the shift toward public relations in the tourism industry, at least as is reported here, is due in large part to the events of 9/11, which created a crisis for the industry. Crisis communication has a rich tradition of theory and research, with a practical focus. That tradition and focus changed on 9/11. The results of 9/11 have implications for crisis management and communication that must not be ignored. Organizations must continue to proactively plan for crises, but they must also

think the unthinkable, which Mitroff (2004) refers to as critical thinking. Critical thinking–thinking the unthinkable–is the essence of crisis leadership. When crisis leadership is enacted in an organization, crisis management and communication are just a part of the organization's proactive efforts at eliminating or mitigating crisis. Indeed, Mitroff argues that if crisis leaders are truly able to think the unthinkable, then many crises will be avoided entirely. The problem is that most managers cannot think the unthinkable. It is not whether managers have the ability to think critically, but whether they have the courage and the will to do so. The results of 9/11 and the results of this investigation demonstrate that crisis leadership must be adopted in organizations so that crisis management and crisis communication theory and practice can be advanced.

Implications for Managers

An organization cannot successfully provide quality service to its varied publics without the implementation of a well-orchestrated public relations program (Fall, 2000a, 2000b, 2004; Kinser & Fall, 2005; Stacks & Carroll, in press; Heath, Leth & Nathan, 1994). In support of this premise, several lessons can be learned from this study and lead to the following three recommendations. First, tourism managers should continue to carefully and consistently assess WHO their primary target markets are–and then to keep abreast of their target audiences' wants and needs. By doing so, tourism managers can more clearly define messages that answer the primary question in the mind of all potential receivers: "what's in it for me?" As well, they can better determine the most appropriate information source (communication channels) for dissemination of such messages.

Second, results from this study support the recommendation that tourism managers should to take a step back and think about what and how they want to promote their destinations during times of unrest. In the case of the terrorist attacks, travel managers realized they needed to be sensitive to the emotional and psychological states of travelers. Therefore, they opted for softer, subtler, less self-promotional oriented messages to encourage travel to visit their destinations.

The need to regroup and retool communication programs during a crisis situation leads to the third recommendation: tourism managers need to continuously engage in environmental scanning and other research-related activities on a regular basis. In the aftermath of a crisis, ongoing monitoring is critical; but an organization needs to be concerned with more than just the immediate post-crisis stage. In the case of a crisis of the 9/11 magnitude, in which the residual negative financial affects are still lingering four years later, it is vital that tourism managers continue to keep their hands on the pulse of their traveling public. Launching periodic primary research (e.g., conducting surveys, in-depth interviews, focus groups) and keeping themselves up-to-date by means of secondary research (e.g., examining results from reports conducted by Travel and Tourism Industry Association of America, Yankelovich Travel MONITOR, and other market research firms) will enable managers to revamp communication campaigns that are both captivating and successful.

Limitations of the Study

This study has some limitations that should be noted. First, it was launched in the summer, which is one of the busiest periods for CVB managers. This timing issue probably diminished the response rate. Second, as with any self-administered survey, one can never be sure if the appropriate person actually completed the questionnaire. Third, the results have limited generalizability to convention and visitors bureaus. Finally, other research data collection methods should be considered when launching research directed at CVB managers. These managers receive a constant flow of email messages. Therefore, an on-line survey disseminated via e-mail may get buried among the barrage of other messages, therefore diminishing the survey's return rate.

CONCLUSION

Suggestions for Future Research

Examining post-September 11 terrorist attacks communication strategies employed by CVB managers represents just a small aspect of other ways the travel/tourism industry has worked so assiduously to bring travel levels back to pre-September 11 stature. And, destination organizations represent only one segment of the industry. Other segments should be further investigated, ranging broadly in scope from food and beverage to accommodations, to transportation and various entertainment facilities. Finally, although leisure travel is a prosperous market, when a crisis hits it affects all markets–including business travel. Hence, future studies related to crisis communication should examine the measures taken to target business travelers, conventioneers, and corporate meeting planners. But what is even as important as determining *how* these entities have re-strategized their crisis communication and promotional programs is *why*–and analyzing what has worked effectively and what has not from a crisis management perspective. Unfortunately, no one is immune from crisis situations; however, the post-crisis windfall may be dramatically diminished if handled properly and efficiently during the actual situation at hand. Case study analyses are invaluable research methods in this regard.

Related directly to this study, the researchers anticipate disseminating the survey five years from now to determine how communication programs have since been further adjusted. We will determine if post-crisis communication management continues to stay in the forefront or if it has gone by the wayside, thereby supporting the "out of sight, of out mind" philosophy. Respondents will also be asked to determine what has worked well–and not so well–regarding their ongoing marketing and public relations strategies and tactics over the past five years. Further, they will be asked to elaborate and explain why some of these techniques worked better than others. Evaluation methods will also be included in this follow up analysis.

The results from this study demonstrate how CVB managers effectively incorporated marketing and public relations crisis communication strategies in the aftermath of the 9/11 terrorist attacks. Results from this study reinforce a dominant message: one cannot assume that programs that were successful pre-9/11 will continue to be appropriate post-9/11.

In an industry where the fall-out and residual effects are still evident, marketing and public relations crisis management strategies continue to contribute to the ongoing efforts to revitalize the travel/tourism industry.

REFERENCES

Allen, W.M., & Caillouet, R.H. (1994). Legitimation endeavors: Impression management strategies used by an organization in crisis. *Communication Monographs, 61*, 44-62.

Andereck, K., & Caldwell, L. (1993). The influence of tourists' characteristics on ratings of information sources for an attraction. In M. Uysal & D. Fesenmaier (Eds.), *Communication and channel systems in tourism marketing* (pp. 171-189). New York: The Haworth Press, Inc.

Barton, L. (2001). *Crisis in organizations II*. Cincinnati: South-Western Publishing Company.

Batterman, R.L., & Fullerton, J.F. (2002). Collective bargaining after September 11: What about job security and workplace security. *Cornell Hotel & Restaurant Administration Quarterly, 43*(5), 93-108.

Benoit, W.L. (1995). *Accounts, excuses and apologies*. Albany, NY: State University of New York Press.

Caywood, C., & Stocker, K.P. (1993). The ultimate crisis plan. In J. Gottschalk (Ed.), *Crisis-response: Inside stories on managing image under siege*. Detroit: Gale Research Inc.

Cohen, E.A. (2002). Collective bargaining regarding safety and security issues. *Cornell Hotel & Restaurant Administration Quarterly, 43*(5), 109-118.

Coombs, W.T. (1995). Choosing the right words: The development of guidelines for the selection of the "appropriate" crisis-response strategies. *Management Communication Quarterly, 8*(4), 447-476.

Coombs, W.T. (1999). *Ongoing crisis communication: Planning, managing, and responding*. Thousand Oaks, CA: Sage Publications.

Coombs, W.T. (2000). Designing post-crisis messages: Lessons for crisis-response strategies. *Review of Business, 21*(3/4), 37-41.

Chura, H. (2002). The new normal. *Advertising Age, 73*(10), 1.

DeFleur, M., & Ball-Rokeach, S. (1975). *Theories of mass communication*. NY: David McKay.

Enz, C.A., & Canina, C. (2002). The best of times, the worst of times: Differences in hotel performance following 9/11. *Cornell Hotel & Restaurant Administration Quarterly, 43*(5), 41-51.

Enz, C.A., & Taylor, M.S. (2002). The safety and security of U.S. hotels: A post-September 11 report. *Cornell Hotel & Restaurant Administration Quarterly, 43*(5), 119-136.

Fall, L.T. (1996). The crisis of Hurricane Hugo as it relates to public relations. Chapter 10. *Earth, Wind,*

Fire and Water: Approaching Natural Disaster. Open Door Publishers.

Fall, L.T. (2000a). An exploratory study of the relationship between human values and information sources within a tourism framework. *Journal of Hospitality & Leisure Marketing, 7*(1), 3-28.

Fall, L.T. (2000b). *Segmenting pleasure travelers on the basis of information source usefulness and personal value importance*. Unpublished doctoral dissertation, Michigan State University, Michigan.

Fall, L.T. (2004). A public relations segmentation study: Using Grunig's nested segmentation model and Yankelovich's generational influences model to distinguish vacation traveler publics. *Journal of Hospitality & Leisure Marketing, 11*(1), 5-30.

Fesenmaier, D., & Vogt, K. (1992). Evaluating the utility of touristic information sources for planning midwest vacation travel. *Journal of Travel & Tourism Marketing, 1*(2), 1-18.

Fink, S. (1986). *Crisis management: Planning for the inevitable*. New York: American Management Association.

Fodness, D., & Murrray, B. (1998). A typology of tourist information search strategies. *Journal of Travel Research, 37*(2), 108-120.

Fodness, D., & Murrray, B. (1999). A model of tourist information search behavior. *Journal of Travel Research, 37*(3), 220-230.

Frisby, E. (2002). Communicating in a crisis: The British tourist authority's reponses to the foot-and-mouth outbreak and 11 September, 2001. *Journal of Vacation Marketing, 9*(1), 89-100.

Hearit, K.M. (1995). "Mistakes were made": Organizations, apologia and crises of social legitimacy. *Communication Studies, 46*(1 & 2), 1-17.

Heath, R.L., Leth, S.A., & Nathan, K. (1994). Communicating service quality improvement: Another role for public relations. *Public Relations Review, 20*(1), 29-41.

Hopper, P. (2001). Marketing London in a difficult climate. *Journal of Vacation Marketing, 9*(1), 81-88.

Kinser, K., & Fall, L.T. (2005). Lions and tigers and bears, oh my! An examination of membership communication programs among our nation's zoos. *Journal of Hospitality & Leisure Marketing, 12*(1/2), 57-77.

Klein, J.S., Pappas, N.J., & Herman, M.I. (2002). The userra: Workers' employment rights following military service. *Cornell Hotel & Restaurant Administration Quarterly, 43*(5), 75-83.

Litvin, S.W., & Alderson, L.L. (2003). How Charleston got her groove back: A CVB's response to 9/11. *Journal of Vacation Marketing, 9*(2), 188-197.

Massey, J.E. (2001). Managing legitimacy: Communication strategies for organizations in crisis. *Journal of Business Communication, 38*(2), 153-183.

Massey, J.E. (2002). The airline industry in crisis. In J. Biberman, & A. Alkhafaji (Eds.), *Business research yearbook, 9* (pp. 727-732). Saline, MI: McNaughton & Gunn, Inc.

Massey, J.E. (2003). Managing organizational images: Crisis response and legitimacy restoration. In D. Millar & B. Heath (Eds.), *Crisis communication: A rhetorical approach* (pp. 233-246). New Jersey: Lawrence Erlbaum Associates.

Massey, J.E. (2005). The airline industry in crisis: Analyzing the response to the September 11th attacks on the U.S. *Journal of Hospitality and Leisure Marketing*, 12(1/2), 97-114.

Massey, J.E., & Larsen, J. (in press). Crisis management in real time: How to successfully plan for and respond to crisis. *Journal of Promotion Management*.

Massey, J.E., Simonson, K., Ward, D., & Campbell, A. (2004, June). United Airlines' image restoration strategies: A discourse of renewal. In *Conference on Corporate Communication, 2004 Proceedings* (pp. 249-258).

McCombs, M., & Shaw, D.L. (1972). The agenda-setting function of mass media. *Public Opinion Quarterly*, 36(2), 176-187.

Meyers, G.C., & Holusha, J. (1986). *When it hits the fan: Managing the nine crises of business*. Boston: Houghton Mifflin.

Mitroff, I.I. (2004). *Crisis leadership: Planning for the unthinkable*. Hoboken, NJ: John Wiley & Sons.

Mitroff, I.I., & Anagnos, G. (2001). *Managing crises before they happen: What every executive and manager needs to know about crisis management*. New York: AMACOM.

O'Neill, J.W., & Lloyd-Jones, A.R. (2002). One year after 9/11: Hotel values and strategic implications. *Cornell Hotel & Restaurant Administration Quarterly*, 43(5), 53-64.

Pearson, C.M., & Clair, J.A. (1998). Reframing crisis management. *Academy of Management Review*, 23(1), 59-76.

Ries, A., & Ries, L. (2002). *The fall of advertising and the rise of PR*. New York: Harper Business.

Rao, S., Thomas, E., & Javalgi, R. (1992). Activity preferences and trip-planning behavior of the U.S. outbound pleasure travel market. *Journal of Travel Research*, 30(3), 3-12.

Seeger, M.W., & Ulmer, R.R. (2001). Virtuous responses to organizational crisis: Aaron Feuerstein and Milt Cole. *Journal of Business Ethics*, 31, 369-376.

Sherwyn, D., & Sturman, C. (2002). Job sharing: A potential tool for hotel managers. *Cornell Hotel & Restaurant Administration Quarterly*, 43(5), 84-91.

Snepenger, D., & Snepenger, G. (1993). Market structure analysis of media selection practices by travel services. In M. Uysal & D. Desenmaier (Eds.), *Communication and channel systems in tourism marketing* (pp. 21-36). New York: The Haworth Press, Inc.

Sproule, C.M. (2002). The effect of the USA patriot act on workplace privacy. *Cornell Hotel & Restaurant Administration Quarterly*, 43(5), 65-73.

Stacks, D.W., & Carroll, T.B. (2005). Travel-tourism public relationships: One step forward, two steps back. *Journal of Hospitality & Leisure Marketing*, 12(1/2), 3-8.

Stafford, G., Yu, L., & Armoo, A.K. (2002). Crisis management and recovery: How Washington DC hotels responded to terrorism. *Cornell Hotel & Restaurant Administration Quarterly*, 43(5), 27-40.

Stark, M. (2002). Research resurgence. *Brandweek*, 43(16), 21.

Ulmer, R.R., & Sellnow, T.L. (2002). Crisis management and the discourse of renewal: Understanding the potential for positive outcomes of crisis. *Public Relations Review*, 28, 361-365.

A Study of Crisis Management Strategies
of Hotel Managers
in the Washington, D.C. Metro Area

Larry Yu
Greg Stafford
Alex. Kobina Armoo

SUMMARY. The 9/11 terrorist attack on the Pentagon in Washington, D.C. had a devastating impact on the local hospitality industry, and tested hotel managers' preparedness for crisis management under great uncertainty and time compression. This study examines how hotel general managers handled catastrophic events, analyzes and compares empirically the impact of the terrorist attack on the human and financial aspects of the hotel industry. General managers operating hotels with different affiliations, sizes and in different locations in the Washington, D.C. Metro Area were surveyed to ascertain their crisis management and recovery strategies. The study offers an insight into crisis management strategies as performed by hotel general managers in the Washington, D.C. Metro Area and identifies strategies that can be emulated and formulated into future hotel crisis management plans. *[Article copies available for a fee from The Haworth Document Delivery Service: 1-800-HAWORTH. E-mail address: <docdelivery@haworthpress.com> Website: <http://www.HaworthPress. com> © 2005 by The Haworth Press, Inc. All rights reserved.]*

KEYWORDS. 9/11 terrorist attack, crisis management, hotel general manager, Washington, D.C. Metro Area

INTRODUCTION

Tourism destinations face potential events that may disrupt and destruct business operations on a short-term basis. The terrorist attacks of September 11, 2001 on the United States, the SARS epidemic spreading to many parts of the world and the taxi bombing in front of the J.W. Marriott Hotel in Jakarta, Indonesia had calamitous impact on the tourism industry in the affected countries (Schneider, 2001; Waldie, 2003; Kelley, 2003). These devas-

Larry Yu is Associate Professor, Department of Tourism and Hospitality Management, School of Business, The George Washington University, 600 21st Street, NW, Washington, D.C., 20052 (E-mail: lyu@gwu.edu). Greg Stafford is affiliated with Collective Cognition Consulting, 20034 Valhalla Sq., Ashburn, VA 20147 (E-mail: gstaffo@gwu.edu), and is a Doctoral Student at George Washington, University's Executive Leadership Doctoral Program. Alex. Kobina Armoo is Assistant Professor, School of Hospitality Management, Baltimore International College, 17 Commerce Street, Baltimore, MD 21202 (E-mail: kobinaarmoo@msn.com).

[Haworth co-indexing entry note]: "A Study of Crisis Management Strategies of Hotel Managers in the Washington, D.C. Metro Area." Yu, Larry, Greg Stafford, and Alex. Kobina Armoo. Co-published simultaneously in *Journal of Travel & Tourism Marketing* (The Haworth Hospitality Press, an imprint of The Haworth Press, Inc.) Vol. 19, No. 2/3, 2005, pp. 91-105; and: *Tourism Crises: Management Responses and Theoretical Insight* (ed: Eric Laws, and Bruce Prideaux) The Haworth Hospitality Press, an imprint of The Haworth Press, Inc., 2005, pp. 91-105. Single or multiple copies of this article are available for a fee from The Haworth Document Delivery Service [1-800-HAWORTH, 9:00 a.m. - 5:00 p.m. (EST). E-mail address: docdelivery@haworthpress.com].

Available online at http://www.haworthpress.com/web/JTTM
© 2005 by The Haworth Press, Inc. All rights reserved.
doi:10.1300/J073v19n02_08

tating events highlight the importance of crisis management for tourism destinations and business organizations. Destinations and organizations must manage sudden crises as efficiently as possible in order to regain control over operations, minimize the impact of the crisis and quickly return post-crisis business to normalcy. This paper reviews prior crisis management studies and outlines the different types of business crises and the evolution of a major crisis. It examines and analyzes how hotel managers in the Washington, D.C. metro area managed an unprecedented business crisis caused by the 9/11 terrorist attacks. It identifies and compares crisis management carried out by managers of hotels of different sizes, affiliations and locations. The experience and lessons learned from handling this unprecedented business crisis can serve as a guideline for formulating future crisis management plans for the hotel industry.

CONCEPTUAL BACKGROUND

Defining Crisis

A crisis is defined as a situation that has reached a critical phase or a turning point for better or worse, and it is simply characterized by a certain degree of risk and uncertainty (Fink, 1986). Figure 1 shows the relationship between the probability of the occurrence of an event and the degree of the impact of the event once it occurs. Each destination or business organization faces different types of events or crises in their tourism business. Frequently occurring events (e.g., mechanical or maintenance breakdowns or employees calling in sick) can be pre-

dicted or anticipated with relative accuracy. Therefore, the impacts of these events can be minimized (e.g., by a well-planned maintenance schedule or staff schedule). However, crisis occurs when a low-probability, high-impact event strikes. Though such an event occurs rarely, it causes greater damage to business operations, not only because of its severity, but also because of its unexpectedness.

Due to the nature of its low-probability occurrence, three distinctive aspects characterize a crisis: suddenness, uncertainty, and time compression (Lerbinger, 1997). Crises are rarely occurring events which are unfamiliar where and when they occur, and therefore cannot be easily traced and analyzed for preventative purposes. Hotel and destination management are typically unprepared for their impact. Therefore, when a crisis occurs, management of destinations or businesses cannot predict the likely timing of its occurrence, and thereby, be prepared for the crisis. A crisis normally occurs suddenly, even when some early warning signs are detectable. Tourism administrators and business managers are under great pressure to make quick and effective decisions in order to minimize financial and human costs and to maintain effective communication with the business community and the general public. Time is compressed. In order to avoid being swept up in the momentum of the crisis, managers must make decisions based on inputs that are sometimes incomplete, inadequate or even inaccurate. Decisions must be made even as the details of the crisis continue to unfold. A balanced attitude toward the needs of all stakeholders and strong decision-making networks appear to reduce the potholes on the uncertain decision pathways which managers must traverse swiftly.

Types of Crisis Threatening Tourism Business

Various types of crises may disrupt and cause disastrous impact on tourism operations. These crises may be characterized into two broadly defined types: those that arise externally and those that are internal and self-inflicted. Crises are further divided into three broad categories and nine specific types as illustrated in Figure 2.

FIGURE 1. Crisis Defined by Probability of Occurence and Impact of an Event

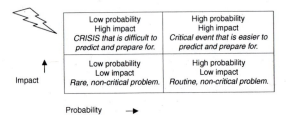

	Low probability High impact CRISIS that is difficult to predict and prepare for.	High probability High impact Critical event that is easier to predict and prepare for.
	Low probability Low impact Rare, non-critical problem.	High probability Low impact Routine, non-critical problem.

Impact ↑

Probability →

Source: Adapted from Leonard D. Goodstein, Timothy M. Nolan, and J. William Pfeiffer, 1992.

FIGURE 2. Types of Tourism Business Crises

Major Factors	Specific Environment	Types of Crises	Examples of Crises
External Factor	Physical Environment	Natural Disaster	Mudslide damages a hillside resort; hurricane destroys beachfront properties.
		Technology Failure	Oil spill contaminates a resort beach and prevents tourists from visiting the resort.
	Human or Social Environment	Confrontation	Union strike disrupts normal operations; special interest group boycotts restaurant food.
		Malevolence	Terrorist attack; food is poisoned through product tempering; hackers introduce a virus into computer reservation systems; street crime.
		Epidemic	Mad cow disease and foot and mouth disease raise concerns of food safety and health problems; SARS epidemic spreads through human contact.
		War/Politics	Second gulf war prevents many international tourists to the Middle East region; recent political upheaval diminishes tourism to Haiti, Venezuela and many African countries.
Internal Factors	Management Failure	Skewed Values	Cruise ships dump waste oil into the ocean, ranking short-term costs over concern for the environment.
		Deception	Restaurant knowingly serves spoiled or contaminated food items.
		Misconduct	Corporate executives embezzle funds or receive kickbacks.

Sources: Adapted from Otto Lerbinger, 1997; Stafford, Yu, and Armoo, 2002. Original exhibits ©Cornell University. Used by permission. All rights reserved. Crisis Management and Recovery: How Washington D.C. Hotels Responded to Terrorism. *Cornell Hotel and Restaurant Administration Quarterly*, 43, No. 5, pp. 27-40.

Physical environment refers to crisis caused by natural disasters, which have always been a threat to the tourism industry. For example, the Izmit earthquake in Turkey in 1999 had a destructive effect on the local tourism industry (Beirman, 2003). Technology failure refers to accidents, caused by human application of science and technology, which pollute or degrade natural environment for tourism activities. For instance, an oil spill from an oil tanker can affect not only marine life, ruin fish spawning sites, but also contaminate beaches and prevent tourists from visiting resorts.

Human and social environment includes confrontation, malevolence, epidemic and war. Confrontation is characterized by disagreement between two parties, typically unions and management, or business organizations and consumers. For example, employee strikes and consumers' boycotts of certain products and services are commonly used confrontational tactics that often cause short-term crises for businesses.

Malevolence refers to the criminal acts or extreme tactics developed by individuals or groups either against a business organization or an entire industry. Crises of malevolence may be generated by street crimes; product-related criminal acts such as product tampering, extortion, corporate espionage, and terrorism. These extreme measures aim to destroy a company's business or a country's economic system.

Epidemic is the sudden outbreak of a virus that infects and kills humans or farm animals. It scares visitors away from the infected areas and causes many people to avoid food products that are produced either from the animal or come from the infected country. The devastating impact of SARS epidemic on the tourism industry in China, Hong Kong, and Canada from April to June in 2003 represents a recent crisis caused by a deadly epidemic. The foot and mouth disease in the United Kingdom, in early 2001, was another epidemic crisis that disrupted operations of fast food restaurants and catering/culinary organizations in the U.K. and its neighboring countries.

War always disrupts any form of travel business and social activities. Military conflict, whether it is an internal conflict such as a civil war or an external conflict between two countries immediately stops the flow of travel to the warring destinations. The devastating effects of wars or internal political conflicts on once vibrant tourism industries have recently been seen in Iraq and much of the Middle East, many African nations, Haiti, Venezuela, Nepal, the Balkan region and many other parts of the world.

Management failures are crises caused by internally self-inflicted factors, such as skewed values, deceptions and misconduct. These factors normally lead to scandals and have serious public relations implications (Cohn, 2000). Unreasonable financial expectations and failures of corporate governance are the main causes of these unethical or sometimes criminal actions of corporate executives. Though these crises tend to be short-term, and are public relations sensitive, several recent corporate failures also resulted in bankruptcy and destruction of owners' and shareholders' value in the company.

Crisis Management

Crisis management is the planning for, responding to and recovering from a crisis. It is the skill of removing much of the risk and uncertainty inherent in low-probability and high-impact events so that tourism administrators and business managers can achieve more control over management operations (Fink, 1986). Therefore, crisis management, in its most basic form, implies being prepared before the crisis strikes, effectively execute the crisis management plan during the crisis, and quickly recover to normalcy after the crisis.

To be fully prepared for and effectively manage a crisis, it is essential to understand the four stages of a crisis (Fink, 1986):

- Pre-crisis stage
- Acute crisis stage
- Chronicle crisis stage
- Crisis resolution stage

Pre-crisis stage is the early warning stage of the occurrence of a potential crisis. Some warning signs may be detected at this stage. Early detection and action can prevent potential disasters to business operations. If early warning signs are recognized, but they are not acted upon for whatever reason, they still give tourism administrators and business managers a sense of what might happen. Such exposure assists managers in preparing for the next crisis stage (Albrecht, 1996).

The second stage of a crisis is described as an acute crisis stage, a stage defined as a point of no return. At this stage, some damage (sometimes very severe) has already been done to the business. How much additional damage may occur depends on the destination and business organization's speed, intensity and effectiveness in controlling and managing the crisis.

Chronicle crisis, the third stage, is a period of self-analysis and recovery. Damage, losses and costs are examined and analyzed, and planned recovery strategies are evaluated, modified and executed. Great effort is made to return business operations to normalcy as early as possible. The lingering effect of the crisis is usually determined by the destination's level of preparation. Companies without a crisis management plan reported suffering lingering effects of a chronicle crisis as much as two and a half times longer than companies that were prepared with a crisis management plan (Fink, 1986, p. 86).

The last stage is the crisis resolution stage. This stage is measured by the return of activities and sales to pre-crisis levels. At this stage, the operations of the business organization should have returned to normalcy or near normalcy. The goal of the organization and the destination then becomes one of converting this turning point into opportunity. Figure 3 attempts to illustrate the crisis stages for the 9/11 terrorist attacks on the U.S. in 2001.

This study examines how the hotel industry in the Washington, D.C. Metro Area handled the acute crisis and chronicle crisis stages after the 9.11 terrorist attacks by surveying the general managers who personally managed the unprecedented business crisis. It identifies and analyzes how Washington, D.C. Metro Area hotels attempted to find creative solutions to minimize profit loss by using various market-

FIGURE 3. Stages of Crisis Applied to the 9/11 Terrorist Attacks on Washington, D.C., 2001

Crisis Stages	9/11 Terrorist Attacks on Washington, D.C.
Pre-crisis stage	Pre 9/11, 2001 Warning signs: Al-Qaeda operatives learning to fly commercial jets in the U.S.; chatter increased by Al-Qaeda sleeping cells; FBI lost track of suspected terrorist operatives.
Acute crisis stage	September 11- October, 2001 Terrorist attack on the Pentagon; making sure that guests, employees and properties were safe; rescue and relief efforts to assist the injured and victim families, reassuring the public that D.C. was open for business; making crucial decisions to conserve cash and reallocate human resources.
Chronicle crisis stage	November 2001-April 2002 Recovery marketing initiatives: gradually targeting the local, regional, national and international markets; hotel occupancy returning to pre-crisis level.
Crisis resolution stage	Tourist business returning to normalcy since April, 2002.

ing and sales techniques in light of much reduced demand and altered patterns/sources of demand as well as reducing costs, while protecting assets and remaining sensitive to the well-being of customers and staff. It compares and identifies the crisis management and recovery strategies developed and pursued by hotels of different sizes, ownerships, affiliations and locations. The experience and lessons gained from handling this unprecedented terrorist attack serve as useful guidelines for formulating crisis management plans for future hotel operations.

RESEARCH METHODS

This study examines and compares crisis management by hotel managers in the Washington, D.C. Metro Area, namely Washington, D.C., northern Virginia and suburban Maryland. A survey instrument was designed to solicit information from hotel general managers about crisis management strategies employed by the individual hotels in the aftermath of the 9/11 terrorist attacks on Washington, D.C. The first version of 50-question, four-page survey questionnaire was pre-tested with four general managers from hotels of different affiliations and sizes in Washington, D.C. Their input was incorporated in the revised version of a shorter two-page survey questionnaire, which consisted of 3 parts. The first part sought basic information on the location, affiliation and size of the hotels. The second part consisted of 33 questions concerning crisis management decisions made by the general managers during the acute crisis and chronicle crisis stages. Respondents were asked to indicate their level of involvement by selecting "Active," "Somewhat active" or "Inactive" for the 33 questions. The third part was made of three open-ended questions. The first two questions asked each general manager to share their short-term and long-term recovery strategies respectively. The third question asked respondents to indicate when they would expect the tourism industry to bounce back to pre-9/11 levels. The survey was conducted during April 2002.

Survey questionnaires were sent to 88 members of the Washington, D.C. Hotel Association by email and they were requested to return the completed survey within two weeks. One hundred, four members of the Virginia Hotel Association and 98 members of the Maryland Hotel Association were selected for this survey using systematic random sampling method. Randomly selected hotel general managers in northern Virginia and suburban Maryland were contacted by mail or fax and were requested to return the completed survey in two weeks. After the two-week deadline, a follow-up email reminder, phone calls or fax letters were utilized, and the final responses yielded a total of 79 completed usable survey returns. The response rate was 24.5 percent.

Two types of statistical analysis were conducted for this study. Descriptive analyses of the data were performed to examine the location, size, ownership and affiliation of the sample hotels. Since the data were measured on a nominal scale, a comparison of crisis management by hotel location, affiliation and size was analyzed by Chi-square test to determine statistical differences.

RESULTS AND DISCUSSION

Of the 79 hotels in this survey, 22 are in Washington, D.C., 26 in suburban Maryland (Montgomery and Prince George Counties), and 31 in northern Virginia (the cities of Alexandria, Arlington, and Falls Church). In terms of hotel affiliations in the sample, 32% are franchised hotels, 28% are brand-managed properties, 15% are independently operated hotels with representation, and the remaining 25% are independently operated hotels without representation. The hotel size was categorized into three groups: (i) "small"–less than 200 rooms, (ii) "mid-size"–between 200 and 499 rooms, and (iii) "large"–more than 500 rooms. Among the sample hotels, 33% are "small" properties, 42% are "midsize" properties and 25% are "large" properties.

Table 1 reports Chi-square statistics for questions measuring crisis management of human resources. The sudden decline of hotel business forced hotel owners and managers to make hard decisions to conserve cash by reducing operating costs. The hardest decision was to either reduce the work schedules or lay off many of the 75,000 hotel employees in Wash-

TABLE 1. Comparison of Crisis Management of Human Resources by Location, Affiliation and Size

Question	Location	Affiliation	Size
	χ^2	χ^2	χ^2
Reduce staffing level below prior staffing guidelines	15.323*	8.904	1.433
Cross-utilized staff in multiple job functions and/or ask managers to cover line shifts	.344	.323	1.838
Flexible use and/or mandated use of vacation time, personal leave and sick leave	6.804	2.050	7.125
Reduce or eliminate employee benefits	4.880	4.528	4.761
Outsourcing services previously handled by property staff	.248	1.833	.688
Helping rescue worker/victim family	.777	3.438	1.115
Provide special relief services or funds for displaced workers	2.633	8.064	1.814

Note: Significant at 1% level.

ington, D.C. (Schneider, 2001; Sheridan, 2001). As Table 1 reveals, the only significant difference was found in the question of reducing staffing levels below prior staffing guidelines by location, but not by affiliation and size. On the issue of staff reduction, 72.7% of the Washington, D.C. hotels were very actively involved in reducing staffing levels, while only 13.3% of suburban Maryland and northern Virginia hotels indicated respectively that they were very active. Clearly, the terrorist attack had a particularly significant impact on hospitality employment in the capital city, forcing many hotels in Washington, D.C. to engage in some amount of staff reduction.

To effectively manage hotel operations, all the hotels were either active or somewhat active in cross-utilizing line employees in multiple job functions or asking managers to cover line work shifts. The majority of the hotels encouraged employees to make flexible use and/ or mandated the use of vacation time, personal leave, and sick leave. No statistical difference was detected for all categories for these two questions. As for reducing or eliminating employee benefits to cut costs, only 18.2% of the Washington, D.C. hotels were active in this program, 6.7% of the northern Virginia hotels did so, and none in suburban Maryland pursued this practice. Most hotels did not reduce employee benefits. The majority of the hotels were also inactive in outsourcing services previously handled by property staff. Considering the help given to rescue workers and families of victims, in the form of donated rooms, meals and/or cash contributions, there was no significant difference among the general man-

agers when considered by location, hotel affiliation and hotel size. The involvement in this activity by the general managers was quite evenly distributed.

Table 2 illustrates crisis management of financial and investment decisions. As room occupancy rates in the Washington, D.C. Metro Area plummeted to below 40% immediately after the terrorist attack, hotel owners and managers faced critical decisions of meeting debt obligations and keeping their operations afloat. For the question of restructuring hotel capitalization, the responses revealed that 45.5% of the Washington, D.C. hotels, 73.4% in northern Virginia, and 73.3% in suburban Maryland indicated that there was some form of activity related to restructuring their capitalization. The test results, however, show a significant difference among hotels when compared by affiliations at the 10% significance level. Only 27.3% of brand-managed hotels and 10% of the independent hotels without representation were very active in restructuring capitalization of their hotels. However, 77% of franchised hotels and 71.4% of independent hotels with representation reported somewhat active involvement in restructuring hotel capitalization.

On the issue of deferred capital improvement programs, a statistically significant difference was found only when compared by the size category, but not by location and affiliation. It is revealing to note that 30.8% of "small" hotels, 10% of mid-size hotels, and none of the "large" hotels were very active in deferring capital improvement programs. However, 61.1% of "mid-size" hotels, 23.1% of "small" hotels,

TABLE 2. Comparison of Crisis Management of Financial Decisions by Location, Affiliation and Size

Question	Location	Affiliation	Size
	χ^2	χ^2	χ^2
Restructure capitalization of the hotel	10.814**	10.786***	1.787
Defer capital improvement program	4.305	1.481	11.240**
Partial closure of the hotel	14.554*	6.801	2.758
Reduce hours of services and/or hours of operations of facilities	5.631	4.313	5.504
Renegotiate pricing and/or terms of contract services and/or frequently purchased goods with purveyors	3.739	6.058	4.683
Defer preventive maintenance and routine non-critical product care	10.503**	5.546	4.002
Eliminate non-critical expenses	6.524	1.793	3.154
Reduced specified quality levels of guest products, food products and/or some other routine purchases	10.325**	3.955	6.159
Reduce amenities and services	6.278	4.009	6.580

Notes: *Significant at 1% level.
** Significant at 5% level.
*** Significant at 10% level.

and 20% of "large" hotels were somewhat active in deferring capital improvement programs.

A significant difference was noted in the question on partial hotel closure by location due to the drastic decrease of reservations. While no hotel in suburban Maryland and northern Virginia reported being very actively engaged in partial closure of their properties, 36.4% of the Washington, D.C. hotels did. Meanwhile, 9.1% of the Washington, D.C. hotels, 6.7% of the suburban Maryland hotels and 26.7% of the northern Virginia hotels were somewhat active in partial hotel closure. The rest of the hotels in the three locations remained open; however, majority of the hotels reduced their operating hours and/or services.

There was an evenly distributed response to the questions on renegotiating terms of contracts/services and prices for frequently purchased goods with purveyors. Therefore, there is no significant difference for this question by all the three categories. Concerning the deferral of preventive maintenance and routine non-critical product care, a significant difference was determined by the location category. None of the hotels in suburban Maryland, only 6.7% of hotels in northern Virginia and 18.2% of D.C. hotels were very active in deferring such programs. However, 80% of suburban Maryland hotels and 53% of hotels in northern Virginia reported that they were somewhat active in deferring preventive maintenance; 63.6% of

the Washington, D.C. hotels were inactive in deferring preventive maintenance.

Most of the Washington, D.C. hotels (72.3%) reported that they were either very active or somewhat active in eliminating most non-critical expenses such as decorations, employee awards, manager expense accounts, training, travel, etc. Only 33.3% of hotels in both suburban Maryland and northern Virginia had done the same. A statistical significance was found regarding reducing specified quality levels of guest products, food products and/or some other routine purchases by location. While 45.5% of the Washington, D.C. hotels indicated that they were either very active or somewhat active in reducing the specified quality levels of such purchases, only 13.3% of northern Virginia hotels reported very active or somewhat active reduction of specified quality levels of purchase, but none in suburban Maryland. The majority of the hotels reported that they did not reduce hotel amenities and services in order to cut costs; therefore there was no significant difference in reducing amenities among hotels by location, affiliation and size.

Crisis management strategies for business recovery performed by hotel general managers are reported in Table 3. The first three questions asked the hotel general managers about their involvement in lobbying the federal, state and local governments for assistance. No statistical difference was found among the ho-

TABLE 3. Comparison of Crisis Management for Business Recovery by Location, Affiliation and Size

Question	Location	Affiliation	Size
	χ^2	χ^2	χ^2
Lobby for reopen airport/attraction	3.589	4.137	6.258
Lobby for tourism stimulating package	1.525	4.305	1.440
Lobby for tax relief	26.382*	5.014	5.374
Marketing recovery campaign with local tourism organization	11.617**	8.256	9.430***
Strategic marketing with other travel sector	2.098	5.478	6.536
Forming marketing alliances with hotels in same area, or in same company/brand	13.936*	5.964	3.041
Increase brand marketing initiatives	11.064**	6.792	2.598
Promote guest loyalty programs	10.160**	2.854	4.292
Special pricing	6.738	2.934	4.549
Direct sales	.637	2.081	1.092
Redeploy sales staff for new market segment opportunities	9.499***	2.845	3.500
Redirect marketing resources toward local/regional market opportunities	14.191*	13.555**	4.002
Increase discounting rates and/or bundled value-added features	6.507	5.822	2.489
Increase investment with non-fly travel organizations (AAA, Amtrak)	4.376	8.091	4.980
Increase investment in internet-related travel opportunities	5.818	6.455	3.858
Special value pricing in restaurant and catering programs	7.502	3.999	2.645
Sharply curtail marketing expenses	4.065	8.366	4.276

Notes: *Significant at 1% level.
** Significant at 5% level.
*** Significant at 10% level.

tels by location, affiliation and size on the issue of lobbying (1) the federal government for the reopening of the Ronald Reagan National Airport and Washington, D.C.'s major tourist attractions, such as the U.S. Capital and the White House, and (2) the federal, state and local governments for economic stimulus packages to boost tourism to the nation's capital.

However, significant differences were observed in the involvement of general managers in lobbying the government for tax relief for their operations. It was found that no general managers in Washington, D.C. had been actively involved in lobbying for tax relief, 27% had been somewhat actively involved, and the remaining 73% did not take part in any tax relief lobbying activity. All the general managers in suburban Maryland indicated that they participated actively in lobbying the government for tax relief. In northern Virginia, there was a polarized distribution with 53% of the general managers being actively involved in lobbying for tax relief and the remainder inactive.

The next fifteen questions dealt with marketing and promotion activities deployed by hotel management for returning the business to normalcy. For the question of strategic marketing alliances or increased investment made by hotel owners and management in forging strategic marketing alliances with local convention and tourism marketing organizations, a significant difference was found by location at 5% significance level and by size at 10% significance level. Only 9% of the hotels in Washington, D.C., 6.7% of those in suburban Maryland reported inactivity, and 20% of the hotels in northern Virginia were inactive in forging strategic marketing alliances. When compared using the size of the hotel, it was observed that 5.6% of the mid-sized hotels, 10% of the large hotels, and 23% of the small hotels were inactive in forging strategic marketing alliances with local convention bureaus and tourism marketing organizations.

As for the hotels' efforts in forging strategic marketing alliances with travel related businesses such as travel companies and destination marketing organizations, no significant difference was found in this activity by hotels in the three categories. However, a significant difference was identified by using the hotel's location as an independent variable for the question asking hotels about their efforts in forming marketing alliances with hotels in the same area, in the same company and/or in the same brand. No significant difference was found when affiliation and size were used. In Washington, D.C., 27.3% of the hotels were actively involved in strategic marketing alliance with other hotels in the same area and company, 45.4% were somewhat active and 27.3% were inactive. In suburban Maryland, 86.7% of the hotels reported either active or somewhat active strategic marketing efforts with hotels in the same area and the same company, while 13.3% report being inactive. Among the hotels in northern Virginia, 73.3% were active and 26.7% were inactive as far as strategic marketing alliances are concerned.

It is interesting to note that no statistical difference was found among hotels regarding increasing brand marketing initiatives by using the affiliation and size categories. The difference was found among hotels using the location category. In Washington, D.C., 45.5% of the hotels were inactive in forging such strategic marketing alliance, while 13% of hotels in both suburban Maryland and northern Virginia were inactive. Concerning increasing guest loyalty programs as a recovery strategy, all the hotels in suburban Maryland reported being "somewhat active," while in northern Virginia most of the hotels (93.4%) were active or somewhat active in implementing this program. In Washington, D.C., 91% of the hotels were actively or somewhat actively deploying this program. Therefore, there was a significant difference among the hotels in pursuing this activity as a recovery strategy in the three locations. However, no significant difference was found in this activity when analyzed using affiliation and size categories.

The questions on special pricing and increased direct sales as recovery activities yielded no significant difference among surveyed hotels by location, affiliation and size. Over 92% of the hotels were either actively or somewhat actively providing special pricing to attract transient customers and were re-

doubling their efforts in direct sales, regardless of their location, affiliation and size. When asked if the hotel management had redeployed sales staff and/or other marketing resources to take advantage of new market segment opportunities, all the hotels in D.C. and suburban Maryland responded as either actively or somewhat actively making the redeployment, while 20% of the hotels in northern Virginia did not make any redeployment adjustments. Therefore, a statistical difference was noted for the location category at 10% significance level, but no difference was found for the affiliation and size categories.

To the question of redirecting marketing resources toward local/regional market opportunities rather than national/international market opportunities, a significant difference in approaches of the hotels in the three locations was observed. The majority of the D.C. hotels (90.8%) indicated some form of activity. In suburban Maryland, 80% were very active in promoting the local and regional markets and the other 20% were somewhat active. In northern Virginia, 33.3% were very active, 60% were somewhat active and 6.7% were inactive. However, no significant difference was found when compared by affiliation and size categories.

No significant differences were found for the last five questions in Table 3 as recovery strategies pursued by the general managers. The results of the analysis show that the majority of the hotels were very actively and somewhat actively pursuing these strategies to increase sales and return business to normalcy.

RECOVERY ASSESSMENT AND LESSONS LEARNED

The recovery strategies pursued collectively by the Washington, D.C. tourism industry yielded positive results. The hotel industry was hardest hit during the last four months of 2001, with city-wide hotel occupancy declining by 42.34% in September, 26.86% in October, 15.93% in November and 8.11% in December compared to the same periods of 2000 (Table 4).

After continuous declining hotel occupancy in the first quarter of 2002, occupancy rate in April surpassed pre 9/11 level by 6.87%. Since then hotel performance in Washington, D.C.

TABLE 4. Washington, D.C. Hotel Performance Before and After 9/11 Terrorist Attacks, 2000-2003 Hotel Occupancy Rate 2000-2003

	2000	2001	% Change	2002	% Change	2003	% Change
January	50.97%	57.01%	11.85%	51.79%	−9.16%	54.33%	4.92%
February	65.56%	68.55%	4.57%	67.47%	−1.58%	64.58%	−4.28%
March	81.11%	82.77%	2.04%	76.88%	−7.11%	74.11%	−3.59%
April	84.78%	81.16%	−4.27%	86.74%	6.87%	73.93%	−14.77%
May	82.95%	78.74%	−5.08%	78.41%	−0.41%	76.12%	−2.92%
June	81.74%	79.95%	−2.19%	77.42%	−3.17%	79.45%	2.63%
July	76.65%	74.10%	−3.32%	71.21%	−3.91%	77.11%	8.29%
August	71.46%	66.62%	−6.78%	64.34%	−3.42%	63.88%	−0.72%
September	79.37%	45.77%	−42.34%	69.62%	52.12%	73.20%	5.14%
October	81.06%	59.29%	−26.86%	75.41%	27.19%	79.24%	5.08%
November	67.25%	56.54%	−15.93%	58.76%	3.93%	63.19%	7.54%
December	50.13%	46.06%	−8.11%	46.06%	−0.02%	48.35%	4.98%

Hotel ADR ($) 2000-2003

	2000	2001	% Change	2002	% Change	2003	% Change
January	134.21	177.32	32.12%	130.85	−26.21%	132.39	1.18%
February	143.01	156.17	9.20%	143.05	−8.40%	145.59	1.77%
March	153.64	167.81	9.23%	153.86	−8.32%	162.70	5.75%
April	162.42	168.91	4.00%	170.10	0.70%	155.56	−8.54%
May	161.12	164.88	2.33%	164.57	−0.19%	162.84	−1.05%
June	150.03	155.10	3.38%	149.12	−3.86%	151.77	1.78%
July	131.63	132.14	0.38%	128.35	−2.87%	131.13	2.17%
August	128.99	124.48	−3.49%	121.00	−2.80%	118.84	−1.79%
September	159.72	149.25	−6.55%	164.85	10.45%	158.00	−4.15%
October	168.03	149.95	−10.76%	165.12	10.12%	159.06	−3.67%
November	153.78	140.34	−8.74%	141.45	0.79%	143.49	1.45%
December	137.87	125.49	−8.98%	128.70	2.56%	131.62	2.27%

Hotel RevPar ($) 2000-2003

	2000	2001	% Change	2002	% Change	2003	% Change
January	68.40	101.09	47.78%	67.76	−32.97%	71.93	6.16%
February	93.76	107.06	14.18%	96.51	−9.85%	94.02	−2.58%
March	124.62	138.89	11.45%	118.28	−14.84%	120.58	1.94%
April	137.70	137.09	−0.44%	147.54	7.62%	115.01	−22.05%
May	133.65	129.82	−2.87%	129.04	−0.60%	123.95	−3.94%
June	122.63	124.01	1.12%	115.45	−6.90%	120.59	4.45%
July	100.90	97.92	−2.95%	91.40	−6.66%	101.12	10.63%
August	92.17	82.92	−10.04%	77.85	−6.12%	75.91	−2.49%
September	126.77	68.31	−46.12%	114.77	68.01%	115.66	0.78%
October	136.20	88.91	−34.73%	124.53	40.06%	126.04	1.22%
November	103.42	79.35	−23.27%	83.12	4.75%	90.68	9.09%
December	69.11	57.81	−16.36%	59.27	2.54%	63.64	7.37%

Source: Compiled from monthly *STAR Summary Report*, Smith Travel Research, 2000-2004.

has been consolidating, improving significantly from the last four months of 2001. All the three hotel performance indicators (occupancy, ADR and RevPar), were close to pre-9/11 levels by the end of 2003. Recovery strategies examined in this study were clearly implemented by hotels of different ownerships, affiliations, sizes and locations to stabilize business operations, amidst a series of subsequent bio-terrorism events, a weak economy, the Sniper rampage, SARS fears, a hurricane, one of the worst snowstorms of the century, the "War on Terrorism" and the frequently heightened terror alert in 2002 and 2003. Some noteworthy differences do exist among individual hotels and among hotels in different locations, brand-affiliations and sizes. It is beyond the scope of our project to isolate the effects of those differences on the recovery of individual hotels or clusters of hotels. However, the common ground of crisis management strategies across all three parts of the DC Metro region is surprisingly strong considering that there are completely separate state jurisdictions and, more importantly, independent hotel associations and regional marketing groups in each area. Overall, Washington, D.C. Area hotels found ways of creatively controlling, communicating, cooperating and collaborating to improve performance in the wake of the 9/11 terrorist attacks much more rapidly than the rest of the country despite encountering a virtual continuous string of crises or at least major unexpected business obstacles.

Figure 4 shows seasonal-adjusted hotel occupancy for the three study areas by using 12-month moving-average method from 1998 to 2003. The six-year trendline illustrates clearly the dip in occupancy in the last four months of 2001 for D.C., suburban Maryland and Virginia. After a period of consolidation in 2002, occupancy slowly rebounded for these study areas, with D.C. showing slightly quicker recovery. It is interesting to note that occupancy rates in the metro areas of Maryland and Virginia demonstrated an almost identical trend from 1998 to 2003 as the two trend lines became intertwined into one.

Figure 5 displays hotel performance by average daily rate in these three study areas as well as the national average from 1998 to 2003. Obviously, hotels in the Washington

D.C. metro area outperformed the national average, with ADR in D.C. almost doubling the national average. The impact of 9/11 terrorist attacks on ADR in D.C. was cancelled out by the phenomenal ADR increase in the first quarter of the year which was stimulated by presidential inaugural activities. ADR for these three study areas have been stable in the last two years despite the constant disruptive political, climatic and epidemic events since the 9/11 terrorist attacks. Such positive performance could be attributed to the effective crisis management strategies implemented by individual hotel management and coordinated by the hotel industry in the Washington, D.C. Metro Area.

This unprecedented crisis tested the preparedness and management strategies necessary for reacting to a major business crisis. Lessons learned from this crisis can be summarized as follows: (1) expect the unexpected; (2) take care of people; (3) adjust the financial and operational business structure; (4) know your customers and market to the right customers at the right time; and (5) build relations and then networks and then communities of common concern.

Our innocence has been erased and hotel general managers will never be able to excuse a future terrorist event directed against a destination, its citizens or innocent tourists as an unthinkable event, something which he or she could not have reasonably anticipated. In fact, the litany of crises which the Washington, D.C. tourism industry has experienced since 9/11 reinforces very clearly that managers had best learn to live and manage in an environment where crises and severe unexpected events may not be quite so unusual. In such an environment mindfulness about people, facilities, and events inside hotels and destinations and similar locations enhances the possibility of preventing crises. An understanding of how past crises have been managed successfully and a plan which can be executed swiftly and keeps everyone informed may aid in preventing crises. Additionally, such a plan will certainly mitigate the impact of crises when they do occur. Likewise, ready availability and familiarity with emergency and crisis response equipment and information is vital.

FIGURE 4. Twelve-Month Moving Average of Hotel Occupancy in D.C., Suburban MD and VA, 1998-2003

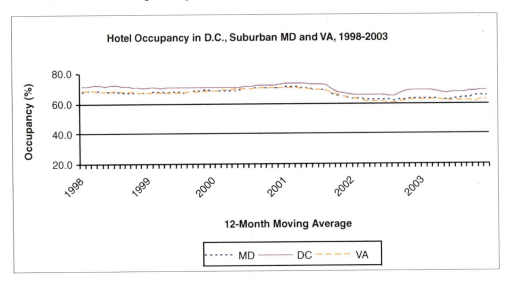

Source: Compiled from monthly *STAR Summary Report*, Smith Travel Research, 1999-2004.

FIGURE 5. Comparison of Hotel Average Daily Rate, 1998-2003

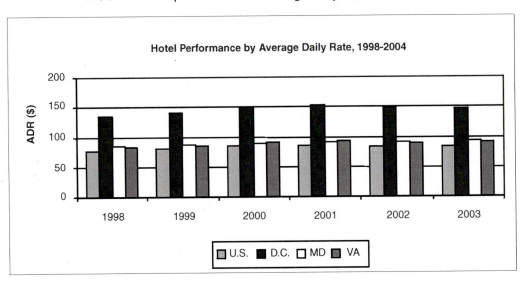

Source: Compiled from monthly *STAR Summary Report*, Smith Travel Research, 1999-2004.

The most immediate and important toll of a terrorist act is human. At the crisis response stage customers, employees, and of course friends and families of victims require information, direction, assistance and compassion. Although hotels in the Washington D.C. Area were devastated by the 9/11 crisis, most hotels assisted in some manner with housing families of victims, meals for relief workers, donations to victim foundations and much more (an amazing level of generosity and community involvement which has continued through the series of additional crises which have rocked Washington, D.C. over the past few years). As the reality sets in that far fewer customers will visit a destination and stay in hotels, general managers must find ways to reduce payroll costs. However, most hotels in the Washington D.C.

Area recognized that customers will return and employees will be needed again. Most hotels reduced hours, encouraged cross-utilization of staff, job sharing and other creative work designs, forced vacation benefits, eliminated or reduced perks and incentives before they began outright staff layoffs. Very few hotels cut basic employee benefits such as health care coverage despite several months of severe business damage from the 9/11 terrorist attack.

Hotels typically operate with low current ratios and therefore sudden swings in revenues must be met with drastic operating cost reductions. Hotel general managers were forced to resize their business and enable much more flexibility to accommodate the dramatically reduced demand and much greater volatility of demand levels for several months after 9/11. Almost every hotel implemented contingency operation plans and sought concessions from purveyors and contractors to eliminate non-essential expenses. Many hotels took advantage of relatively low interest rates and recapitalized properties, others deferred non-critical maintenance and/or capital programs, and others, particularly some of the larger D.C. hotels, shut down hotel room sections or outlets. Most hotel general managers were faced with walking the fine line between asset protection, customer comfort and safety, caring for their staff and conserving enough cash to stay in the game.

Many customers who checked out of Washington, D.C. Area hotels on 9/11 or cancelled reservations in the days and weeks after 9/11 would not return for many months or even years, if ever. New customers would begin to arrive soon: defense and security agency personnel, National Guard and Coast Guard personnel to protect the city, environmental clean up specialists, media and others. Hotels which quickly redeployed their sales and marketing efforts toward these new markets were less damaged than others. Loyalty programs and special pricing for target markets were tactics employed by most hotels to aid in recovery. Internet channels were used to promote distress inventory and special packages. Unlike many major cities with large state financial support, Washington, D.C. had to cobble together a marketing fund based mostly on the

donations of private organizations. The most critical marketing lessons for DC were the following: (1) when funds are scarce find ways to work together–through brand marketing cooperatives, area hotel cooperatives and, most especially, through providing greater support to destination marketing organizations; (2) pressure the largest organizations based in the destination (in the case of Washington, D.C. that is the federal government) to conduct their meetings and other travel activities at home; (3) do not use marketing funds until the target markets are ready to travel, which for Washington meant very close to home at first, then markets within an easy drive, then fly in domestic travel and youth groups, and now almost three years after 9/11 Washington, D.C. hotels and destination marketing organizations are beginning to reach out to international tourism.

The Washington, D.C. Area's very strong hotel associations and destination marketing organizations with dynamic leadership were instrumental in an effective crisis response and recovery effort. When the crisis happens, strong, cooperative relationships with competitors proved invaluable as a source of information and support for most hotel general managers in D.C.'s tightly knit hotel community. Reliable and timely information initially from first responders and then from government agencies is vital. Having a clear spokesperson communicating with emergency and government agencies, then back to hotels and ultimately to the general public proved to be a very efficient approach in Washington, D.C. Although most of their colleagues in Maryland and many in Virginia sought some form of tax relief, most D.C. hotel general managers did not spend time lobbying for business tax relief (although many lobbied for unemployment benefit extensions) or tourism stimulus packages. D.C. hotel managers generally believed such initiatives were unlikely to succeed and were secondary to recovery. Most hotel general managers in all parts of the Washington, D.C. Area did recognize that reopening Washington, D.C.'s tourism infrastructure (airports, museums, key buildings and attractions), which required an extensive and persistent lobbying effort at many levels was crucial to recovery. Today the Washington, D.C. hotel community is actively engaged in the city's and federal government's emergency response network and has participated in a variety of emergency response exercises. The destination marketing organization has an extensive crisis response plan in place to respond at all levels to virtually every type of disaster which might occur. Broadly, the hotel industry and hotel general managers are connected in a larger community of dialogue and practice with other industries, local and federal government, and emergency services organizations to help prevent future crises and minimize the impact of crises when they do occur.

Every hotel organization, regardless its size, location and affiliation, should develop: (1) a rich understanding of how specific crises affecting the tourist industry and other organizations have been responded to and recovered from; (2) a state of mindfulness about conditions that may lead to future crises deeply and pervasively throughout its membership; and (3) a carefully defined crisis response and recovery which is networked with the larger community crisis management plan. A process of acculturation and training for handling crises formally and informally should be conducted throughout the organization on a regular basis, much as managers might build a customer service culture and train against a service plan and goals.

CONCLUSION

The 9/11 terrorist attack on the Pentagon and various crises that followed had an immediate and devastating impact on the hotel industry in the Washington, D.C. Metro Area. Room sales decreased drastically due to the closure of the airport and major tourist attractions, the anthrax cleanup publicity and tourists' perception of safety in the nation's capital. A terrorist attack of such magnitude tested the local hotel industry's ability to manage the crisis and recover from the unexpected attack.

In the light of the unprecedented nature of the 9/11 attacks, hotels in the Washington, D.C. Metro Area, regardless of location, affiliation and size, worked closely with local tourism and convention authorities to lobby government to reopen tourist facilities and at-

tractions to stimulate tourist activities in the area. The only significant difference was that all sampled general managers in suburban Maryland lobbied actively for government tax relief, while 53% of general managers in northern Virginia and none in Washington, D.C. were actively involved in government tax relief lobbying. It is ironic that, even though Washington, D.C. was hit the hardest by the 9/11 attack, 73% of its general managers did not participate at all in any effort to lobby for tax relief. It seems that the farther away a hotel property was from the Washington, D.C., the more active the general managers was in lobbying for tax relief. However, this significant difference to is attributed to Washington, DC general managers' recognition of initiatives likely to succeed and order of importance for recovery.

All the hotels focused on marketing strategies and sales promotions to boost room and food and beverage sales. However, in selecting specific marketing and sales strategies, there were some variations by hotel locations and sizes. By location, it was found that more Washington, D.C. hotels and suburban Maryland hotels were active in working with convention bureaus and tourism marketing organizations. Also, by size of hotel, it was observed that more mid-sized and large hotel categories worked closely with convention and other tourism marketing organizations. In addition, more hotels in suburban Maryland and northern Virginia actively forged marketing strategic alliances than those in Washington, D.C. The alliances were formed with other hotels within their respective areas, under the same ownership, and/or in the same brand. Most of these differences were attributed to the variance in dynamics of the sub-markets.

Also, more hotels in suburban Maryland and northern Virginia actively increased brand-marketing initiatives immediately after the 9/11 attacks. However, Washington, D.C. hotels were more actively engaged in developing guest loyalty programs, to entice repeat business, than the hotels in northern Virginia and suburban Maryland. Most hotels in Washington, D.C. and suburban Maryland actively redeployed sales staff to explore new market segment opportunities and redirected marketing resources toward local and regional market opportunities.

In deploying cost cutting measures to conserve cash, there are some significantly different activities pursued by the hotels in the three locations, by affiliation and by size. When considered by location, more suburban Maryland (73.3%) and northern Virginia (73.4%) hotels chose to restructure the capitalization of their hotels, than those in Washington, D.C. (45.5%). When considered by type/classification, more franchised hotels and independent hotels without a representative chose to restructure their hotels' capitalization. More small hotels deferred capital improvement projects.

As for reducing staffing levels below prior staffing guidelines, the majority of Washington, D.C. hotels reported active reduction of staff immediately after the terrorist attack; and more Washington, D.C. hotels had to partially close their facilities due to lack of reservations. In addition, Washington, D.C. hotels were more active in reducing specified quality levels of guest products, food products and/ or some other routine purchases. But more hotels in suburban Maryland (80%) and northern Virginia (61%) indicated active deferment of preventive maintenance and routine non-critical product care.

This study demonstrated that hotel management in Washington, D.C., suburban Maryland and northern Virginia shared many similar strategies in dealing with the unexpected and disruptive crisis of the 9/11 terrorist attacks. They also differed in some ways of deploying strategies for crisis management and business recovery. The experience gained through the management of this crisis will greatly enhance the awareness and preparation for similar crises in the future, and will greatly improve the management effectiveness in handling such a crisis.

This study has a limitation in its small sample size that might have caused non-response bias. After the 9/11 terrorist attack, general managers were extremely busy with crisis and recovery management. Every effort was made to ensure the high rate of survey return. The final return rate fell short of what was originally expected. However, the sample illustrated a relatively balanced distribution of hotels in the three study areas and by affiliation and property size and it can serve as an insight into the crisis and recovery management activities by the local hotel industry.

REFERENCES

Albrecht, S. (1996). *Crisis management for corporate self-defense: How to stop a crisis before it starts.* New York: American Management Association.

Beirman, D. (2003). *Restoring tourism destination in crisis: A strategic marketing approach.* St. Leonards, New Zealand: Allen & Unwin.

Cohn, R. (2000). *The PR crisis bible.* New York: Truman Talley Books.

Fink, S. (1986). *Crisis management: Planning for the inevitable.* New York: American Management Association.

Goodstein, L.D., Nolan, T.M., Pfeiffer, J.W. (1992). *Applied strategic planning: An introduction.* San Francisco: Jossey-Bass/Pfeiffer.

Kelley, J. (2003, August 6). Bomb kills 14 in Indonesia. *USA Today*, p. 1A.

Lerbinger, O. (1997). *The crisis manager: Facing risk and responsibility.* Mahwah, New Jersey: Lawrence Erlbaum Associates, Publishers.

Schneider, G. (2001, September 19). Aftershocks rock local economy: Travel, tourism jobs bear brunt of cuts. *The Washington Post*, pp. A1 & A25.

Sheridan, M.B. (2001, October 31). Wall Street to Washington, layoffs shatter lives. *The Washington Post*, pp. A1 & A21.

Stafford, G., Yu, L., & Armoo, A.K. (2002). Crisis management and recovery: How Washington, D.C. hotels responded to terrorism. *Cornell Hotel and Restaurant Administration Quarterly*, 43(5), 27-40.

Waldie, P. (2003, May 14). Renewed SARS fears deal tourism heavy blow. *Global and Mail*, p. B1.

Privation as a Stimulus to Travel Demand?

Bob McKercher
Ray Pine

SUMMARY. It is widely recognised that crises induce hardship that can affect tourism demand. The end of a period of privation may result in a strong rebound in tourism demand that is proportionate to the intensity of the hardship felt by residents: the response to mild privation may be mild tourism recovery, while the response to deep privation may be intense tourism recovery. This paper examines the recovery of the Hong Kong outbound tourism market in the immediate post-SARS period. The authors conclude that travel is a cathartic experience that can help the overall healing process. *[Article copies available for a fee from The Haworth Document Delivery Service: 1-800-HAWORTH. E-mail address: <docdelivery@haworthpress.com> Website: <http://www.HaworthPress. com> © 2005 by The Haworth Press, Inc. All rights reserved.]*

KEYWORDS. Privation, demand, recovery, crisis

INTRODUCTION

Tourism crises have been defined as events that disrupt the tourism industry at regular, though unpredictable intervals (Sonmez, Apostolopoulos & Tarlow, 1999; Faulkner, 2001). They can affect destinations, source markets, or in the case of trans-national events, both destinations and source markets simultaneously. Most of the research on crises has focussed on the destination, documenting impacts and outlining strategies used to facilitate speedy recovery (Barton, 1994; Durocher, 1994; Beirman, 2003; Faulkner, 2001; Glaesser, 2003). Source markets have, by contrast, received little attention. Yet, in many ways, crises affecting source markets have far more widespread impacts on tourism flows than destination-specific crises, for if the flow of tourists is disrupted, all destinations wholly or partially reliant on that market will suffer. Further, destinations cannot recover until or unless the source markets begin to travel again. The end of a crisis, especially one that causes great privation among the citizenry, may be a stimulus for a rebound period of higher than normal consumption. History provides ample evidence of similar experiences at a macro level. The endings of the First and Second World Wars were followed by periods of excess in the west, notably the Roaring Twentys and the Baby Boom and the emergence of a mass consumer society in the 1950s, respectively.

Bob McKercher (E-mail: hmbob@polyu.edu.hk) and Ray Pine are affiliated with The School of Hotel and Tourism Management, The Hong Kong Polytechnic University, Hung Hom, Kowloon, Hong Kong, SAR.

[Haworth co-indexing entry note]: "Privation as a Stimulus to Travel Demand?" McKercher, Bob, and Ray Pine. Co-published simultaneously in *Journal of Travel & Tourism Marketing* (The Haworth Hospitality Press, an imprint of The Haworth Press, Inc.) Vol. 19, No. 2/3, 2005, pp. 107-116; and: *Tourism Crises: Management Responses and Theoretical Insight* (ed: Eric Laws, and Bruce Prideaux) The Haworth Hospitality Press, an imprint of The Haworth Press, Inc., 2005, pp. 107-116. Single or multiple copies of this article are available for a fee from The Haworth Document Delivery Service [1-800-HAWORTH, 9:00 a.m. - 5:00 p.m. (EST). E-mail address: docdelivery@haworthpress.com].

The authors explore the impact of the end of privation on tourism demand by examining the Hong Kong outbound tourism market during and after the SARS crisis. The 2003 outbreak of Severe Acute Respiratory Syndrome (SARS) induced the temporary collapse of Asian tourism. One of the key reasons was that the short haul markets of Hong Kong, Chinese Taipei, Singapore and the People's Republic of China stopped travelling. Forecasts conducted during the midst of the epidemic predicted that these markets would not recover for at least a year. Yet, within a month after the lifting of the final travel advisory, tourist flows had returned to near normal levels.

MARKET RECOVERY AND PRIVATION

Neither the recovery of tourism markets nor the subject of privation and tourism have been examined in detail in the tourism literature. The relationship between the recovery of destinations and markets is, or should be, axiomatic, for destinations cannot recover until source markets begin to travel again. Thus, while market recovery has not been explored widely, insights into this area can be gained by examining the literature on destination recovery. Privation can be considered within the context of social crisis triggered by an event.

Market Recovery

Destinations tend to recover more quickly from single events that occur randomly (Mansfeld, 1999; Sonmez et al., 1999; Faulkner & Vikulov, 2001; Pizam & Fleischer, 2002) than long duration or repeated crises (Leslie, 1999; Mansfeld, 1999; Pizam & Fleischer, 2002). The psychological proximity of source markets to the location of the event can also impose a significant dampening effect on the rate of recovery (Clements & Georgiou, 1998). Events that occur in physically or psychologically remote places far from media coverage have much less effect than events that occur in well-known destinations or that have a deep, personal effect on tourists. Slow recovery, therefore, is related to the perception of risk that in turn affects the travel decision making process (Sonmez & Graefe, 1998). Tourists may alter their travel plans, substitute destinations and, in extreme cases, postpone travel (Sonmez et al., 1999; Cook, 2002).

Markets also likely exhibit similar behaviours. They are likely to recover faster when affected by single crises that occur randomly and are seen to have a clear end point. Conversely, open ended crises may lead to a slower recovery, as evidenced by the ongoing recession felt by destinations that are reliant on the US outbound market since the September 11, 2001 attacks (TBR, 2002; TIA, 2002, 2003). Likewise, psychological proximity may accelerate or retard the speed of recovery. But as far as markets are concerned, psychological impact relates more to the impact on core values of the society than the geographic proximity of the event. The September 11th terrorist attack represented an attack on American values and way of life. As such, it was and still is a psychologically proximate event to most Americans, even though the event was restricted to two cities.

Interestingly, Mansfeld (1999) asserts that mature destinations tend to recover more slowly than destinations in the rapid growth phase of their life cycles. He argues that demand and faddism prompt tourists to replace an insecure destination image with a secure one more rapidly in new or expanding destinations. Building on this idea, one could postulate that the newly emerging tourism markets may recover more quickly than mature markets. Two possible reasons are offered. First, the novelty and excitement of tourism among the population ·that is exploring the world for the first time may counterbalance risk perception once the immediate threat passes. By contrast, experienced tourists may adopt a more cautious approach to travel. Second, the absolute growth in international tourism demand by first-time travellers may mask caution shown by more experienced tourists in emerging source markets.

A third set of dynamics may also apply to small jurisdictions like Hong Kong or Singapore. Destination recovery literature assumes that tourists still travel, but that they substitute "safe" destinations for crisis-affected ones. In extreme cases, tourists may substitute domestic travel for international travel, as evidenced again in the US, where domestic tourism benefited from 9/11 (Craver, 2002) as Americans substituted road travel for air travel (Schmeltzer, 2002). However, domestic tourism is not a viable option for geographically small jurisdictions, especially if they are subjected to the same crisis. As such, travel may cease altogether rather than being redirected elsewhere.

Privation–SARS, the Social Crisis

Privation is typified by a period of externally induced hardship that causes people to modify normal behaviour patterns. Some evidence exists that a short, sharp period of hardship produces a period of dramatically increased tourism consumption, while an extended period of hardship induces a much more cautious approach to tourism (Frechtling, 1982). Safety and security represent only part of the bundle of issues producing soft travel demand (TIA, 2003, 2002; TBR, 2002; McKercher & Hui, forthcoming). Concerns about the economy, financial scandals, falling consumer confidence and consumer concerns about not having enough time or money to travel may also exacerbate social crises. As discussed below, SARS was as much a social crisis as it was a medical crisis.

The world became aware of SARS in late February, 2003, when a medical school professor from Guangdong Province in south China visited Hong Kong to attend a family wedding. He was ill on arrival and once there, his condition deteriorated rapidly (Benitez, 2003a). He admitted himself to hospital where he subsequently died, but not before infecting 12 other people staying at the same hotel, as well as health-care workers who attended to him. Seven of these infected guests returned to their places of residence in Canada, Vietnam and Singapore, where they introduced the disease to their home countries. Ultimately, Hong Kong reported a total of 1,755 cases with some 299 deaths. Globally, almost 81,00 cases were reported, with 774 people succumbing to SARS (WHO, 2003a). SARS was confirmed in 33 countries, but the outbreak was most severe in the People's Republic of China and Hong Kong, where 84 percent of all cases were recorded (WHO, 2003a).

The impacts on global tourism are well known and need not be documented here in detail.

The WTTC (2003) reported that the crisis was perhaps the most dramatic prolonged shutdown of the industry on record. Only the 9/11 events in the United States provide a reference point and the SARS impact is 5 times greater. McKercher (2003), in a posting first made on TRINET and then subsequently published elsewhere, reported that tourism in most Asian destinations had declined by 80% or more.

What is less well-known is that SARS exerted a profound period of deep privation on the people of Hong Kong. Life as they knew it came to a virtual standstill. Worse still, it was seen as an open ended crisis with no signs of abatement. The situation was exacerbated by the seemingly out of control epidemic in China and the failure of the Central Government to acknowledge the severity of the outbreak. At first, the disease seemed to be confined to a small number of individuals, their close families and friends and health care workers looking after them. However, the discovery of a large and almost simultaneous cluster of probable cases among residents of a housing estate, followed quickly by revelations that it had spread widely through the community, heightened concerns. Media reports suggested that up to three-quarters of the world's population could have been infected, overwhelming the ability of the health-care sector to cope with this disease (Benitez, 2003b).

Uncertainty about the cause, vectors of spread, the most effective means of containing the disease and the best treatments created an unprecedented level of hysteria. People were scared to leave their homes (Shellum, 2003) and, consequently, their normal daily routine stopped. When they did leave their homes, up to 80% wore surgical face masks (Lakshmanan, 2003). In particular, they avoided going to places where the public normally congregates. As one reporter observed, "schools have closed, and those who could have fled the city. Others are working at home and avoiding public places, giving the ordinarily cheek-by-jowl city a deserted, ghostly feel" (Lakshmanan, 2003).

Restaurant takings collapsed by at least one-third. A consumer survey conducted by the authors and reported in the local media concluded that 68% of the populace stopped going out for dinner during the height of the outbreak

(The Standard, 2003). Attendance at cinemas fell by a minimum of 80%, shopping centres emptied (Leung, Wong & Wong, 2003) and visitor numbers at local recreational theme parks plummeted by 70% or more (Li, 2003). Public swimming pools were closed and even some Easter church services were cancelled (Benitez, 2003c). Schools were closed for over a month after a handful of students were confirmed to have contracted the disease. Concerts by the Rolling Stones, Santana and Andy Williams were cancelled as were visits by touring opera and theatre companies. Local performances by Canto-pop stars were also postponed indefinitely.

The feeling of panic turned to one of helplessness and isolation when the World Health Organization (2003b) issued a general travel advisory on March 15, 2003, followed in short order by specific travel advisories against Hong Kong (April 2, 2003), China and Toronto (April 24) and Taiwan (May 8). They, in turn, triggered a domino effect of responses from non-infected areas that were designed to keep their countries SARS-free, but in doing so, effectively stopped international tourist arrivals. The cumulative effect made residents of affected jurisdictions feel like social pariahs, unwelcome anywhere. The Thai government ordered tourists from affected areas to wear masks for the entire duration of their visit or face up to six months' imprisonment. It also warned them that if one passenger on an arriving flight showed SARS-like symptoms, all passengers would be quarantined for two weeks (Shamdasani, 2003). Malaysia issued a travel ban on all visitors from SARS-infected countries. A number of cities in China issued similar travel bans that were also quietly lifted. Singapore imposed an automatic 10-day quarantine period on returning residents who visited infected countries. Taiwan imposed a similar 14-day quarantine period on incoming passengers (Tang & Chan, 2003). Countries around the Asia Pacific granted powers of quarantine to immigration staff. Hong Kong and Chinese tourists were denied hotel accommodation in Rome, entry to trade fairs in New Zealand, the United States and Switzerland and a group of Hong Kong tourists was denied access to a cruise in Hawaii. Some destinations stopped processing visa applications.

Even if people wanted to travel, it was becoming increasingly difficult to leave, as most major airlines either stopped flying to Hong Kong or halted non-stop flights in order to save flight crews from being exposed to SARS (Lo & Cheung, 2003). At its peak, more than 110 countries issued measures restricting the movement of Mainland Chinese tourists (Doran, Cheng & AFP, 2003).

Indeed, something akin to a siege mentality affected the entire populace, with recovered patients stating that they were being treated like lepers (Law, 2003). Residents of Amoy Gardens, the locus of the first widespread infection in the community, were quarantined in holiday camps located in country parks (Moy, 2003a), prompting email campaigns spreading fears that sewage from these camps would contaminate Hong Kong's water supply (Phillips, 2003). Foreign domestic helpers were urged to report employers who denied them a rest day and refused to let them leave their flats for fear of being exposed to the virus (Chow, 2003). The daily count of new infections and the death toll opened the evening television news for over two months. Newspapers devoted special sections to SARS, providing a running tally of infections, deaths, recoveries and names and addresses of housing estates where new infections were recorded. Television ads imploring people to wash their hands regularly and to stop spitting on sidewalks were run constantly. The fines for spitting and other hygiene related offences were tripled from $500 to $1,500. A prank web-based message by a 14 year-old boy that Hong Kong's borders would be sealed led to panic buying of rice, noodles and other staples. The government had to take the unprecedented step of denying the rumour and subsequently pursued charges against the adolescent instigator of the prank.

A study conducted by the Chinese University of Hong Kong showed a dramatic increase in mood disorders, including headaches, insomnia, fatigue, depression, anxiety and an inability to concentrate (Moy, 2003b). Housewives in particular were most vulnerable. This study also revealed emerging obsessive compulsive behaviour amongst 20 percent of the population who were now washing their hands more than 15 times a day to relieve their anxiety.

On top of everything else, Spring 2003 was one of the coldest and wettest in recent memory, contributing to the overall sense of gloom. The Easter long weekend was the first prolonged spell of fine weather, with sunshine and temperatures in the mid-20s. Tens of thousands of people inundated country parks, beaches and outlying islands. The media described it as an unprecedented exodus from urban areas (Michael & Wu, 2003), as crowds, sometimes doubling previous records, discarded their face masks, left home quarantine and began to reclaim their lives. Indeed, Easter represented the psychological turning point in the battle against SARS. Coincidentally, the number of new cases began to decline shortly afterwards and by early May had fallen to fewer than 10 a day.

The social crisis induced must be placed in the broader context of the ongoing social and economic problems affecting Hong Kong since 1997. Prior to the SARS outbreak, Hong Kong suffered a double dip recession and unemployment levels reached all time records of almost 9 percent of the workforce. There had been almost 50 consecutive months of deflation, a collapse in the housing market (prices fell by 70% from their 1997 highs), and one in four homeowners was in negative equity. The Region faced a structural budget deficit. All in all, SARS was an unnecessary social burden on an a community already facing unprecedented hardship.

METHOD

The authors sought to examine empirically the impact of SARS on outbound travel over time. Two rounds of telephone interviews were conducted with the same cohort of Hong Kong residents: the first between April 23 and 26, 2003 at the height of the SARS outbreak; and the second between July 2 and 4, some six weeks after the Hong Kong travel advisory was lifted and two weeks after Hong Kong was officially declared SARS-free by the World Health Organization. A representative sample of 1,010 Hong Kong residents was interviewed, using a modified random digit dialling (mRDD) strategy of residential telephone numbers. Prospective respondents were filtered to select Hong Kong residents aged 18 or above and to ensure the individual had been continuously living in Hong Kong territories for two years.

These criteria met the operational definition of a "Hong Kong resident" as used by the Hong Kong Polytechnic's Computer- Assisted Survey Team (CAST), the agency that conducted the interviews. Protocols developed by CAST in relation to "re-dials" and "follow-ups" were followed. The sample size and method produced a margin of error (sampling error) of less than 3.1%. The same 1,010 individuals were contacted again in July.

A total of 503 people completed both rounds, providing the total paired-sample size. This sample reflected Hong Kong's demographic profile. The majority of respondents were aged 45 or below (32% less than 36, 34% 36-45). Most had a high school education or less (21% more than high school, 45% had completed high school). The typical household had three people living in it. About 51% of the sample earned US$31,000 or less per annum, while one-third earned between US$31,001 and US$62,000 per annum, $40,000 per month), with the balance (15%) earning more than US$62,000. No statistically significant differences were noted between the profile and characteristics of individuals who participated in both surveys and those who participated in only the April survey.

The survey instrument was prepared in English and translated into Chinese. The Chinese version was vetted by the organisation contracted to conduct the interviews. Minor revisions were made to align it more with the intent of the original English questions. Interviews were conducted in Cantonese. Open-ended responses were translated into English. The first part of the questionnaire sought information on dining behaviour. The findings of this aspect of the study will be published separately elsewhere. The second part examined travel behaviour, intentions and attitudes to determine the extent to which SARS affected behaviour. In addition, standard demographic questions were asked.

ANALYSIS

Context

The Hong Kong Polytechnic University has been conducting domestic travel surveys since 2000. During that time, researchers have been able to track outbound travel activity during the previous 12 months and future travel intentions over the upcoming 12-month period. A brief summary of these findings will help place the results of the SARS surveys in context. Generally, Hong Kong residents are active travellers, with around two-thirds taking at least one overnight pleasure trip outside of Hong Kong each year. Most of these individuals travel to the immediate hinterland regions of Macau and Guangdong Province in China, but about one-third of the population travels beyond this region. While actual travel activity has remained largely unchanged over the three-year period, a softening of travel intentions has been noted as Hong Kong residents adopt a wait and see attitude about travel. Travel intentions are recorded on a seven-point Likert scale with the end points reflecting "definitely will not travel" to "definitely will travel." The percent of respondents who answered in the "very likely" or "definitely will" travel categories declined from 34% to 12% between December, 2000 and December, 2002, while the proportion of respondents who said they would "likely" travel increased from 14% to 36%. Hong Kongers prefer short break, short haul travel. The preferred destinations are Southeast Asia, China, Chinese Taipei, Japan and Korea, which collectively accounted for about 80% of the person trips taken. The median trip duration is 5 days, with 72% of all trips involving a single destination.

It Is Darkest Just Before Dawn– April, 2003 Survey Results

In some ways, the timing of the April survey was fortuitous for it assessed public opinion at, what turned out to be, the depth of the crisis. The outbreak had gone unchecked for almost two months and by April 24, 1,488 people were diagnosed with SARS and an average of 30 or more new cases were confirmed each day. Few people realised that the worst was almost over. Within days of the completion of the survey, the number of new cases fell to fewer than 10 and within a month the travel advisory against Hong Kong would be lifted. Indeed, by April 24, 85% of all local cases had already been confirmed. But, of course, no one knew that at the time.

Table 1 shows international travel had virtually ceased. The vast majority of people who planned to travel either cancelled their trips outright or postponed them until at least the end of August. Residents felt that air travel was no longer safe, in response to two incidents of air travel related transmission of SARS during the initial outbreak phase. Further, there was a widely held belief that, even if they could fly, most if not all destinations were unsafe. This perception was fuelled in part by the belief, later substantiated, that China was hiding the severity of its outbreak and in part by the imposition of onerous entry conditions imposed by other destinations, leading many Hong Kongers to fear they could be jailed, quarantined, denied entry or deported. More than half of the respondents felt that all destinations were unsafe and those who identified specific

TABLE 1. Attitudes to Travel (April 24 Survey)

Question	%
Took an overnight pleasure trip outside of Hong Kong, Macau or Guangdong Province between March 1 and April 24, 2003 (n = 503)	2.0
Of those who intended to travel, has SARS forced you to change your travel plans (n = 279)	Yes–84.2 No–15.8
How have plans changed (n = 232)	Cancel trip–74.2 Postpone until August–19.8 Other–6.0
Is air travel safe during the SARS (n = 424)	Yes–3.4 No–96.6
Are some destinations safer than others (n = 433)	All are unsafe–50.8 Some safer–38.1 All are safe–11.1
Specific Unsafe Destinations (other than "all unsafe") (n = 134)	China–80.5 SE Asia–6.0 Canada–3.7
Safe destinations (n = 127)	Japan–29.9 Europe–23.6 Australia/NZ–11.0 USA–7.1 Macau–7.1 SE Asia–3.2
Likelihood of taking an overnight pleasure trip between April and June 2003 (n = 501)	"Definitely"/"Very likely"–1.2 Likely–9.8 Unsure to very unlikely–43.3 Definitely will not–45.7
Which month do you think it will be safe to travel again? (n = 495)	Before August 2003–4.8 Before October 2003–14.2 Before January 2004–33.9 Before March 2004–34.5 After March 2004–41.8 Don't know–58.2

countries singled out China and Southeast Asian countries. By contrast, Japan and Europe were most likely to be identified as safe destinations by the small number of people who ventured such opinions.

More importantly, Hong Kong residents were unsure if or when the situation would improve. When asked when it would be safe to travel again, over half the respondents answered "don't know." What was certain was that recovery would not occur quickly. Virtually none said travel would be safe before July, 2003. Of those who identified a specific month, half felt travel would not be safe until at least November, some seven months after the survey was conducted, with a significant minority stating it would take more than a year. Most people believed that there would be little or no outbound tourism from Hong Kong for the duration of 2003.

Rapid Recovery–July, 2003

By July, 2003 this situation had changed dramatically. The WHO travel advisory was lifted on May 23 and Hong Kong was declared SARS free on June 23. Other travel advisories had also been lifted or were expected to be lifted shortly. Even the apparently rampant outbreaks in Mainland China and Taiwan Province were under control. Whereas in April, virtually no one expected to travel before July, by the time the second survey was undertaken, one out of every seven respondents had already taken an overnight pleasure trip outside of the region (Table 2). Some travel was stimulated by low cost airfare or travel packages offered by the industry. More importantly, though, consumer confidence had returned. The travel packages were able to capitalise on latent demand that simply did not exist two months earlier. The vast majority of residents felt that air travel was now safe and most felt destinations were once again safe to visit. Generic fear of the safety of all destinations was replaced by specific concerns about destinations where SARS was still present.

Travel intentions had also recovered, and indeed, exceeded those recorded in the December 2002 background survey. By July, 15% said they would "very likely" to "definitely" travel and more than 42% said they were "likely" to

TABLE 2. Results of July, 2003 Survey

Question	%
Took an overnight pleasure trip outside of Hong Kong, Macau or Guangdong Province between March 1 and July, 2003 (n = 503)	13.5
Likelihood of taking an overnight trip now compared to before the SARS outbreak	More likely–27.3 As likely–57.0 Less likely–15.8
Is air travel safer now than during SARS (n = 427)	Yes–82.9
Are some destinations safer than during SARS (n = 416)	All are unsafe–10.6 Some safer–38.0 All are safe–51.4
Unsafe destinations (n = 130)	China–69.2 Taiwan Province–17.7 SE Asia–7.7 Canada–4.6
Which month do you think it will be safe to travel again (n = 355)	Now–49.6 Before October 2003–73.0 Before January 2004–94.6 Before March 2004–98.9 After March 2004–1.1
Likelihood of taking an overnight pleasure trip between July and December, 2003 (n = 502)	"Definitely"/"Very likely"–15.4 Likely–26.7 Unsure to very unlikely–46.6 Definitely will not–11.4
Likely main destination of trip (among those who were likely or better to travel) (n = 200)	China–31.5 Japan–22.5 SE Asia–19.0 Europe–10.0 Australia/NZ–5.5 USA–2.5 Taiwan province–3.5

"definitely" travel by December. Only 11% said they would definitely not travel. Importantly, more than one-quarter of respondents said they were more likely to travel now than before the outbreak. A separate study of visitors to a travel show also suggested the nature of post-SARS trips had changed. Residents indicated a high propensity to enjoy health and spa related trips and also to spend more on travel (Travelwirenews.com, 2003).

A paired-sample comparison between the two survey periods illustrates the extent of the change in mood (Table 3). Consumer confidence in the safety and desirability of travel showed an across-the-board recovery. SARS clearly dampened interest in outbound travel, with a strong majority (69%) of April's respondents indicating they were less likely to travel than before the outbreak. By July, the vast majority of them now stated they were as likely (51%) to travel or more likely to travel (31%). Future travel intentions were also measured. Whereas the vast majority of respondents

TABLE 3. Paired-Sample Comparisons

Variable	Test Score	Sig.
Likelihood of taking a trip April (by July) vs. June (by December)	t = −17.411	p < .001
Likelihood of taking an overnight pleasure trip now than before SARS	Chi Sq = 18.248	p = .001
% of respondents who felt air travel was unsafe in April and now felt it was safe in July (n = 256)	84.4%	
Are some destinations safer?	Chi Sq = 24.244	p < .001
Mean number of months before travel is safe again	t = 42.938	p < .001

(79%) suggested they were unlikely (points 1 to 3 in the seven-point scale) to travel in the immediate period following the April survey, by July, 42% of the same people had changed their opinion and suggested they would probably travel (points 5 to 7 on the scale). People who had attained higher education levels were most likely to express the greatest change in opinion about the likelihood of travel, although no such differences were noted by age or income group.

The comprehensive recovery of consumer confidence was shown in responses to the question about when it would be safe to travel. The April survey revealed a great deal of uncertainty or pessimism, but by July the consensus was that travel was now safe. This change in public opinion occurred across the population, irrespective of the opinion expressed in April. Respondents who originally felt travel would probably be safe in August, October December, January or who were initially unsure when travel would be safe were equally likely to feel it was safe now. The only exception came from that group of respondents who felt it would take at least a year before travel was safe. They were somewhat more cautious, with the majority suggesting that they should wait until August. Moreover, no differences were noted by socio-demographic group, reinforcing the belief that an "across the board" recovery had occurred.

Likewise, the perception of the safety of air travel had also changed dramatically, with almost all who expressed concerns during the midst of the outbreak now feeling that it was safer. A similar pattern was noted in attitudes to the safety of destinations. Again, over 83% of participants who felt all destinations were unsafe in April now believed that either all were safe (49.4%) or that some destinations were safer than others (34.4%).

DISCUSSION AND CONCLUSIONS

The SARS outbreak was a difficult time for the 99.8% of Hong Kong residents not infected by the influenza. Fear and panic induced wholesale behaviour modification, as once outgoing Hong Kongers cloistered themselves at home and work and enveloped themselves in face masks and surgical gloves. Most chose to avoid social situations that put them at risk. In addition, the global reaction to SARS turned Hong Kongers into virtual prisoners in their own community. The outbreak, coupled with five years of continuous economic recession, subjected residents to a period of severe privation most had never felt before.

The April, 2003 survey revealed a near complete collapse in consumer confidence as the crisis appeared to be deepening. By July, however, the storm had passed and the negative mood was replaced by optimism and a renewed desire to travel. Tourism recovered quickly and may have recovered even more quickly had airlines been able to reintroduce capacity. Demand, as measured by future travel intentions, had also rebounded to levels above those identified prior to the outbreak. It would appear, therefore, that short duration, intense crises that suppress travel demand may be matched by an even stronger rebound in demand once the situation is resolved.

Further, just as SARS demonstrated the economic importance of tourism to Asian economies, so too did it demonstrate that travel is a core aspect of people's lives and can no longer be considered as a discretionary activity. Unlike 15 to 20 years ago when travel was placed in the context of other discretionary activities, like the purchase of a mink coat, where the purchase decision for one, by necessity, means forsaking the purchase decision for the other item (Mill & Morrison, 1985), today travel is considered as a core purchase by a significant segment of the Hong Kong populace. While the nature of the trip may change depending on the prevailing economic and social conditions, one-third of the populace will take at least one international pleasure trip a year. A one-off crisis like SARS may cause a postponement in travel plans, but once it passes, pent-up demand will be released in a flood of exceptional consumption.

The study, therefore, raises a number of issues for Destination Marketing Organizations (DMOs) to consider about how best they can attract affected markets. Faulkner (2001), in his framework for disaster management, stresses the importance of managing both the media and the message effectively during the midst of a crisis. A number of commentators and academics in Hong Kong feel that many destinations mishandled the crisis, possibly to their long-term detriment. The effective ostracization of Hong Kongers during the midst of SARS has caused some people to reconsider visiting traditional destinations. Alternatively, destinations like Japan, Korea and Australia that took a more measured approach appear to be beneficiaries of post-SARS travel. Thus, it is essential to control the message during a crisis to ensure that it does not leave a lingering post-crisis negative impact on tourists.

Both the crisis management literature and this study suggest that markets will rebound quickly once the immediate crisis abates. This study, further, suggests that the magnitude of the rebound is in direct proportion to the extent of privation felt by affected individuals. Tremendous opportunities exist for DMOs to capture a significant share of this pent-up demand. While destination marketers must move quickly and assertively, the study reaffirms the importance of timing. There is little merit in running promotional campaigns during the crisis, for the market is simply not receptive to them. However, public sentiment changes almost instantaneously once the crisis passes. DMOs, therefore, must have promotional campaigns "in the can" and be ready to launch them at short notice.

Low-price promotional fares may be an appropriate strategy to stimulate demand in the immediate aftermath. Such campaigns may only be needed for a short period of time as pent-up demand is so great that tourists will be willing to pay competitive market rates once consumer confidence returns. Instead, the communications message and the product offered are more important than the price. "Welcome

back" campaigns will appeal to the emotions of markets that have felt isolated during the crisis. Likewise, indulgent- and spa-style holidays will also prove to be popular as they will help the emotional healing process.

This study suggests that travel represents a healthy, cathartic response to privation. It enables people to escape both physically and emotionally from the event and in doing so to help the healing process. Travel, therefore, appears to serve a deeper personal and social need, especially in collectivist societies like Hong Kong. The world closed its doors on the HKSAR. The end of a period of deep privation, coupled with the renewed welcoming of Hong Kong tourists, has spawned post-SARS optimism amongst the community. While painful in the short run, the end of a period of deep privation may actually provide longer-term benefits to the travel industry.

REFERENCES

Barton, L. (1994). Crisis management: Preparing for and managing disasters. *Cornell Hotel & Restaurant Administration Quarterly, 35*(2), 59-65.

Beirman, D. (2003). *Restoring tourism destinations in crisis: A strategic marketing approach.* Cambridge: CABI International.

Benitez, M. (2003a, March 20). Guangdong doctor may have triggered pneumonia outbreak at Kowloon hotel. *South China Morning Post*, p. A1.

Benitez, M. (2003b, September 27). Virus unchecked would have affected billions: Professor. *South China Morning Post*, p. C3.

Benitez, M. (2003c, April 4). Holy rites scrapped to stop SARS from spreading. *South China Morning Post*, p. C3.

Chow, C.Y. (2003, May 10). Maids urged to report errant bosses. *South China Morning Post*, p. C4.

Clements M.A., & Georgiou, A. (1998). The impact of political instability on a fragile tourism product. *Tourism Management, 19*(3), 283-288.

Cook, S. (2002). *Dr. Suzanne Cook, SVP of research travel industry association of America, provides insight for summer 2003 travel forecast.* Retrieved November 20, 2003, from *http://www.tia.org/Press/speechrec.asp?Item=58.*

Craver, R. (2002). *Impact of terrorist attacks on North Carolina tourism was softer than expected.* Retrieved August 15, 2003, from *http://hotel-online.com/News/2002_Jul_08/k.HPT.1026227531.html.*

Doran, H., Cheng, A. & AFP. (2003, May 14). World closes the door on China over virus. *South China Morning Post*, p. A3.

Durocher, J. (1994). Recovery marketing: What to do after a natural disaster? *Cornell Hotel and Restaurant Administration Quarterly, 35*(2), 66-71.

Faulkner, B. (2001). Towards a framework for disaster management. *Tourism Management, 2*, 135-147.

Faulkner, B., & Vikulov, S. (2001). Katherine, washed out one day, back on track the next: A post-mortem of a tourism disaster. *Tourism Management, 22*, 331-344.

Frechtling, D. (1982). Tourism trends and the business cycle: Tourism in recession. *Tourism Management, 3*(4), 285-290.

Glaesser, D. (2003). *Crisis management in the tourism industry.* Oxford: Butterworth-Heinemann

Lakshmanan, I. (2003). *Hong Kong's fear of SARS spreading faster than the disease itself: 80% residents wearing surgical masks.* Retrieved October 24, 2003, *http:// www.hotel-online,com/News/PR2002_2nd/Apr03_ SARSUpdate.html.*

Law, N. (2003, May 2). Stop treating us like lepers, pleads infected nurse. *South China Morning Post,* p. C1.

Leslie, D. (1999). Terrorism and tourism: The northern Ireland situation–A look behind the veil of certainty. *Journal of Travel Research, 38*, 37-40.

Leung, A., Wong, K., & Wong, B. (2003, April 3). Double hit for HK with travel and war. *South China Morning Post,* p. A2.

Li, S. (2003, May 2). Ocean park losing $15m a month due to outbreak. *South China Morning Post,* p. C1.

Lo, J., & Cheung, J. (2003, April 5). Major airlines halt non-stop HK flights. *South China Morning Post,* p. A1.

Mansfeld, Y. (1999). Cycles of war, terror and peace: Determinants and management of crisis and recovery on the Israeli tourism industry. *Journal of Travel Research, 38*(August), 30-36.

McKercher, B. (2003). *SIP (SARS Induced Panic) a greater threat to tourism than SARS (Severe Acute Respiratory Syndrome).* Available from the e-Review of Tourism Research site, *http://ertr.tamu.edu/.*

McKercher, B., & Hui, E.L.L. (forthcoming). Tourism, economic uncertainty terrorism and outbound tourism from Hong Kong. *Journal of Travel and Tourism Marketing.*

Michael, P., & Wu, E. (2003, April 21). SARS fear fuels exodus to HK parks and beaches. *South China Morning Post,* p. C1.

Mill, R.C., & Morrison, A.M. (1985). *The tourism system: An introductory text.* Englewood Cliffs, NJ: Prentice Hall.

Moy, P. (2003a, April 2). Camps are likely to be short on holiday spirit. *South China Morning Post,* p. C3.

Moy, P. (2003b, May 19). SARS fuels surge in anxieties. *South China Morning Post,* p. C1.

Phillips, H. (2003, April 4). Sai Kung mother stirs fears over camps' sewage. *South China Morning Post,* p. C3.

Pizam, A., & Fleischer, A. (2002). Severity versus frequency of acts of terrorism: Which has a larger effect on tourism demand? *Journal of Travel Research, 40*, 337-339.

Schmeltzer, J. (2002). *More American families opt for road-trip vacations.* Retrieved August 15, 2002, from *http://hotel-online.com/News/2002_Jul_19/k.TBT. 1027084549.html.*

Shamdasani, R. (2003, April 3). Three more die as countries around the world take drastic steps to halt SARS. *The South China Morning Post,* p. A2.

Shellum, S. (2003). *Pressure cooking: Florian Trento, Executive Chef at the Peninsula Hong Kong, explains how he and his team coped during the bleakest days of the SARS crisis.* Retrieved August 8, 2003 from *http://hotel-online.com/News/PR2003_2nd/ Jun03_SARSPressure.html.*

Sonmez, S., & Graefe, A.R. (1998). Influence of terrorism risk on foreign tourism decisions. *Annals of Tourism Research, 25*(1), 112-144.

Sonmez, S., Apostolopoulos, Y., & Tarlow, P. (1999). Tourism in crisis: Managing the effects of terrorism. *Journal of Travel Research, 38*, 13-18.

Tang, J., & Chan, C. (2003, May 14). Taipei likely to drop travel restrictions. *South China Morning Post,* p. A3.

The Standard. (2003, May 15). Restaurants lose $300m a week. *The Standard,* p. A-8.

Travelwirenews.com. (2003). *SARS affected travel habits and choice of destinations of Hong Kong travellers.* Retrieved October 21, 2003, from *www.eturbonews.com.*

TBR. (2002). *Traveller confidence returning: Concerns over the economy's health is primary reason consumers are avoiding travel.* Retrieved April 25, 2003, from *http://www.hotel-online.com/News/PR2002_3rd/ Aug02_TBRSurvey.html.*

TIA. (2002). *TIA's traveler sentiment index declines in third quarter 2002.* Retrieved April 25, 2003, *http:// www.hotel-online.com:80/News/PR2002_3rd/Sept02_ TIAIndex.html.*

TIA. (2003). *TIA travel outlook–Focusing US travel and tourism in the context of war.* Retrieved April 25, 2003, from *http://www.hotel-online.com:80/News/ PR2003_1st/May_03_TIAOutlook.html.*

WHO. (2003a). *Summary table of SARS cases by country, 1 November 2002-7 August 2003.* Retrieved August 20, 2003, from *http://www.who.int/csr/sars/ country/2003_08_15/en/.*

WHO. (2003b). *Situation Updates.* Retrieved November 20, 2003, from *http://www.who.int/csr/sars/ archive/en/.*

WTTC. (2003). *Special SARS analysis: Impact of travel and tourism* (Hong Kong, China, Singapore and Vietnam reports). World Travel and Tourism Council.

Japanese Tourism and the SARS Epidemic of 2003

Malcolm Cooper

SUMMARY. This paper chronicles and analyses the reactions of the Japanese tourist industry and tourists towards one of the major crises affecting world tourism during 2003, Severe Acute Respiratory Syndrome (SARS). Secondary sources are used to build up a picture of the impact of the SARS event on tourist flows to and from Japan during the period of the crisis and its management. The material is also framed, for both theoretical and practical purposes, within the existing tourism disaster management literature. In this way a more systematic attempt can be made, in the aftermath of the SARS outbreak, to place the impact of this event within a wider context. *[Article copies available for a fee from The Haworth Document Delivery Service: 1-800-HAWORTH. E-mail address: <docdelivery@haworthpress.com> Website: <http://www.HaworthPress.com> © 2005 by The Haworth Press, Inc. All rights reserved.]*

KEYWORDS. SARS, tourist responses, government responses, industry responses, media responses

INTRODUCTION

After the lifting of restrictions on overseas travel in 1964, the number of Japanese travelling abroad as tourists increased very quickly, reaching 17.82 million in 2000 (Figure 1), and making Japan one of the most important individual world source markets for international tourists. However, Figure 1 also shows that the reaction of Japanese tourists to previous "crises" (in 1991 the First Gulf War, in 1997-8 the "Asian Economic Crisis," and in 2001 9/11 as it is popularly known) that might affect their safety is consistently one of short-term avoidance of affected areas or particular modes of travel. Most recently this is seen in a reduction in the number of Japanese travelling overseas to 16.22 million in 2001 (rising to about 16.5 million in 2002) resulting from the terror-

FIGURE 1. Japanese Outbound Tourism 1964-2003 (Millions)

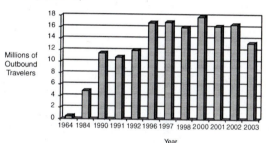

Source: Japan Tourism Marketing Co. (2004).

ist attacks in the USA of September 2001 (Table 1). However, while 9/11 contributed to a reduction of only 9% in Japanese outbound travel from the previous year of 2000, in 2003 the total of outbound travellers fell by 24.3%

Malcolm Cooper is Professor of Tourism Management and Environmental Law, Graduate School of Asia Pacific Studies, Ritsumeikan Asia Pacific University, Beppu, Japan (E-mail: cooperm@apu.ac.jp).

[Haworth co-indexing entry note]: "Japanese Tourism and the SARS Epidemic of 2003." Cooper, Malcolm. Co-published simultaneously in *Journal of Travel & Tourism Marketing* (The Haworth Hospitality Press, an imprint of The Haworth Press, Inc.) Vol. 19, No. 2/3, 2005, pp. 117-131; and: *Tourism Crises: Management Responses and Theoretical Insight* (ed: Eric Laws, and Bruce Prideaux) The Haworth Hospitality Press, an imprint of The Haworth Press, Inc., 2005, pp. 117-131. Single or multiple copies of this article are available for a fee from The Haworth Document Delivery Service [1-800-HAWORTH, 9:00 a.m. - 5:00 p.m. (EST). E-mail address: docdelivery@haworthpress.com].

TABLE 1. Japanese Out and Inbound Tourism 2001-2003

Tourist Numbers / Month/Year	Outbound	Inbound	% Change on previous Year Outbound	% Change on previous Year Inbound
August 2001	1,791,166	433,490	1.8%	2.3
September	1,331,411	354,578	−20.6%	−6.6
October	925,142	403,181	−39.2%	−9.2
November	860,698	354,484	−43.8%	−6.4
December	1,037,934	369,047	−27.5%	2.1
January 2002	1,125,330	392,588	−17.4%	−5.7
February	1,193,791	400,081	−20.5%	12.2
March	1,434,275	434,034	−11.0%	8.2
April	1,240,563	460,377	−9.5%	2.3
May	1,279,403	438,537	−6.4%	12.3
June	1,244,200	441,123	−14.8%	9.3
July	1,420,406	516,013	−11.0%	7.5
August	1,668,593	484,771	−6.8%	11.8
September	1,643,681	401,407	23.5%	13.2
October	1,483,874	471,813	60.4%	17.0
November	1,396,561	404,537	62.3%	14.1
December	1,392,127	393,682	33.2%	6.7
January 2003	1,262,094	450,857	20.4%	14.8
February	1,318,859	394,869	10.5%	−1.3
March	1,256,784	456,614	−12.4%	5.2
April	719,127	354,054	−42.0%	−23.1
May	567,832	288,562	−55.6%	−34.2
June	662,259	352,431	−46.8%	−20.1
July	968,000	515,692	−31.9%	N/C
August	1,285,000	550,380	−23.0%	13.5
September	1,358,511	457,574	−17.3%	14.0
October	1,295,142	527,859	−12.7%	11.9
November	1,259,963	444,435	−9.8%	9.9
December	1,327,133	N/A	−4.7%	N/A

Source: Japan Tourism Marketing Co. (2004). N/C is No Change; N/A is Not Available.

in the 3 months of the so-called SARS "crisis," and overall by 13.3 million or 19.5% for the year (Table 1). Despite the sequence of demand-dampening impacts observable in the data of Figure 1 and Table 1, including a range of terrorism incidents around the world, two Gulf Wars, the lingering after-effects of the collapse of the Japanese "bubble" economy, and the ongoing impact of airline route and capacity restructuring resulting from earlier adverse economic influences, Japan remains a very important generator of overseas travellers even in times of "crisis," with several markets reliant very heavily on what Japanese tourists do during each one.

The Iraqi and SARS "crises" of late 2002/early 2003, coming on top of the earlier ones, thus clearly combined to produce a further slump in demand from Japanese tourists for overseas travel during the middle months of 2003 (Table 1). However, the impact of such crises on inbound travel has been much less important; in late 2001 inbound travel volumes declined by less than 10% and recovered more quickly than outbound, indicating that Japan's international visitor source markets were not much affected by the 9/11 crisis (Table 1). The SARS and Iraqi crises did produce a different picture, but one in the case of SARS that probably more reflects Japan's proximity to the worst affected areas even though it had no cases itself, and in the case of Iraq reflected more the reluctance of Americans to travel during the "emergency." The major reductions in inbound markets were in travellers from Canada, USA and Mexico, while those from the Pacific (Oceania), including Australia and New Zealand, were virtually not affected (Japan Tourism Marketing Co., 2004). However, this decline in numbers of travellers was even more short-lived than that of Japanese outbound flows, indicating that once reliable information about the likelihood of contracting SARS or being affected by the Iraqi conflict while to/from or in Japan was available to Japan's major tourist markets, the "crisis" threat quickly evaporated.

TOURISM AND DISASTER (CRISIS) MANAGEMENT

The SARS "epidemic" of 2002-2003 infected just 8,096 people (Table 2); of these 774, or 9.6%, died (World Health Organisation, 2004). The People's Republic of China was hit the hardest; SARS was first discovered in the southern province of Guangdong in mid-November 2002. Nearly three months later, the Chinese Ministry of Health reported that there had been 300 cases of an "acute respiratory syndrome" in the province, which ultimately rose to 5,327 for the country as a whole, or 66% of all the cases reported and confirmed as being SARS. China faced international criticism for failing to report the full scale of this outbreak initially and comprehensively to the World Health Organisation (WHO). From there the disease spread across the world to some 28 countries as detailed in Table 2. For a chronology of SARS see BBC News Online, *Timeline: SARS virus* (2003b).

The Potential of SARS to Disrupt Tourism

Nevertheless, for the world community and its tourism industry in early 2003 the SARS "epidemic" was a disaster of potentially huge proportions; coming closely as it did in the wake of earlier crises and initially being an unknown disease. In terms of the definitions commonly used in the tourism disaster literature (Faulkner, 2001), it impacted on the Asia Pacific tourism community with such severity that exceptional measures were necessary (Carter, 1991), and the disease epitomised all the essential ingredients of a disaster, as identified by Fink (1986) and Faulkner (2001). Most notably, it involved:

- A triggering event (here a disease with no immediately known origins, disease vectors, or cure), which was potentially so significant that it challenged the existing structure, routine operations and survival of tourism businesses and the whole regional tourism network;
- The epidemic presented businesses and Governments with a high threat situation, involving a short decision time and an element of surprise and urgency;
- There were perceptions of an inability to cope amongst the health services directly affected;
- It represented a turning point in the evolution of the tourism destinations of the Asia-Pacific Region, and others worldwide, especially if they recorded visitors who had contracted the disease (as the longer term impact was unknown); and
- At the height of the epidemic, and in the period afterwards, both the management environment and personal circumstances of those involved could be described as "fluid, unstable, and dynamic" (Fink, 1986, p. 20).

How the tourism sector adjusts to disaster situations has not received a great deal of attention in tourism management research, even though as Faulkner noted in his seminal work on this topic, it is arguable that all destinations face the prospect of either a natural or human-induced disaster at some time in their history (Faulkner, 2001). The vulnerability of

TABLE 2. Number of SARS Cases Worldwide in 2003

Country	SARS Cases	Fatalities	Methods used to Combat SARS on Entry of Visitors
China–PRC	5,327	349	Information, thermal imaging (outbreak area travellers only), personal declaration, quarantine of suspects
China–Hong Kong	1,755	299	Information, thermal imaging, personal declaration, quarantine of suspects
China–Taiwan	346	37	Information, thermal imaging, personal declaration, quarantine of suspects
China–Macao	1	0	Information, thermal imaging, personal declaration, quarantine of suspects
Canada	251	43	Information, personal declaration, quarantine of suspects
Singapore	238	33	Information, thermal imaging, personal declaration, quarantine of suspects
Vietnam	63	5	Information, thermal imaging, personal declaration, quarantine of suspects
Philippines	14	2	Information, personal declaration, quarantine of suspects
Thailand	9	2	Information, thermal imaging (outbreak area travellers only), personal declaration, quarantine of suspects
Malaysia	5	2	Information, flight checks, personal declaration, quarantine of suspects
France	7	1	Information, personal declaration, quarantine of suspects before flights, passenger manifest demand
South Africa	1	1	Information, personal declaration, quarantine of suspects
USA	27	0	Information, personal declaration, quarantine of suspects
Mongolia	9	0	Information, personal declaration, quarantine of suspects
Germany	9	0	Information, personal declaration, quarantine of suspects
Australia	6	0	Information, personal declaration, quarantine of suspects
Sweden	5	0	Information, personal declaration, quarantine of suspects
United Kingdom	4	0	Information, Alert Levels, personal declaration, quarantine of suspects
Italy	4	0	Information, personal declaration, quarantine of suspects
India	3	0	Information, personal declaration, quarantine of suspects
South Korea	3	0	Information, personal declaration, quarantine of suspects
Indonesia	2	0	Information, personal declaration, quarantine of suspects
Kuwait	1	0	Information, personal declaration, quarantine of suspects
Colombia	1	0	Information, personal declaration, quarantine of suspects
Spain	1	0	Information, personal declaration, quarantine of suspects
Switzerland	1	0	Information, personal declaration, quarantine of suspects
New Zealand	1	0	Information, personal declaration, quarantine of suspects
Romania	1	0	Information, personal declaration, quarantine of suspects
Japan	0	0	Thermal imaging, personal declaration, quarantine of suspects
TOTAL	8,096	774 (9.6%)	*Note that Japan financed Asian Development Bank Infectious Diseases SWAT Team for affected Asian countries*

Source: http://www.who.int/csr/sars/country/table2004_04_21/en/, based on data as at December 2003 and on country reports of activities relating to SARS at entry points (e.g., http://www.asean-disease-surveillance.net/ASNSARS_Indonesia.asp).

many tourist destinations to such disaster events has however been noted by several authors (Murphy & Bayley, 1989; Drabek, 1994; Burby & Wagner, 1996). Despite this, tourism businesses and organisations are generally unprepared for disaster situations even in high-risk areas (Cassedy, 1991; Drabek, 1992, 1994), while many have played down the actual or potential impacts of disasters for marketing reasons (Cammisa, 1993; Murphy & Bayley,

1989). The latter reaction is particularly important with the SARS "epidemic," in that as an epidemic it did not really happen except perhaps in the originating country, China (including Hong Kong and Taiwan), but it certainly triggered safety considerations and confusion within a number of tourism markets in the Asia-Pacific Region and the rest of the world. In all of the affected areas outside the PRC, Hong Kong and Taiwan, the numbers involved were small, and the tendency of press reports to exaggerate the impacts of disasters in tourism areas accounted for much of the labelling of SARS as an epidemic and as a disaster (see for example Japan Times, 2003a).

Even so, it is unlikely that tourism businesses and organisations could have "planned" for SARS in order to offset its impact, which does put it squarely within the definition of a "disaster" (Faulkner, 2001). Certainly, it had been well recognised prior to 2002 that difficulties relating to respiratory illness were likely, and would most likely originate in Asia, given the increasing ability of influenza viruses to mutate and the difficulties of monitoring this in such a vast region. And in addition to this, as Gro Harlem Brundtland said in the aftermath, the world had to rely on old-fashioned methods of isolating sufferers to combat the reality of SARS, there not being "an answer to everything, and that there was neither a medicine or a vaccine in this case" (BBC News Online, 2003a).

While furthering the theoretical analysis of tourism disaster management is not in the scope of this paper, some aspects of the existing framework must be discussed, in order that the Japanese data on the impact of SARS can be fully evaluated. In his introduction to *Towards a Framework for Tourism Disaster Management*, Faulkner (2001, p. 244) makes the point that, to the casual observer exposed to the media that currently inform our daily lives, it appears that we live in an increasingly disaster prone world. In also observing that our environment appears to have become increasingly "turbulent and crisis prone," Richardson (1994) has suggested this might be so not only because we have become a more complex and crowded world, but also because we now have more powerful technology that has a real capacity to generate disasters, which complicates the process of isolating cause and effect relationships. For this reason, the boundaries between natural disasters and those induced by human action are becoming increasingly blurred, and this situational element needs to be taken into account in any analysis of such phenomena (Capra, 1996; Keown-McMullan, 1997). However, crises and disasters also have potentially positive (e.g., stimulus to innovation, recognition of new markets, etc.) as well

as negative outcomes. This is well illustrated by the SARS epidemic, which galvanised many tourism organisations in the Asia Pacific Region to advertise their attractions heavily, while calling for health-related safety measures being brought up-to-date (Japan Association of Travel Agents, 2003c). The reaction of potential tourists was also positive in a sense: Japanese tourists have exhibited a propensity to shift travel away from areas of difficulty in the past and go elsewhere (but not stop travelling); the domestic travel data for the period show that this was also true of the SARS crisis.

Another approach to defining disasters has been proposed by Keller and Al-Madhari (1996, p. 20), who applied arbitrary statistical benchmarks. Their data purported to show that disasters could be defined in terms of a threshold number of fatalities (10), damage costs (US $1 million) and number of people evacuated (50). On the basis of this definition, the SARS epidemic would certainly qualify as a disaster. This approach has the appeal of providing an unambiguous statistical definition of disasters; however, it loses sight of the qualitative factors referred to above, which are present in disaster situations irrespective of whether or not the fatality, damage cost and evacuation thresholds are reached (Faulkner, 2001).

Asia-Pacific Community Responses to SARS

From a sociological perspective, the immediate response to a disaster situation has been observed as including several phases (Booth, 1993, pp. 102-103):

- Shock at both the individual and the collective level, where the unexpected nature of the event and the severity of its impacts may cause stress and a sense of helplessness and disorientation, but also mobilisation in response;
- Denial or defensiveness, evasion or strategic withdrawal, where the crisis is not acknowledged;
- Acknowledgement, representing a turning point whereby the community accepts the reality of the crisis or change; and

- Adaptation, where the community learns from the crisis, develops new ways of coping and rebuilds.

This sequence of phases is observable in the SARS context, but their individual importance clearly depended on the extent of damage caused by the disaster, the probability and frequency of recurrence and the adaptability of the impacted communities. Community resilience (Granot, 1995) is very important in the level of adaptability shown by a tourism market, and this is well illustrated by the combination of SARS with pre-existing economic difficulties and terrorism in the Asia Pacific context. A number of Asia Pacific destinations were very badly hit in the short-term by the SARS epidemic, but their long-term adaptation will depend on these other factors, as the epidemic itself was of short duration.

Richardson's (1994) analysis of crisis management in organisations provides another perspective on community adjustment capabilities by distinguishing between "single" and "double loop" learning approaches. In the former, the response to disasters involves a linear reorientation "more" or less in keeping with traditional objectives and traditional responses (Richardson, 1994, p. 5). Alternatively, the double loop learning approach challenges traditional beliefs about what society and management is and should do. This approach recognises that management systems in fact can themselves engender the ingredients of chaos and catastrophe, and that managers must also be more aware and proactively concerned about organisations as the creators of crises. If we accept this distinction, it is possible to see the emerging disquiet over the role of the media and the World Health Organisation in the SARS saga as reflecting concern over their role as "creators" of the crisis (Japan Times, 2003e).

The WHO and Media Responses to SARS and Their Impact on Tourism

That the world health system was initially unresponsive with respect to the SARS epidemic, and then did not know what to do, is not open to question. From National Governments (PRC) to local hospitals the level of difficulty in coming to terms with the disease was strikingly obvious. To be fair, however, the degree to which emergency services and other organisations can be prepared for such disasters has been questioned by Huque (1998), who noted that policies and decision-making structures that govern an organisation's activities in normal times may not be appropriate in disaster situations. Bureaucratic structures and power relationships restrict the ability of organisations to respond promptly and effectively to emergency conditions, and this in itself constitutes a barrier to inter-agency cooperation.

Once the new disease had been recognised as a potential disaster of global proportions, the World Health Organisation (WHO) issued each weekday a tabular report of the "Cumulative Number of Reported Probable Cases" on their website. By definition, the numbers of cumulative cases in any outbreak of disease will always increase and there will continue to be additional deaths and new cases until the outbreak is eradicated. However, for tourism authorities and the public perception of the progress of the disease, the focus on these figures provided a negatively distorted view of the current state of the outbreak at any one time, the progress that had been made in containing it, and its likely short-to-medium term course. An indication of how the public perception of SARS was mishandled is to be found in the fact that a key measure progress in fighting it was buried in the WHO's daily reporting in the form of the number of "current probable cases" (Asia Transpacific Journeys, 2003). While data for current probable cases was published daily, a more accurate picture of the SARS outbreak would have been provided if these had been reported as prominently as the figures for cumulative cases, new cases, and deaths. When the data for current probable cases during the so-called crisis is analysed, it is clear, contrary to media coverage and the WHO's primary reporting, that the SARS outbreak had significantly diminished in geographic reach and numbers of active cases very quickly (Figure 2).

Not only that, but as of September 3rd, 2003 there had been just 82 SARS related deaths outside of the region of PRC (including Hong Kong and Taiwan), a total that had not changed from March. While in no way wishing to trivialize the impact of SARS, when compared to the reported annual US death rate of over 35,000 from influ-

FIGURE 2. Weekly New SARS Cases, April-June 2003

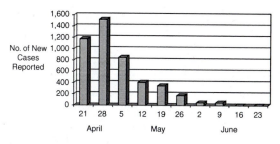

Source: World Health Organisation (2004).

enza, it is obvious that the risk of contraction and/or death through other forms of viral infection in the US and other countries is in fact far greater than the risk of contraction and/or death through SARS infection for any international traveller. The World Health Organisation now suggests that the rapid containment of SARS in 2003 is a back-door testament to the efficient response of health systems worldwide–and is justification for its swift and decisive action in issuing a global alert in March (WHO, 2003). That this alert also came about because there has for many years been a growing *fear* among infectious disease specialists, aided by media speculation, that the increase in global air travel through tourism could assist a disastrous spread of a new and lethal infection is not acknowledged at time of writing.

On the role of the media in disasters in the USA, for example, Quarantelli (1996) has observed:

- Understanding in the mass media of disaster preparedness planning is generally poor;
- Some of the coordination problems attributed to emergency services agencies are also evident in the press as "local mass media systems consider disasters in their own community as 'their' disasters" and "this is sometimes manifest in tension between local mass media and national network staff members";
- There is a tendency for selective reporting focusing on the activities of formal organisations (with whom the media has established links), rather than emergent and informally organised volunteers that may have better information;

- Television, in particular, is prone to perpetuate disaster myths, such as the persistence of disruption, panic, looting, etc.

In the tourism context, it has been noted that the impacts of disasters on the market are often out of proportion with their actual disruptive effects because of exaggeration by the media (Cassedy, 1991; Murphy & Bayley, 1989), or denial by the destination (Cammisa, 1993). Media reports have the potential to have a devastating impact on disaster-affected destinations because pleasure travel is a discretionary item and, within the mind of the consumer, the "quest for paradise can suddenly transform into a dangerous journey that most travellers would rather avoid" (Cassedy, 1991, p. 4). Also, by virtue of the power of the media and the tendency for negative images to linger, the recovery of destinations usually takes longer than the period required for the restoration of services to normalcy. This has been observed in a number of case studies, including the 1987 Fiji Coup, the 1989 San Francisco Earthquake, the 1989 Tiananmen Square incident (Cassedy, 1991), and the SARS epidemic of 2003 (Japan Times, 2003c).

Both the reaction of the WHO and the media over the SARS epidemic provided justification for the fear of health authorities that they would not be able to cope with disease outbreaks made more dangerous by mass tourist travel (at least initially, if a particular disease proves impossible to detect and therefore makes it difficult to hold carriers at traditional entry barriers to a country). But when this fear was coupled with the lack of quick solutions as identified by Gro Harlem Brundtland, and the role of the media in portraying the crisis, the end result was that SARS Panic, rather than SARS itself, is in fact what had a devastating effect on many businesses worldwide, especially businesses in the tourism sector. In fact, the real situation was as outlined above–that very few actual cases occurred, that those that did were in fact usually successfully treatable, and that sufficiently effective screening techniques were very quickly put into place or reinforced at entry points to reduce the likelihood of the disease spreading amongst the wider travelling public (see Table 2 for details). The standard screening process has always relied on information distribution and personal declarations of health status, backed up by thermal imaging and quarantine of suspected cases where appropriate or necessary because of the sheer volume of travellers, and denial of carriage/entry for travellers from areas of severe outbreak. All these techniques have been available to entry points for many years (except for thermal imaging), and have been used many times to control the movement of people across a country's borders; they simply needed to be reconfirmed as likely to be effective in the context of SARS.

THE JAPANESE EXPERIENCE

It is now possible to examine closely the Japanese experience with SARS and its aftermath. In the beginning the response in Japan was that of many other countries; little was known about the reports of a new strain of acute respiratory disease, and little comment was therefore made. Once it became known in February-March of 2003 that this disease was likely to be more difficult to contain and treat, measures were quickly developed and put in place to counteract it. At no time did it appear that Japan itself would have any local cases of the disease (whatever it actually was)–the reactions now described revolved around making sure that travellers did not import it.

At the invitation of the Japan Association of Travel Agents (JATA), infectious disease specialists from the International Medical Centre of Japan participated in a study session held on Tuesday, April 15, 2003, during the height of the international concern over SARS. Including representatives from the mass media and other interested parties, more than 100 people attended the study session, to learn more about SARS itself and the current situation. A TV crew was also on hand to report on the event. JATA Director & Secretary General Ishiyama opened the event by saying to the assembly, "This study session is being held to ensure that those in the tourism business have both an adequate understanding and accurate information about SARS. It is vital that everyone be able to separate out what is correct and important from the avalanche of information coming in every day" (JATA, 2003a). His introduction

was followed by updates on SARS, a preliminary definition of the disease, its suggested clinical progress and pathogenic agents, the route of infection, how hospitals are dealing with SARS patients, and what information should be made available to travellers. Dr. Shinozuka, Managing Director of the Japanese Society of Travel Medicine, then addressed the gathering, suggesting that: "Infectious disease specialists and those in the tourist industry are faced with the greatest difficulties now. More than SARS itself, they must deal with the fallout from fear and rumours. As we seek a swift solution to the cause and treatment, we must all be assiduous about disseminating accurate information." In other words, as early as April 2003 Japanese experts had clearly understood one of the biggest problems with the SARS outbreak; its tendency to induce hysteria in both the media and health authorities, and thus amongst the travelling public. Amid the hope all around that a solution would be swiftly found, experts fielded such questions as: "How many patients have recovered completely?" "What areas have been confirmed with documented cases of SARS?" and "Is there any end in sight?" amongst others (JATA, 2003a).

The Impact of SARS on Japanese Travel Patterns

As noted earlier, the major impact of SARS in the Japanese context, assuming that the disease did not take hold in Japan, was always going to be on the number of Japanese willing to take holidays abroad, or on the number of foreign visitors to Japan, especially to/from the areas of greatest incidence of the disease. Referring back to Table 1 and Figure 1, it is easy to see that a similar pattern to that of all other recent crises occurred; many Japanese simply stopped travelling overseas. While these data are not to be accounted for solely by the impact of SARS, given the contemporaneous Iraqi conflict, the pattern of reduction in demand at times of crisis is very clear. That it was very short is also clear. The main impact occurred in the three months of April-June, and by July the market was already recovering. Nevertheless a reduction of up to 55% in the number of Japanese travelling overseas in any one month is significant and, given the numbers, was likely to severely affect the destinations involved.

Tables 3 and 4 detail the impact of this decline in demand on the destinations most affected. These data show that, as expected, China (with Hong Kong and Taiwan) and the other main SARS affected destinations suffered most, but also that other destinations were not immune. Part of the reason for not travelling to say Australia in this context is that much of Japanese tourist travel is routed through Singapore, an infected area, and part of course of the reason for not travelling to the United States and Europe was the additional reaction against the likelihood of terrorism. SARS, as well as other factors, therefore had a powerful impact on Japanese outbound tourism for the period of April to August 2003, especially for destinations in the rest of Asia. The sales results for April through August were influenced strongly by the reinforcement of the travel advisory on SARS issued by the Ministry of Foreign Affairs issued in March 2003. This resulted in heavy cancellation of package tours at the five

largest travel agencies (surveyed by JATA at the beginning of July 2003), severely impacting travel to China and other Asian destinations. Agency bookings to Asian destinations overall were 33.3% (April), 13.2% (May), and 12.5% (June) of those of the previous year, while those to Chinese destinations dropped to 28.1%, 1.0%, and 1.5% (JATA, 2003c).

Bookings for longer-haul destinations in Oceania, Hawaii and Europe for April through July, while largely unaffected by SARS, were however affected by war and terrorism, as well as reduced airline capacity and the overall Japanese economic situation. Bookings for Oceania destinations stood at 75.3% in April, compared with the same time the previous year, Hawaii destinations were at 70.7%, and European destinations were at 64.5%. Booking levels for domestic tours however showed large increases on the previous year. Bookings for all domestic destinations were up 113.1% (July), 108.4% (August), and 122.1% (September), indicating that some at least of the pent-up demand for travel was being absorbed in the domestic market.

TABLE 3. Japanese Outbound Travellers to Asia, February-August 2003

Month	Hong Kong		PRC China		Taiwan		Korea	
	Number	% Change Previous Year	Number	% Change Previous Year	Number	% Change Previous Year	Number	% Change Previous Year
Feb	99,453	6.0	262,500	38.0	90,785	20.8	172,960	2.4
March	102,959	−20.2	269,100	12.5	96,909	1.3	179,336	−16.3
April	15,546	−85.5	97,800	−54.8	33,624	−56.1	120,315	−34.9
May	10,918	−90.5	54,400	−78.2	7,623	−90.1	87,036	−51.0
June	21,088	−80.6	75,400	−67.2	8,520	−88.3	83,235	−33.3
July	59,442	−46.1	150,100	−37.1	34,862	−52.0	123,887	−41.8
Aug	77,871	−36.2	N/A	N/A	49,281	−39.7	48,488	−40.6
	Thailand		Malaysia		Singapore			
Feb	118,607	8.2	28,328	29.8	50,434	2.2		
March	103,938	−12.7	21,613	−44.0	54,455	−20.5		
April	58,344	−37.6	8,704	−70.6	12,482	−74.6		
May	39,053	−54.5	7,239	−76.8	7,041	−86.1		
June	44,435	−48.8	7,933	−65.1	13,997	−74.5		
July	66,116	−33.5	9,349	−73.1	28,606	−57.0		
Aug	N/A	N/A	11,718	−74.2	42,988	−49.8		

Source: Japan Tourism Marketing Co. (2004)

TABLE 4. Japanese Outbound Travellers to North America, Europe and Oceania, February-August 2003

Month	Canada		USA		Hawaii		Guam	
	Number	% Change Previous Year	Number	% Change Previous Year	Number	% Change Previous Year	Number	% Change Previous Year
Feb	17,662	6.7	271,259	2.7	120,488	9.1	54,676	−20.2
March	25,173	9.3	242,016	−24.8	103,009	−16.0	52,728	−33.5
April	17,829	−44.1	148,093	−40.8	64,702	−36.0	34,039	−36.3
May	13,395	−62.6	178,809	−38.5	71,836	−39.7	31,597	−49.6
June	16,085	−58.6	201,672	−32.6	84,096	−30.9	33,765	−48.2
July	20,949	−58.0	253,542	−16.8	98,436	−20.9	51,857	−21.5
Aug	N/A	N/A	N/A	N/A	131,531	−11.0	64,520	−22.1
	Germany		Spain		Australia		New Zealand	
Feb	77,657	6.7	55,799	39.7	58,900	4.2	16,362	−5.8
March	87,263	−1.1	55,602	4.2	59,900	−13.5	17,024	−6.1
April	68,773	−32.6	35,471	−35.0	43,600	−24.4	11,088	−17.4
May	83,730	−25.9	28,796	−47.0	29,500	−41.6	6,058	−42.8
June	98,228	−21.7	30,174	−43.5	29,500	−41.2	4,378	−36.0
July	105,871	−15.7	33,499	−12.6	45,700	−26.2	9,630	−27.7
Aug	N/A	N/A	40,878	−6.6	56,400	−18.4	11,951	−18.5

Source: Japan Tourism Marketing Co. (2004).

The Reaction

It was acknowledged early on by the Japanese government that the rapid spread of SARS presented a menace, not only in Asia but also throughout the world. In order to overcome this imminent threat to human security, the international community was called upon by the World Health Organisation to take immediate action:

1. To halt the spread through disinfection and isolation, and effective care for people affected by SARS;
2. To strengthening national and regional capabilities of surveillance, prevention and control; and
3. To tackle the economic and social outcomes caused by the disease.

And Japan responded. Under the first of these measures, assistance was extended with the dispatch of Disaster Relief Expert Teams to Vietnam and China (March and May, 2003 respectively), and the provision of medicines, medical equipment and operational funds for China, Mongolia, and Southeast Asian countries (April/May). For the second, Japan proposed to assist the WHO in developing the extensive network of experts and administrators needed in order to control communicable diseases, and for the third, Japan proposed to enhance international cooperation needed in order to support the recovery of economic activities as well as to alleviate negative impacts to everyday life. The Japanese authorities were reacting to the following key concepts:

- The early clinical features of SARS are not specific enough to reliably distinguish it from other respiratory illnesses;
- Risk of exposure is the key to considering the likelihood of a diagnosis of SARS;
- Most patients with SARS disease have a clear history of exposure to another SARS patient or to a setting where SARS transmission is occurring;
- SARS is usually localized and often limited to healthcare settings or households;
- A cluster of atypical pneumonia in healthcare workers may indicate undetected SARS transmission;

- In a setting of extensive SARS transmission, the possibility of SARS should be considered in all persons with a fever or lower respiratory tract illness, even if an epidemiological link cannot be readily established;
- Up-to-date information on the transmission of SARS globally is needed to accurately assess exposure risks;
- Contact tracing is resource intensive yet critical to containment efforts as it allows early recognition of illness in persons at greatest risk;
- Frequent communication among public health officials and healthcare providers, real-time analysis of data, and timely dissemination of information are essential for outbreak management;
- Swift action to contain disease should be initiated when a potential case is recognized, even though information sufficient to determine case status may be lacking.

Having set up these initiatives, the Japanese authorities insisted upon the same measures to control travellers as adopted by other countries on the advice of the WHO. Travel advisories were issued covering all affected destinations. At all Japanese diplomatic and consular missions in the People's Republic of China, and offices of the Interchange Association (Taiwan) in Taipei and Kaohsiung, for example, an interview sheet was collected from all applicants at the time of the receipt of a visa application. In cases that responses on the interview sheet indicated that this was necessary, the applicant was requested to submit a certificate from a doctor indicating SARS non-infection. At the Embassy in Beijing and the Consulates-General in Guangzhou and Shanghai, applications for visas were only accepted through designated travel agencies (this measure could also be implemented according to necessity in the other missions in China and the Interchange Association offices in Taiwan).

On all flights departing from the whole of the PRC, Hong Kong, Taiwan and Korea (only for those who got on board in China, Taiwan or Hong Kong and were proceeding to Japan via Korea), and Toronto, a questionnaire was distributed to passengers and collected upon arrival. Those passengers who had any of the SARS symptoms, such as high fever or breathing difficulty, or a history of close contact with a person suspected of having SARS in the last 10 days, were requested to submit a contact address and telephone number in Japan (at the same time, a "health card" was also handed over). For those who did not fall into any of these categories, only a "health card" was distributed. Doctors of national hospitals were dispatched to the quarantine offices of each airport. All aircraft passengers, irrespective of the origin of departure, were subjected to a temperature (thermal imaging) check upon arrival at each airport. For shipping from affected areas, including PRC China, Hong Kong and Taiwan in particular, and with the cooperation of shipping companies, the same questionnaire was distributed to all passengers and crewmembers, and a temperature check was also carried out. For cargo ships, instructing the captain to carry out a temperature check of crewmembers and report health conditions by radio accurately to port quarantine officers strengthened quarantine measures.

As part of its normal business practice, JATA stays in touch with the changing travel market in order to better assess prevailing business conditions by carrying out a quarterly survey of market trends among member companies, indexed by types of travel, destination and customer segment. Some of the comments relating to the SARS epidemic from these surveys are reproduced here to indicate the response of the Japanese travel industry to the crisis (JATA, 2003c):

The overseas travel advisory suggesting restraint in visiting SARS infected regions put a hold on package tours to China and Hong Kong. The epidemic has, in combination with economic factors, had an indirect impact on other countries/regions as well, putting a chill on overall demand for overseas travel. (Overseas travel wholesaler, August)

Because of the company ban on business travel between April and June, the climate was not conducive for planning incentive travel or proposing a shift to domestic travel. (JATA in-house, August, 2003)

On the whole, the travel market is recovering; in particular, demand for Eastern and Central European destinations among the 50 and over age group stands out. Demand for China appears to have returned as well. (Second Tier Retailer, in June)

The situation remains favourable for European destinations, which were largely unaffected by SARS, while reservations for the Asian region continue to recover little by little. (Second Tier Retailer, August)

The new Chinese short-term stay visa exemption will greatly contribute to increased demand, and it appears demand for such destinations as Asian beach resorts and Vietnam will also return. (First Tier Retailer, August)

The government also developed a *Visit Japan Campaign*, which began at the end of July 2003 in Taiwan and on August 5 in Hong Kong. While primarily directed towards boosting Japan's inbound tourism, this program was also partly designed to remove lingering concerns among local authorities still apprehensive about accepting visitors from those SARS affected areas (Japan Times, 2003b). Other Japanese organisations introduced varying degrees of control over the movement of their employees and their families. In the case of the Universities, for example, both staff and students intending to travel to China, Taiwan, Singapore or Hong Kong during study breaks or for research and conference purposes were told that they would be quarantined for 10 days on return and therefore should not undertake the trip unless it was absolutely necessary.

In the overseas tourist destinations themselves, Japanese companies and government representatives also suffered from the impact of SARS and the subsequent reaction from Japanese tourists. In Canada, for example, tour companies on Prince Edward Island (1,600km from Toronto) found that SARS was deterring many Japanese from travelling to Canada largely due to impressions gained from the media (Japan Times, 2003a). In Singapore, Sumihiro Hirai, President of JETRO Singapore, the Japanese Government's External Trade Relations Organisation, noted on the 29th of October that 84.3% of Japanese firms operating in Singapore in May, 2003 felt the effects of

SARS on their businesses (Japan Times, 2003e). Much of the effect of SARS was caused by travel advisories issued by governments throughout the world, which actually took the practical form of travel restrictions for most concerned tourists, public organisations and governments. When the Japanese Government's version of these was lifted at the end of May, 2003 with regard to Singapore, for example, Japanese business became very much more optimistic concerning travel and the flow of goods, and the same scenario was observed in other destinations.

Within Japan both public and private health authorities undertook the following measures, with private business following suit to a greater or lesser degree where appropriate (health sections in the larger concerns, for example, instituted monitoring and quarantine programs):

- Education of clinicians and public health workers on features that could assist in early recognition of SARS and on guidelines for reporting SARS cases;
- Development of tools to identify, evaluate, and monitor contacts of SARS patients;
- Establishment an efficient data management system linking clinical, epidemiological and laboratory data on cases of SARS disease and allowing rapid sharing of information;
- Identification of surge capacity for investigation of cases and identification, evaluation, and monitoring of contacts in the event of a large SARS outbreak.

On the wider front of political and economic responses, the following were implemented:

- On 24 April 2003 the Government introduced a thermal imaging system at Narita International Airport in its effort to check for SARS. Travellers entering Japan from Hong Kong; Beijing; and Guangdong were also encouraged to complete health declaration forms as part of standard operating procedures for the containment of infectious diseases (ASEAN Disease Surveillance Net, 2004);
- On 28 April 2003 the Japan International Cooperation Agency announced that it

would provide 357.8 million yen in aid to seven Asian nations to help them battle SARS. The Philippines would receive 43.5 million yen and Mongolia 28 million yen. Cambodia, Lao PDR, Myanmar, and Thailand would also receive support. The seven nations would use the money to buy medication and equipment that can be used to test suspected patients' blood, and protective clothing for medical and airport quarantine staff to stop the spread of the disease. The PRC would receive 2,600 biohazard safety suits and 20,000 high-performance face masks;

- On 29 April 2003 the Government advised students studying in Beijing to return home and extended its travel advisory to cover the entire PRC, as concerns grew over one of the regions worst hit by SARS. The Foreign Ministry had already issued a warning for Beijing previously, telling Japanese travellers to postpone all nonessential trips to the capital;

- On 2 May 2003 the Ministry of Health, Labour and Welfare adopted a policy to quarantine those who are suspected of suffering from SARS before their infection is confirmed. The Health Ministry authorized teams of experts mainly from the National Institute of Infectious Diseases to survey the contacts of any patient and their cohabiting family members since returning to the country. The Government also announced it would use public funds to cover examination costs for people suspected of suffering from SARS. Meanwhile, more than 1,000 beds were secured in hospitals nationwide and almost all of the 47 prefectures prepared action plans for a possible outbreak of SARS;

- Also on 2 May 2003 the Development Bank of Japan announced that it was considering the extension of low-interest emergency loans to two air carriers, Japan Airlines System Corp. and All Nippon Airways Co. This move was in response to the Government's call for the bank to consider giving concessional loans to the two air carriers, which suffered a plunge in passengers following the outbreak of SARS;

- On 4 May 2003 the Ministry of Economy, Trade and Industry (METI) extended state-backed trade insurance coverage to losses at Japanese companies' overseas operations caused by the outbreak of SARS. METI took the measure in response to a number of inquiries from companies received at the Ministry as well as at Nippon Export and Investment Insurance, an independent administrative body that manages the insurance program. METI plans to include SARS damages in the program's overseas investment insurance, a type of trade insurance that covers foreign assets such as stockholdings and real estate held by Japanese companies;

- On 7 May 2003, the Foreign Ministry upgraded its travel risk advisory for Taipei, China, urging Japanese travellers to consider postponing non-essential trips to the island because of the SARS epidemic.

Throughout the term of the "crisis," travel agents, hotels, local transport and tourist information sources in Japan continued to stress that there was no outbreak in Japan, that it was still possible to travel to overseas destinations (especially those that were free of the disease like Australia and New Zealand) in safety, and that urgent and effective measures had already been taken to ensure travellers' well-being. While there was no overall panic sale of airline seats or hotel rooms such as occurred in destinations like Singapore and Thailand, there were discount periods and other inducements offered to both domestic and international travellers.

DISCUSSION AND CONCLUSIONS

In summary then, with the SARS outbreak officially declared at an end for 2003 at the time of writing, the worst seems to be over, yet many in Japan have cautioned that it is too early to relax vigilance against SARS (JATA, 2003b). Asian health officials fear that SARS may make a comeback during the 2003-2004 flu season (Japan Times, 2003d), and since the main part of this paper was written it has done so to a limited extent in China as a result of biological contamination at a testing laboratory

(Guardian Unlimited Special Report, 2004). Regional business also remains concerned because SARS "created a new scenario that most (business) planners would not have thought of: *denial of access to people*" (Goh Moh Heng, Executive Director, Disaster Recovery Institute Asia, quoted in Japan Times, 2003c, p. 9), and in some cases even forced companies to segregate employees.

The response of the Japanese inbound tourist market was generally the same as that observed for outbound tourists: to avoid the destinations labelled as SARS infected areas. Partly this was due to governments making travel to these regions difficult to justify (in terms of travel advisories and restrictions on re-entry), but it mainly conformed to the personal avoidance patterns apparent in earlier data. Recovery of overall traveller numbers, however, is generally quite rapid, once the implied threats are reduced, and is proving to be so for SARS affected travel to and from Japan. The crisis, which peaked in May 2003, is estimated to have caused billions of dollars in economic damage; for example, Japan Airlines System posted a record annual loss for 2003-2004, citing as primary causes the SARS and avian flu epidemics, which deterred air travellers. The company reported a net loss of ¥88.6 billion for the business year that ended March 31, 2004, compared with net profit of ¥11.6 billion a year earlier, but is forecasting ¥36 billion profit in the business year through March 2005 (International Herald Tribune, 2004). This pattern is repeated throughout tourism and related industries in both Japan and destination markets wherever there is some degree of reliance on the overseas tourism market, and yet in hindsight the reaction that caused such losses bears all the hallmarks of an overreaction. While it is easy to make such a comment after the event, the crisis' true genesis lay partly at least in the "I told you so" reactions of the World Health Organisation and the media on the nature of respiratory diseases likely to arise in Asia. Panic characterised the World's reactions to SARS, a powerful distorting feature of "disasters" that should be given more prominence in the tourism literature.

REFERENCES

ASEAN Disease Surveillance Net. (2004). *SARS–Standard Operating Procedures*. Retrieved July 9, 2003, from *http://www.asean-disease-surveillance.net/ASNSARS_Indonesia.asp*.

Asia Transpacific Journeys. (2003). *Comparative WHO Data for Cumulative Cases and Active Cases of SARS*. Retrieved July 9, 2003, from *http://www.asiatranspacific.com/admin/book/index.aspx?pageID*.

BBC News Online. (2003a, June 23). *SARS epidemic 'tailing off'*. Available from the BBC News Online site: *http://news.bbc.co.uk/*.

BBC News Online. (2003b, September 9). *Timeline: SARS virus*. Available from the BBC News Online site: *http://news.bbc.co.uk/*.

Booth, S. (1993). *Crisis management strategy: Competition and change in modern enterprises*. New York: Routledge.

Burby, R.J., & Wagner, F. (1996). Protecting tourists from death and injury in coastal storms. *Disasters, 20*(1), 49-60.

Cammisa, J.V. (1993). The Miami experience: Natural and manmade disasters 1992-93. In *Expanding responsibilities: A blueprint for the travel industry* (pp. 294-295). 24th Annual Conference Proceedings of Travel and Tourism Research Association, Whistler, BC.

Capra, F. (1996). *The web of life*. London: Harpers Collins Publishers.

Carter, W.N. (1991). *Disaster management: A disaster manager's handbook*. Manila: Asian Development Bank.

Cassedy, K. (1991). *Crisis management planning in the travel and tourism industry: A study of three destinations and a crisis management planning manual*. San Francisco: PATA.

Drabek, I.E. (1992). Variations in disaster evacuation behaviour: Public response versus private sector executive decision-making. *Disasters, 16*(2), 105-118.

Drabek, I.E. (1994). Risk perceptions of tourist business managers. *The Environment Professional, 16*, 327-341.

Faulkner, B. (2001). Towards a framework for tourism disaster management. In, L. Fredline, L. Jago, & C. Cooper (Eds.), *Progressing tourism research–Bill Faulkner* (pp. 244-268). Clevedon: Channel View.

Fink, S. (1986). *Crisis management*. New York: American Association of Management.

Granot, H. (1995). Proposed scaling of communal consequences of disaster. *Disaster Prevention and Management, 4*(3), 5-13.

Guardian Unlimited Special Reports. (2004, May 9). SARS controls could bring curbs on travel. *Guardian Unlimited Special Reports*.

Huque, A.S. (1998). Disaster management and the interorganizational imperative: The Hong Kong disaster plan. *Issues and Studies, 34*(2), 104-123.

International Herald Tribune. (2004, May 7). SARS and avian flu cause Japan Airlines to post record loss. *International Herald Tribune.*

Japan Association of Travel Agents. (2003a). *Over 100 Participate in JATA Sponsored SARS Study Session on April 15, 2003.* Tokyo: Author.

Japan Association of Travel Agents. (2003b). *2003 Overseas Package Tours.* Tokyo: Author.

Japan Association of Travel Agents. (2003c). *6th JATA Survey on Travel Market Trends: Overseas.* Tokyo: Author.

Japan Times. (2003a, July 15). SARS scares off fans of Canada's 'Anne'. *Japan Times*, p. 4.

Japan Times (2003b, August 1). Residents of SARS-hit areas targeted in tourism drive. *Japan Times*, p. 2.

Japan Times. (2003c, October 21). Business Security still at risk: Survey. *Japan Times*, p. 9.

Japan Times. (2003d, October 22). Report on the recent SARS conference, Hanoi, 19-20 October, 2003. *Japan Times*, p. 2.

Japan Times. (2003e, October 30). World Eye Reports, Singapore, Thursday. *Japan Times*, B1.

Japan Tourism Marketing Co. (2004). *Tourism Statistics.* Retrieved July 9, 2003, from *http://www.tourism.jp/english/statistics.*

Keller, A.Z., & Al-Madhari, A.F. (1996). Risk management and disasters. *Disaster Prevention and Management, 5*(5), 19-22.

Keown-McMullan, C. (1997). Crisis: When does a molehill become a mountain? *Disaster Prevention and Management, 6*(1), 4-10.

Murphy, P.E., & Bayley, R. (1989). Tourism and disaster planning. *Geographical Review, 79*(1), 36-46.

Quarantelli, E.L. (1996). Local mass media operations in disasters in the USA. *Disaster, Prevention and Management, 3*(2), 5-10.

Richardson, B. (1994). Crisis management and the management strategy: Time to "loop the loop". *Disaster Prevention and Management, 3*(3), 59-80.

World Health Organisation. (2003). *Severe Acute Respiratory Syndrome (SARS)–Updates.* Available from the World Health Organisation site, *www.who.int/csr/sars/en/.*

World Health Organisation. (2004). *Summary of probable SARS cases with onset of illness 1 November 2002 to 31 July 2003.* Retrieved 2003, from *http://www.who.int/csr/sars/country/table2004_04_21/en/.*

Tourism Industry Employee Workstress–
A Present and Future Crisis

Glenn F. Ross

SUMMARY. Workstress is a pernicious yet little understood problem in many industries, including tourism. It is, moreover, evidencing no signs of abatement, with researchers such as Schabracq, Winnubst and Cooper (2003) suggesting that a number of clearly identifiable trends within organizational life are likely to exacerbate the extent of this problem in the future. This paper presents an examination of stress as a phenomenon of workplace functioning and suggests a model of organizational wellbeing within which stress might be understood. It is suggested that workstress has the ability to cause personal crises, organizational morbidity and mortality, and even financial crisis at a community level should a climate of workstress come to typify a local industry. The paper presents findings from a series of tourism studies that have, either directly or indirectly, sought to gauge employee reactions to elements of tourism industry worklife that were undesirable, unpleasant or even debilitating. The second section of the paper then offers an organizational justice framework wherein stress within the tourism industry may be addressed. Three major industry employment issues are considered: the treatment of disabled workers, workplace malfeasance and its detection, and employee dismissal procedures; each issue is explored within an organizational justice perspective, examining how proactive organizational change may assist tourism employees to avoid or minimize stress and industry organizations to avert a crisis in the form of an entrenched organizational culture of stress. *[Article copies available for a fee from The Haworth Document Delivery Service: 1-800-HAWORTH. E-mail address: <docdelivery@haworthpress.com> Website: <http://www. HaworthPress.com> © 2005 by The Haworth Press, Inc. All rights reserved.]*

KEYWORDS. Stress, tourism employees, management, morale, work satisfaction, organizational wellbeing

INTRODUCTION

There have, over the last few decades, been considerable changes wrought upon organizational life in the tourism world. Employment, for senior managers through to junior staff, is now plainly understood as no longer for life. It is moreover increasingly transitory and subject to major upheavals due in no small measure to socio-economic, health and security factors over which the tourism industry has no control. Hours of work are generally longer, skill levels required are often higher, and frequent company takeovers and accompanying restructurings have become relatively commonplace. Any increase in remuneration or betterment of working conditions has increasingly been tied to demonstrable productivity

---

Glenn F. Ross is Adjunct Associate Professor, School of Business, James Cook University.

[Haworth co-indexing entry note]: "Tourism Industry Employee Workstress–A Present and Future Crisis." Ross, Glenn F. Co-published simultaneously in *Journal of Travel & Tourism Marketing* (The Haworth Hospitality Press, an imprint of The Haworth Press, Inc.) Vol. 19, No. 2/3, 2005, pp. 133-147; and: *Tourism Crises: Management Responses and Theoretical Insight* (ed: Eric Laws, and Bruce Prideaux) The Haworth Hospitality Press, an imprint of The Haworth Press, Inc., 2005, pp. 133-147. Single or multiple copies of this article are available for a fee from The Haworth Document Delivery Service [1-800-HAWORTH, 9:00 a.m. - 5:00 p.m. (EST). E-mail address: docdelivery@haworthpress.com].

Available online at http://www.haworthpress.com/web/JTTM
doi:10.1300/J073v19n02_11

gains. It is also the case that new technologies such as email, text messaging and WAP technologies impose increasing demands on industry staff, requiring of them a response style that is both immediate and constant. The tourism industry workforce is also now, more than ever, comprised of individuals who are typically part of a two-career family, a situation that can pose dilemmas in the struggle to reach a satisfactory balance between work and family life. The industry furthermore now faces a growing awareness of the importance of non-discriminatory work practices; prejudice and discrimination are no longer tolerated within the workplace in many parts of the world, and the tourism industry has had to embrace anti-discriminatory principles and actions; it has, though, also begun to discover the considerable benefits afforded by a workplace that reflects diversity and inclusiveness.

This paper argues that workstress has a high likelihood of occasioning crises within the tourism industry; crises arise when organizational processes engender stress among workers, producing both short-term and long-term dysfunction and disability. Workstress may also be responsible for the appearance of unethical and destructive responses among members of the tourism industry workforce. Such outcomes, it is concluded, will lead to loss of organizational morale, to reduction of individual and organizational productivity, to damage to customer bases, and to a diminution of profits and perhaps even the basic viability of any firm or organization. Finally workstress may eventually cause a reduction in the living standards among many within a tourist destination should a climate of workstress become widespread and entrenched among many tourism enterprises. It is thus suggested that industry workstress is not only a crisis of personal proportions for tourism industry personnel; it can occasion a crisis having organizational and community dimensions, containing the potency to harm many people who, at first blush, may seem to have a relatively minor or indirect relationship with the tourism industry.

The future challenges and potential crises points occasioned by global, societal and organizational changes have now begun to be considered by a number of tourism and hospitality scholars, such as Holjevac (2003), Pizam

(1999) and Woods (1999). A common theme would seem to run through the human resource management views and predictions entertained by these scholars: that there is some cause for both optimism and for caution. Most are buoyant in their views, envisaging an industry wherein employees are regarded as the organization's most important asset; they would receive regular education and training, would be provided with childcare, and would have flexible working arrangements made available to them. Pizam (1999) would see the possibility of employee participation in benefits such as company stock options and profit sharing, being regularly consulted by management as part of the organizational decision-making process. However, the possibility of a less benign future, based upon some present industry practices, is also foreshadowed. Woods (1999) suggests that a number of current management assumptions and practices need modification; he suggests that many tourism organizations fail to realize that their employees are truly human, with all of the emotions, motivations and expectations that this assumption entails. Woods finds that many managers still adopt the erroneous and dysfunctional view that employees need them more than they need the employees; quoting Drucker (1995), Woods argues that organizations ought to market the membership of their particular organization in a manner that is similar to the way that they may successfully market their products. Woods would thus suggest that tourism management needs to inspire a volunteer-like motivation among employees, evoking a positive and spontaneous willingness and commitment to employment in the organization and the industry.

Lashley and Watson (1999), in summarizing hospitality human resource management over recent decades, have called for researchers to critically reflect on the meaning and theoretical underpinnings of research in this domain. They conclude that a great deal of the recent research endeavour has been concerned with a managerial agenda, with the problems facing hospitality organizations, and with providing more effective strategies for employers. The interests of those who work in the industry ought to also be considered, they suggest; they would pose the question as to whether there is always a natural unity of interest as between those who are employers and those whom they employ. They would further call for an awareness of and increased research focus on industry business practice, including those practices that might negatively effect the lives of those who are employed in the industry. This call for the adoption of a relatively new research perspective on the industry and its functioning vis-à-vis workers brings into sharp focus one of the more debilitating workplace difficulties that is increasingly being faced by many employees, that of workstress.

Workstress

The decade of the 1990s saw well-being and health in the workplace emerge as a prominent topic among many researchers and commentators. Stress, fatigue and burnout have come to be regarded as among the most debilitating of workplace afflictions; these are conditions from which very few individuals are immune, whether they be at the level of senior management, skilled professionals or of entry level staff. The tourism industry workplace has now produced a number of studies, demonstrating stress as a serious and costly condition; indeed some commentators would now suggest that the incidence and incapacitating effects of stress have become increasingly more common in many workplaces (Cooper, 1998). It has now been concluded that stress reactions may prevent or disturb an individual's adaptation to the workplace in a profound manner, both at a personal and also at an organizational level; stress will often produce a range of undesirable, expensive and personally debilitating consequences.

Schabracq, Winnubst and Cooper (2003) have concluded that stress often leads to diminished creativity and an arresting of personal and professional development, with negative consequences for work motivation, pleasure and overall well-being. They also hold that it frequently will lead to a severe reduction in the quantity and quality of social interaction, thus producing both conflict and isolation in the stressed employee. The end result of this process can be a drastic reduction in individual competency, and may also lead to physical illness and even premature death in some. Organizations too will suffer as the result of stress

among members. Various researchers such as Cooper and Payne (1991) and Warr (1987, 1995) have concluded that organizations will likely experience low production quality, as well as disruption to that production. Internal conflict, diminished cooperation, strained and ineffectual communication patterns, and overall, a dysfunctional workplace climate wherein competent problem-solving can be largely absent. Such problems, moreover, can then flow on to relationships with clients, with suppliers or with other companies and regulatory authorities; the loss of valuable staff, damage to the corporate image and an escalation of costs relating to employee sick leave and disability payments are yet further consequences of stress among staff. Thus stress is by no means a problem posed only for the individual employee; a tourism organization may also be forced to assume a heavy burden should it become a characteristic of the organization's work climate.

Occupational Wellbeing in Tourism Employment

Commentators such as Cooper (1998) have concluded that terms such as stress usually describe personal situations relating to affliction and discomfort; they generally do not encompass a much wider understanding of occupational wellbeing. This deficiency has led researchers such as Newton (1989) to advocate the adoption of an occupational wellbeing perspective so as to provide a more complete understanding of employees' experiences. Hart and Cooper (2001) suggest that occupational wellbeing encompasses both emotional and cognitive components. Emotions in this workplace arena are regarded as comprising both positive and negative experiences, sometimes termed morale and distress; these might be conceptualized at the level of the individual worker and also at the level of the workgroup. The cognitive component is comprised of dimensions of employee work satisfaction that relate to management, fellow workers, work-role and working conditions; within a tourism/hospitality industry employment context an organizational health focus would involve employee evaluations arising from the process of balancing both the positive and negative perceptions, with each worker reflecting a summary index of work satisfaction regarding their working conditions, work associates, managers and work role. In respect of emotional reactions, each industry employee will likely experience a range of positive affective responses such as pride, enthusiasm for work and heightened motivation to achieve; negative affective responses evoked by an industry workplace will, for some employees, be likely to include anxiety, depression, anger and guilt. Figure 1 contains a model of organizational wellbeing with relevance to service industries such as tourism.

Employee workplace behaviours have been found to be governed by stress, by morale, or by a combination of the two (George, 1996). Absenteeism, it has been revealed, is more likely to be associated by morale levels, that is by lower levels of positive emotions; stress, or negative emotions appears to play no similarly compelling role in this workplace outcome. Hart and Cotton (2003) make the point that stress and morale evidence quite separate sets of instigators, and point out that the factors activating one are quite different in kind to those evoking the other. It is thus concluded that responses to stress and to morale issues among workers may need to involve a range of tailored strategies, some of which may be suitable for an decrease in stress, others for an increase in morale, and yet others for the mitigation of both conditions.

FIGURE 1. Constituents of Organizational Wellbeing

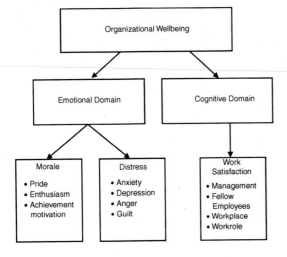

Stress Indicators in the Tourism Workplace

Whilst relatively little research focusing directly on stress within the tourism industry has been completed, in recent years a number of studies have examined various organizational factors that reflect on both the emotional and also the cognitive components of occupational wellbeing. Research in an industry context that have examined factors such as morale, stress and work satisfaction will be examined so as to assess the extent to which they provide insights into the state of occupational wellbeing within the tourism industry. Studies examined will include the attitudes of managers and those of employers, and will encompass topics such as organizational culture, creativity and commitment, perceptions of older employees among industry managers, and foodservice employee job satisfaction and management styles.

Magd (2003) has examined the perceptions of hospitality general managers regarding the benefits, disadvantages and likely future employment prospects of older workers. Whilst managers perceived a number of benefits flowing from the employment of older people, such as self motivation, a lessened proneness to accidents and an ability to produce quality work, they also perceived an inflexibility in regard to workplace change and in the adoption of new technology, higher costs associated with employment, and a lessened ability to work as speedily as other workers. It would thus seem that quite a number of negative assumptions and suppositions are made in regard to older workers, notwithstanding that many of these negative perceptions may not be grounded in reality; a further issue arises here in that more older workers will in the future, as the managers themselves acknowledge in this study, be employed in the industry due to an increasing shortage of younger workers. This may occasion a not uncommon situation wherein a growing number of employees in the older age groups will be regarded as, and perhaps treated as, less than ideal; they may even come to believe it of themselves. Stress issues associated with a diminution of workplace motivation, insecurity and anxiety or anger may be the result. This outcome can be of no benefit either to the employee or to the employer. Within the organizational wellbeing model, as presented in Figure 1, the findings of Magd would reasonably suggest the conclusion that a lessening of morale and an elevation of distress among older industry workers is likely if managers and supervisors were to demonstrate such attitudes within the tourism workplace.

Wong and Pang (2003a, 2003b) have examined both barriers and motivators to creativity among industry managers and supervisors. In regard to creativity motivators, Wong and Pang (2003b) have highlighted a number of primary factors such as transparent policies and processes, support and motivation from senior levels of the organization, recognition for effort and achievement, opportunities for training and development, and autonomy and flexibility; such factors would seem to be basic building blocks for higher levels of morale and thus organizational wellbeing. In regard to creativity barriers, Wong and Pang (2003a) have identified four major dimensions: a low level of commitment to the organization, a fear of change and criticism, the perception of time and work pressures, and finally, rigid rules and company management style. Here both low morale and stress agents have been elucidated; whilst a low level of commitment to the organization may be seen as leading to a morale deficit, fear related to change and criticism, time and work pressures, and rigidity in rules and management methods would all engender levels of stress. These sets of findings would suggest that a diminution of occupational wellbeing, particularly in regard to stress, is likely to have been experienced by a number of individuals in these work contexts.

Lam (2003) has investigated job satisfaction and organizational commitment among foodservice operatives, and reports that new employees seldom find that workrole expectations are met; instead they encounter jobs that lack challenge and meaningfulness, and that does not provide the new worker with any sense of accomplishment. Lam also found that these employees found their coworkers less courteous and helpful than expected; they were moreover offered relatively little opportunity to use their own discretion and decision-making skills in the workplace. The picture revealed is of an industry wherein new employees were disappointed and bored, finding few opportunities for training and development or for pleasant

and effective communication with managers and fellow employees. There is also presented in this study the image of an employment culture of transience, with high staff turnover in this workplace. Such findings would suggest the presence of major morale inhibitors as well as a significant inhibitor of work satisfaction leading to the possibility of stress and indifferent work effort.

Deery and Jago (2001) report a study of perceptions of hotel management styles among employees; this study examined the hypothesis that hotel management has generally become more consultative in their style in recent years. Their findings suggest that, whilst staff overall prefer a decisive management style, they believed that their managers and supervisors were in fact autocratic. The authors report deficiencies in regard to managements' communication skills and also people management skills, articulating a clear need for management to move toward a more consultative style in their interactions with staff. Findings from this study, when considered within an organizational wellbeing framework, would suggest the possibility of a real threat to morale, a distinct possibility of stress, and a clear barrier to work satisfaction for many staff. An autocratic style not only reduces morale and vitiates work satisfaction, but also is likely to produce emotions such as anxiety, anger and perhaps even some incidents of depression. Deery and Jago have found, as did Lam, evidence of both distress and work dissatisfaction, which may be attributed to indifference or ineptitude on the part of industry management.

Only a relatively small number of researchers have directly examined aspects of workplace stress within a tourism industry context. Brymer, Perrewe and Johns (1991); Krone, Tabacchi and Farber (1989); Reynolds and Tabacchi (1993); Tabacchi, Krone and Farber (1991) and Sarabakhash, Carson and Lundgren (1989) have investigated aspects of stress and burnout in the hospitality industry, and have concluded that it is a much more troublesome and debilitating condition than has been commonly realized. Vallen (1993), investigating organizational climate and burnout, reports a strong association between burnout experienced by industry workers and organizations characterized by mistrust, by high levels of employee control, and by a lack of teamwork among employees. Zohar (1994) has concluded that a lack of empowerment among industry personnel is a potent contributor to job stress in the industry, and argues for workrole redesign as a major preventative measure.

Ross (1993a) has found that uncooperative or unpleasant coworkers were regarded by fellow workers as likely to engender stress; work pressure, particularly from managers with an autocratic style, poor working conditions and unsatisfying staff-guest interactions were also found to evoke high levels of stress among industry staff. In an examination of help-seeking responses to stress, Ross (1993b) has found that industry workers, particularly older workers and female workers, were more likely to turn to a spouse, a relative or a close friend than they were to turn to a supervisor or manager. Only in a situation where the cause of the stress was perceived to be in the home would they consider turning to a trusted and approachable supervisor. Management was thus perceived by many to be either the major causal agents of the stress or to be unsympathetic or unapproachable. Ross (1995a, 1995b, 1997) has further found that issues such as workrole difficulties particularly over autonomy, and also dysfunctional workplace communication patterns were regarded by many industry employees as major causes of stress; employees further believed that the most effective way to reduce stress in organizations involved better communication skills on the part of management. Jogaratnan and Buchanan (2004) report that work stress may be evoked in junior hospitality staff by the imposition of unrealistic time pressures. Basic communications skills among managers, particularly as they may engender a culture of trust in an organization, are also seen as of overriding importance among those who are potential industry employees (Ross, 2003). Law, Pearce and Woods (1995) have also concluded that management style can be a major agent of stress among industry employees; such a point receives emphasis by Scott (1998) who, in a study of workplace violence experienced by industry employees, concludes that managers and employers have a clear duty to ensure the workplace is safe and healthy; this study would suggest that employ-ers are not providing such a working environment at present.

It may thus be concluded that industry-focused studies of workstress, workplace creativity, job satisfaction and organizational commitment evidence a common if disturbing theme of dysfunctionality that pertain to tourism management action or inaction. As the organizational wellbeing model would suggest, when morale is descending, distress is escalating and work satisfaction is conspicuously absent, often as the result of management indifference or incompetence, the cognitive and emotional functioning of individual workers will suffer; it is also the case that the efficient functioning of the organization will decline, and often sharply. This is, for any tourism enterprise, a clear portent of impending crisis.

ORGANIZATIONAL JUSTICE

The most effective preventative measure in regards to occupational stress at the organizational level involves the implementation of a culture of organizational justice; the ethical integrity of the organizational is, as Enz (2003) and Simons (2002) assert, the most important determinant of a healthy and productive enterprise. The notion of organizational justice involves each individual worker's perception of the fairness existing within the workplace. This fairness may involve policy matters within a large and complex company or government agency, or might involve specific practices relating to day-to-day functioning such as assignment of appropriate work tasks or the provision of operational autonomy (Crompanzano, 1993; Greenberg, 1996; Brockner & Weisenfeld, 1996).

Issues concerning organizational justice and integrity often arise for employees whenever they perceive that decisions have been reached concerning the allocation of organizational resources. Equity issues in this context, as Greenberg and Tyler (1987) have suggested, play an important role in the way that employees come to shape their attitudes and behaviour toward their managers and employers. A number of commentators such as Greenberg and Tyler (1987) and Bierhoff, Cohen and Greenberg (1986) would hold that the understanding of social justice perceptions within an organization reveals a great deal about the wellbeing of an organization, and also about the wellbeing of the individual members of the workforce. The concept of organizational justice among employees has been understood by way of two separate perspectives: perceptions in regard to the goods, benefits and opportunities that they receive, this being generally termed distributive justice; and the process by which means such as outcomes are reached, commonly referred to as procedural justice.

Furnham (1997) has suggested that the idea of distributive justice may be noted in the writings of Aristotle, particularly the *Nichomachean Ethics* (Tredennick, 1956), and more latterly Homans (1986), whose interest was in the rules of social exchange; rewards, Homans argued, ought to be proportional to personal costs and to individual investment of effort, time and skill. Furnham finds that fairness perceptions in the workplace are founded on relative judgments, with workers comparing their rewards with the rewards received by others. He points out that, in terms of an employee's pay, it is not so much the absolute amount received that is influential in the fairness decision, as the comparison made with the pay of salient others. It is moreover the case that employees generally differentiate between an unfavourable outcome wherein rewards might not be as bountiful as hoped for, and unjust outcomes wherein a precept of equity is perceived to be infracted. Furnham (1997) warns that employees will exhibit a much greater degree of affront and negative affect at the latter outcome.

Procedural justice, according to Deutsch (1975), Leventhal (1976), and Thibaut and Walker (1975), involves means rather than ends in social justice decision-making processes. In this approach employees would be equanimeous in respect of organizational decisions concerning safety issues such as smoking bans or reward issues such as differential pay scales in respect of qualifications or experience, so long as they were convinced that they outcomes were founded upon fair procedures. Furnham (1997) has outlined a set of precepts that are said to be critical in the establishment of procedural fairness in work settings. These include such requirements as all employees being given adequate notification so that they may prepare a case or an appeal, that all employees have a reasonable opportunity to argue their views, that there ought be a shared understanding among workers that outcomes have been based on the best evidence available, and that decisions arrived at be consistent with previous cases of a similar kind. Furnham makes the point that a shared perception of fair procedures in a workplace can lead to the acceptance of managerial decision-making that may seem harsh in the short-term, but in the long-term be necessary for organizational survival. In contrast, it is pointed out that perceived injustice in areas such as staff selection or promotion can have severe negative effects upon an organization and thus upon many staff therein. Employees negatively affected will likely feel aggrieved and may evidence common symptoms of stress such as anxiety, depression or anger.

Future Crises Points in Tourism/Hospitality Industry Employment

Greenberg (1996) suggests that major insights into the efficient functioning of an organization may be gained through an examination of major workplace issues associated with the functioning of justice and equity. Examining fairness in regard to a number of specific organizational topics in industries such as tourism can afford insights into employee experiences and reactions involving job satisfaction, morale and occupational stress. Moreover, the extent to which industry organizations are able to identify critical workplace issues, and also the extent of perceived injustice that may be associated with each, will in large measure determine the extent of stress that might provoke a future crisis for the entire organization. The following sections consider three emergent tourism issues that, if not managed carefully and with the welfare of all employees in mind, will carry major potential to provoke perceptions of unfairness, produce stress among employees, and thence may become the occasion for crisis.

Workplace Malfeasance and Its Detection

Managers in many organizations such as tourism are sometimes faced with unethical and unlawful acts, typically committed by a relatively small number of employees. And whilst the proportion of people may not be sizeable, the effects upon the organization can be considerable. The response of management to this situation will be critical for the well-being of the entire workforce. Organizations are now attempting to deal with issues such as theft, industrial espionage or sabotage by way of integrity testing. These tests, also known as tests of honesty, trustworthiness, counterproductive behavior and dependability, are favoured among the procedures by which organizations attempt to deal with incidents of employee malfeasance, particularly those incidents involving money, means of production, confidential information or merchandise of considerable value. Commentators such as Slora (1989) report that a number of employees in the fast-food industry and also in supermarkets freely admit to having previously been responsible for theft, either of company property or money. Theft is not the only serious concern; it is also estimated that up to 30% of all business bankruptcies may be the produced by the unethical behavior of some workers (Meinsma, 1985). Substance abuse, particularly that involving the consumption of alcohol at work, has been judged to cause losses within the vicinity of $28 billion to US industry (Jones & Wuebker, 1985); unsanctioned extensions of sanctioned work breaks, something that may be deemed a harmless practice in the view of many, have been suggested as occasioning a loss exceeding 50 hours per year for each worker (Jones, 1983). Integrity testing, whether it is in the pre-employment context or on the job, is typically focused on the identification of individuals disposed toward or actually engaging in such practices.

There have now been various attempts to understand some of the causal factors that might play a role in these counterproductive workplace behaviors. Greenberg and Barling (1996), Lasson and Bass (1997) and Murphy (1993) have all suggested a two-factor conceptualization of causality; one taking cognizance of issues associated with the individual worker, and another associated with issues within the work environment. In regard to person-based understandings, researchers have focused upon

attitudes, values and personality traits as they may predispose an individual to engage in unethical behavior in the workplace (Greenberg & Barling, 1996). A number of researchers have sought to examine a range of demographic factors, with Hollinger and Clark (1983) finding that both younger and part-time workers may be somewhat more likely to exhibit unethical behaviors. Other researchers have investigated attitudes displayed by particular groups, such as new workers, who had not yet had time to acquire a large measure of organizational commitment (Murphy, 1993). Murphy has concluded that lower-status and lower-paid employees, those who generally perceive themselves as least likely to share in the formal and legal reward systems of an organization, were the ones less likely to believe that there was a problem with counterproductive workplace behaviors.

An alternative person-based factor involves identifying and developing a construct that concerns employee dispositions toward unethical behavior (Ash, 1991). This approach suggests that lower levels of personal integrity predispose and predict unethical workplace actions. In recent decades much effort has been given over to assembling instruments and techniques by which individuals who would evince values related to unethical behavior might be recognized and understood (Goldstein & Lanyon, 1999). However, these integrity-focused approaches have also attracted much criticism; most of this criticism has concentrated on the psychometric instruments that they seek to employ. Issues involving validity, privacy and adverse reactions among potential and actual workers, many of whom do not engage in such malfeasance, represent the major arguments leveled at this type of approach (Camara & Schneider, 1995; Lilienfeld, Alliger & Mitchell, 1995). Notwithstanding the objections, it is also the case that a number of commentators would not accept the criticisms, and vigorously posit that integrity testing in the workplace does have a valid role in the investigation and prediction of unethical behavior (Mikulay & Goffin, 1998; Ones, Viswesvaran & Schmidt, 1993; Wimbush & Dalton, 1997). It is however the case that those who are advocates of such methods generally do not give serious consideration to the adverse effects of and reactions to integrity testing in many of its present forms.

Another perspective from which unethical workplace behaviors may be examined is that related to the situation or context in which the employee finds himself or herself. This situational perspective examines aspects of the individual's and the organization's circumstances that would more likely evoke unethical workplace behavior. Murphy (1993) argues that counterproductive workplace behaviors are more likely to be manifested when an employee judges them to be in their self-interest. However, if these actions are deemed to militate against their particular self interest, they are believed much more likely not to perform those actions. In any workplace environment, desirability-related issues are said likely to increase the probability of unethical behavior. Desirability outcomes are said to have a payoff for the employee; even though the attainment of money may seem the most desirable outcome, it is by no means the only one in a workplace context. A reaction to stressful work conditions or to managerial style will also alter perceptions of the desirability of outcomes. Personal responses associated with occupational stress, such as anxiousness, resignation or bitterness, by reason of their positive reinforcement effect upon the employee, might also be present; a worker might thus steal a relatively worthless object from a supervisor or manager, knowing that it will likely inconvenience or even anger the superior; it will moreover be done so as to avenge a real or imagined grievance held against that supervisor. A number of studies have now addressed the explanatory value of desirability factors, particularly in regard to domains such as equity (Greenberg, 1990; Lasson & Bass, 1997) and economic need (Hollinger & Clark, 1983).

Within organizational cultures of stress, risk can be a situational factor central in the understanding of unethical workplace behavior; risk here involves the consequences of being apprehended and exposed (Kamp & Brooks, 1991; Hollinger & Clark, 1983). Those suffering high levels of stress often do not care as might other workers; the condition is such that risk is perceived and calculated in a manner different to those not similarly afflicted, who would be less likely to jeopardize

their reputation, employment or freedom in a similar manner. It is also suggested by commentators such as Hollinger and Clark that a pervasive and obvious system of monitoring is crucial such that every employee understands that unethical practices will be observed and dealt with. Monitoring, conclude Hollinger and Clark, can be a potent deterrent; this monitoring system typically includes the provision of guards, of cameras, of audits and also subjects the workplace to computer monitoring in both public and private spaces. Such monitoring may be all-encompassing, and involve various systems of data collection, recording every workplace action and event. These measures have also been vigorously propounded by a variety of commentators in many contexts: Anonymous (1999); Dev, Brown and Dong-Jin (2000); Harris and Heft (1992); Krohe (1997); McCulloch (1996) and Smith (1993). By way of contrast, other commentators, with similar levels of passion and energy, have asserted that measures such as these are pointlessly punitive, have no demonstrable advantage, are clearly counterproductive and are an encroachment upon each individual's personal privacy: Dalton and Metzger (1993), de Paulo, Wetzel, Sternglanz and Wilson (2003), Hough and Oswald (2000), Smithers, Reilly, Millsap, Perlman and Stoffey (1993) and Townsend (1992). Indeed it is the intrusive and all-encompassing nature of surveillance, together with the perceived presupposition of guilt about which commentators warn.

Various issues in respect of organizational trust and occupational stress are thus raised by this monitoring, and are often not readily appreciated by many whose role it is to manage individuals in workplace such as tourism; when employees perceive that they are so little trusted that their management actively monitors their behaviour whilst in the workplace, this mistrust is often reciprocated (Kramer, 1999). Some employees may even respond to this perceived expectation of malfeasance by fulfilling the managerial expectation, but in a manner that they believe might circumvent the surveillance; others are likely to experience a reduction in morale at the obvious lack of autonomy and basic trust. Yet others may experience elevated levels of stress at the high and continuous levels of scrutiny and the implied lack of trust in their integrity. This monitoring in the workplace may very well provide management with a plethora of data regarding their workplace, but may also bring in its wake some deleterious stress-related effects upon employees, upon productivity and profit, and ultimately upon the culture of the organization. Thus managers in industry contexts such as tourism need to carefully consider the possible advantages in detecting the guilty by way of these particular methods, against the possible disadvantages experienced by the more ethical employees, by the organization overall, and perhaps even by the shareholders when profits start to decline.

The Physically Disabled Employee

A potential cause of work stress, as Furnham (1997) has pointed out, will often involve the frustration of normal career progression. When an employee applies for a position for which he or she is qualified and suitable, but is not given serious consideration by reason of prejudice and discrimination, frustration and stress are frequently experienced. Van Hoof, McDonald, Yu and Vallen (1996) argue that discrimination in an organization may be understood as a course of action wherein preferential treatment is offered to members of certain groups or one particular group at the expense of other groups of individuals. Such a practice is said not only to be unlawful and psychologically destructive, but also that it makes no commercial sense. The entertaining of negative stereotypes concerning particular groups, whether they be cultural, gender, age or physical ability groups, will inevitably result in the rejection of able, well-motivated and valuable workers; they moreover hold the potential to become distinct assets to the organization and the entire industry. Van Hoof et al. go on to make the point that discriminatory practices may be understood within an ethical context; indeed they conceptualize and describe this discrimination by means of core ethical precepts such as inequality, unfairness and the denial of equal opportunities.

The tourism industry, like many others, now has developed a realization of the ever-present possibility of discrimination particularly that directed toward disabled travellers. Lucas (1993) and Warr (1995) have written of the discrimination often experienced by older workers in many industries; Wood (1994) clearly adumbrates the potency of factors such as social class, gender and ethnicity in the perpetuation of discrimination in employment practices within the hospitality industry, whereas Tharenou (2001) concludes that, despite the perceived advances made by female employees, many still report encountering discrimination in aspects of organizational life such as glass ceilings with the promotion process. Employees with physical disabilities also encounter such barriers. Peterson and Gonzalez (2000) argue that career development can too often be hampered or terminated for those individuals having a physical disability. It is also evident that previous workplace experiences and limitations encountered by these individuals can result in fewer social and vocational opportunities, and thus a consequent loss of motivation. It is pointed out by Springer (2000) that this group of people is by no means small in number, with almost 20% of the adult population evidencing at least one form of disablement.

It is also the case that disability discrimination comes in varied forms. One subtle and insidious form of physical discrimination than can manifest itself within service industries, particularly in areas such as the appointment of staff to positions dealing directly with the public, involves an individual's physical appearance. Schultz and Schultz (2002) highlight a physical discrimination focusing upon physical attractiveness, which they label beautyism, wherein those employees regarded as more physically attractive are regarded as possessing more desirable personal and social traits, and are seen to be more sociable, dominant and mentally healthy than less physically attractive people. This bias, they point out, leads to clear cases of discrimination, inappropriate appointment and the loss of competent and well-motivated staff that don't fit the stereotype of physical attractiveness. These acts of employee discrimination do not only cause distress and harm to the recipients of this behaviour, but also diminish the ethical integrity and the productive capacity of the organization when competent and dedicated staff are not appointed to a position for specious reasons.

Commentators such as Baum (1995) point out that the demographic structures in a number of western countries are now in the process of major change; the progressive decline in the size of the youth population is said to have a major influence on recruitment within the tourism industry. The contraction in size of this traditional pool of cheap and flexible labour suggests that previously ignored or underutilized groups, such as individuals with a physical disability, will increasingly be seen as suitable, or perhaps necessary, for employment. Baum argues that disabled workers, among others, should be acknowledged as having a number of basic rights, such as the provision of easily understood and publicly accessible criteria relating to promotion and to career development; policies and procedures ought in no way discriminate on the basis of factors such as a physical disability. He regards the provision of such rights as falling within a sustainable perspective of industry employment that makes no assumptions about a staff member based upon status, gender, race, educational background or physical disability. Any organization that is seen not to contain the capacity to acknowledge the potential for growth, for development and for learning in every employee will not function effectively and not be sustainable within the industry.

Relatively little research has been devoted to the understanding of the stressful effects of discrimination upon individual employees who have a physical disability. Whilst there are now a growing number of studies addressing the topic of disability from the perspective of the employer, the organization and the industry (e.g., Kreismann & Palmer, 2001; Lee, 1996; Cleveland, Barnes-Farrell & Ratz, 1997; Jen-Gwo Chen & He Zenheng, 1997), relatively few studies have examined this issue by way of an employee perspective (e.g., Den Uijl & Bahlmann, 2002; Konur, 2002). One investigation that has attempted such an approach among those individuals currently in training for employment was that of Loo (2001), who examined attitudes of management undergraduates toward people with disability. Loo makes the point that such a population will likely be the next generation of professionals and managers who hire and work with employees with disabilities. He has found that whilst respondents did generally express a complex array of attitudes toward the disabled,

a number of attitudes were found to be negative and potentially discriminatory; it was concluded that a need clearly exists to sensitize many management students to issues regarding the abilities and employment potential of people with disabilities. This would also have implications for those students training for careers within tourism industry management; the incorporation within professional ethics' courses of material regarding the stressful effects of discrimination upon groups such as disabled employees would therefore seem of considerable value.

As Baum (1995) suggests, disabled workers are a source of competent and well-motivated industry employees who have often been ignored or suffered discrimination in the workplace. This group, moreover, will represent an increasingly important source of labour in any attempt to avert the coming labour supply crisis occasioned by an ageing population within the western world; the unfolding shortage of younger entry-level employees for industries such as tourism will need to be supplemented from other sources such as people with a disability, many of whom would clearly prove capable employees. The point is therefore made that, in order to avert or ameliorate this coming labour crisis, disability discrimination, a practice that is hurtful, unethical and plainly dysfunctional, needs to be addressed in a thorough and systematic fashion.

Employee Dismissal Procedures

Many global industries such as tourism have, over the last decade or so, undergone processes such as downsizing or restructuring. One major outcome of these processes has been the laying off of staff deemed in excess of requirements (Sahdev, 2004). Commentators such as Cascio (1995) have suggested that changes in the workplace will be even more common in the future as the process of change increases in pace; moreover the painful experiences endured by many employees caught up in these organizational changes are said to endure for periods long after the events themselves. A range of commentators such as Brockner (1994), Brockner and Greenberg (1990), and Konovsky and Brockner (1993) have all concluded that the provision of organizational justice affords ways of ameliorating the damaging personal effects of employment loss, whether it involve those who actually lose their jobs, or those who remain after other workers around them are terminated.

Konovsky and Folger (1991) have found that perceptions of fairness are important determinants in regard to the responses of employees who are laid off. Greenberg, Lind, Scott and Welchans (1995) have also examined this topic, and have concluded that the social treatment experienced by employees during the process of termination influenced their fairness reactions as well as their intentions to seek legal or financial redress from the company. Those workers who believed they were treated unfairly and with little or no dignity were the ones reporting that they would likely take legal action; in contrast, those employees who believed their layoff process did not cause them to suffer a loss of self-respect were found much less likely to sue, less likely to make financial claims or to consider some form of action for recompense. It might thus be concluded that the normally expected anguish occasioned by a termination of tourism employment can be aggravated and made much more stressful by a layoff processes that takes little account of the individual's personal dignity, made already vulnerable by the basic event (Sahdev, 2004). Thus the use of termination methods within the tourism industry that occasion as little stress as possible will have advantages not only for the employees concerned, but also for the organization through the avoidance of possible litigation and financial claims.

Survivors of the layoff process are also vulnerable to stress when fellow employees undergo retrenchment. Brockner and Greenberg (1990) have reported that remaining workers of an organization perceived a greater degree of fairness in a termination process and responded much more positively when management provided sufficient and credible explanations. Brockner and Greenberg (1990) and Brockner (1994) report that perceptions of fairness are engendered in survivors by clearly demonstrated procedural justice mechanisms such as the provision of adequate explanations as to the necessity for the action, and the provision of as much advance notice as was possible. In this manner beliefs in the fairness of the process are optimized, and negative responses such as stress experienced by those remaining will be correspondingly minimized. It may therefore be concluded that managers in industries such as tourism need not only to treat with fairness and with courtesy those who are to be laid off, but also need to be mindful of providing a detailed and cogent explanation of its necessity to those staff that remain within the organization, if they are to mitigate the damaging effects of stress to the employees and also to the tourism organization for which they carry responsibility.

CONCLUSION

Organizational justice influences almost every aspect of the human resource management system, extending from the more formal aspects such as policy and procedure through to the more informal aspects of work life such as the daily interactions that regularly take place between tourism staff and management; in every context and by way of every action an organization is said to present its fundamental ethical principles to its staff. Precepts such as fairness are the building blocks utilized by industry employers in their dealings with those they employ. When the overall interaction is characterized by justice and integrity, job satisfaction and morale are maximized; the presence of justice and integrity in dealings between employer and employee affords the greatest potential for wellbeing within workplaces (Drucker, 2002). However, when suspicion, mistrust or the clear presence of injustice becomes the hallmarks of the relationship, stress is seldom absent (Kramer, 2002). In order to avoid the crisis that this will inevitably bring, tourism organizations need to understand the major precursors to stress, and to proactively intervene, creating conditions wherein tourism industry employees are provided with a workplace that can foster morale and job satisfaction, and one that is less likely to infuse perceptions of unfairness. This remains the most effective procedure to minimize the possibility of a culture of stress developing, with its attendant risks of personal harm and of organizational crisis.

REFERENCES

Anonymous. (1999). NYPD test officer integrity. *Law & Order, 47*, 6-7.

Ash, P. (1991). The theory of planned behavior. *Organizational Behavior and Human Decision Processes, 50*, 179-211.

Baum, T. (1995). *Managing human resources in the European tourism and hospitality industry–A strategic approach.* London: Chapman and Hall.

Bierhoff, H.W., Cohen, R.L., & Greenberg, J. (1986). *Justice in social relations.* New York: Plenum.

Brockner, J. (1994). Perceived fairness and survivors' reactions to layoffs, or how downsizing organizations ends well by doing good. *Social Justice Research, 7*, 345-363.

Brockner, J., & Greenberg, J. (1990). The impact of layoffs on survivors: An organizational justice perspective. In J. Carroll (Ed.), *Advances in applied social psychology: Business settings* (pp. 45-75). New York: Erlbaum.

Brockner, J. & Weisenfeld, B.M. (1996). An integrative framework for explaining reactions to decisions: The interactive effects of outcomes and procedures. *Psychological Bulletin, 120*, 189-208.

Brymer, R.A., Perrewe, P.L., & Johns, T. (1991). Managing job stress in the hotel industry. *International Journal of Hospitality Management, 10*, 47-58.

Camara, W.J., & Schneider, D.L. (1995). Questions of construct breadth and openness of research in integrity testing. *American Psychologist, 50*, 459-460.

Cascio, M. (1995). *Managing human resources.* New York: McGraw-Hill.

Cleveland, J.N., Barnes-Farrell, J.L., & Ratz, J.M. (1997). Accommodation in the workplace. *Human Resource Management Review, 7*, 77-107.

Cooper, C.L. (1998). *Theories of organizational stress.* New York: Oxford University Press.

Cooper, C.L., & Payne, R. (Eds.). (1991). *Personality and stress: Individual differences in the stress process.* Chichester: Wiley.

Crompanzano, R. (Ed.). (1993). *Justice in the workplace: Approaching fairness in human resource management.* Hillsdale, NY: Erlbaum.

Dalton, L.M., & Metzger, M. (1993). Integrity testing for personnel selection: An unsparing perspective. *Journal of Business Ethics, 12*, 147-160.

Deery, M. & Jago, L.K. (2001). Hotel management style: A study of employee perceptions and preferences. *Hospitality Management, 20*, 325-338.

Den Uijl, S., & Bahlmann, T. (2002). A complex problem: Reintegration of partially disabled people in the workforce in the Netherlands. *European Journal of Operational Research, 140*, 413-426.

De Paulo, B.M., Wetzel, C., Sternglanz, W., & Wilson, J.W. (2003). *Journal of Social Issues, 59*, 391-411.

Deutsch, M. (1975). Equity, equality and need: What determines which value will be used as the basis for distributive justice? *Journal of Social Issues, 31*, 137-149.

Dev, C.S., Brown, J.R., & Dong-Jin, L. (2000). Managing marketing relationships. *Cornell Hotel Restaurant and Administration Quarterly, August*, 10-20.

Drucker, P. (1995). *Managing in a time of change.* New York: Penguin.

Drucker, P. (2002). They're not employees, they're people. *Harvard Business Review, February*, 71-77.

Enz, C. (2003). Promoting the human spirit: Key to business success. *Cornell Hotel Restaurant and Administration Quarterly, 43*, 2.

Furnham, A. (1997). *The psychology of behaviour at work.* London: Taylor & Francis.

George, J.M. (1996). Trait and state in affect. In K.R. Murphy (Ed.), *Individual differences and behavior in organizations* (pp. 145-171). San Francisco: Jossey-Bass.

Goldstein, L.D., & Lanyon, R.I. (1999). Applications of personality assessment to the workplace: A review. *Journal of Business and Psychology, 13*, 291-322.

Greenberg, J. (1990). Organizational justice: Yesterday, today, tomorrow. *Journal of Management, 16*, 399-432.

Greenberg, J. (1996). *The quest for justice on the job: Essays and experiments.* Thousand Oaks, CA: Sage.

Greenberg, J., & Barling, J. (1996). Employee theft. In C.L. Cooper & D.M. Rouse (Eds.), *Trends in organizational behavior*, Vol. 1 (pp. 49-64). New York: Wiley.

Greenberg, J., Lind, E.A., Scott, K.S., & Welchans, T.D. (1995). Wrongful termination litigation in response to perceived injustice among layoff victims. *Research in Personnel and Human Resource Management, 8*, 265-301.

Greenberg, J., & Tyler, T.R. (1987). Why procedural justice in organizations? *Social Justice Research, 1*, 127-142.

Harris, M.M., & Heft, L.L. (1992). Alcohol and drug use in the workplace: Issues, controversies and directions for future research. *Journal of Management, 18*, 239-257.

Hart, P.M., & Cooper, C.L. (2001). Occupational stress: Toward a more integrated framework. In N. Anderson, D.S. Ones, H.K. Sinangil & C. Viswesvaran (Eds.), *Handbook of industrial, work and organizational psychology*, Vol. 2 (pp. 93-114). London: Sage.

Hart, P.M., & Cotton, P. (2003). Conventional wisdom is often misleading: Police stress within an organizational health framework. In M.F. Dollard, A.H. Winefield & H.R. Winefield (Eds.), *Occupational stress in the service professions* (pp. 103-138). London: Taylor and Francis.

Holjevac, I.A. (2003). A vision of tourism and the hotel industry in the 21st Century. *Hospitality Management, 22*, 129-134.

Hollinger, R.C., & Clark, J.P. (1983). *Theft by employees.* Lexington, MA: Heath.

Homans, G.C. (1986). *Social behavior: Its elementary forms*. New York: Harcourt, Brace & Ward.

Hough, L.M., & Oswald, F.L. (2000). Personnel selection: Looking toward the future–Remembering the past. *Annual Review of Psychology, 51*, 631-664.

Jen-Gwo Chen, J., & He Zenheng. (1997). Using analytic hierarchy process and fuzzy set theory to rate and rank the disability. *Fuzzy Sets and Systems, 88*, 1-22.

Jogaratnam, G., & Buchanan, P. (2004). Balancing the demands of school and work: Stress and employed hospitality students. *International Journal of Contemporary Hospitality Management, 16*, 237-245.

Jones, J.W. (1983). *Dishonesty, staff burnout, and unauthorized work break extensions*. (Technical Report No. 11). Park Ridge, IL: London House.

Jones, J.W., & Wuebker, L.J. (1985). Pre-employment screening to control hospital crime and counterproductivity. *Readings in Healthcare Risk Management, 8*, 93-96.

Kamp, J., & Brooks, P. (1991). Perceived organizational climate and employee counterproductivity. *Journal of Business and Psychology, 5*, 447-458.

Konovsky, M.A. & Brockner, J. (1993). Managing victim and survivor layoff reactions: A procedural justice perspective. In R. Crompanzano (Ed.), *Justice in the workplace: Approaching fairness in human resource management* (pp. 133-153). Hillsdale, NJ: Erlbaum.

Konovsky, M.A., & Folger, R. (1991). The effects of procedures, social accounts, and benefits level on victims' layoff reactions. *Journal of Applied Social Psychology, 21*, 630-650.

Konur, O. (2002). Access to nursing education by disabled students: Rights and duties of nursing programs. *Nurse Education Today, 22*, 364-374.

Kramer, R.M. (1999). Trust and distrust in organizations. *Annual Review of Psychology, 50*, 625-650.

Kramer, R.M. (2002). When paranoia makes sense. *Harvard Business Review, July*, 62-69.

Kreismann, R., & Palmer, R. (2001). Reasonable accommodation under the ADA: What's an employer to do? *The Cornell Hotel and Restaurant Administration Quarterly, 42*, 24-33.

Krohe, J. (1997). The big business of business ethics. *Across the Board, 34*, 23-29.

Krone, C., Tabacchi, M., & Farber, B. (1989). Manager burnout. *Cornell Hotel, Restaurant and Administration Quarterly, 30*, 58-63.

Lam, T. (2003). Job satisfaction and organizational commitment in the Hong Kong fast food industry. *International Journal of Contemporary Management, 15*, 214-220.

Lashley, C., & Watson, S. (1999). Researching human resource management in the hospitality industry: The need for a new agenda? *International Journal of Tourism and Hospitality Research, 1*, 19-40.

Lasson, E.D., & Bass, A.R. (1997). Integrity testing and deviance: Construct validity issues and the role of situational factors. *Journal of Business Psychology, 12*, 121-146.

Law, J., Pearce, P.L., & Woods, B.A. (1995). Stress and coping in tourist attraction employees. *Tourism Management, 16*, 277-284.

Lee, B.A. (1996). Legal requirements and employer responses to accommodating employees with disabilities. *Human Resource Management Review, 6*, 231-251.

Leventhal, G.S. (1976). Fairness in social relationships. In J.W. Thibaut, J.T. Spence & R.C. Carson (Eds.), *Contemporary Topics in Social Psychology* (pp. 211-240). Morristown, NJ: General Learning Press.

Lilienfeld, S.O., Alliger, G., & Mitchell, K. (1995). Why integrity testing remains controversial. *American Psychologist, 50*, 457-458.

Loo, R. (2001). Attitudes of management undergraduates toward persons with disabilities: A need for change. *Rehabilitation Psychology, 46*, 288-295.

Lucas, R.E. (1993). Ageism and the U.K. hospitality industry. *International Journal of Contemporary Hospitality Management, 15*, 14-23.

McCulloch, M.C. (1996). Can integrity testing improve market conduct? *Market Facts, 15*, 2-15.

Magd, H. (2003). Management attitudes and perceptions of older employees in hospitality management. *International Journal of Contemporary Hospitality Management, 15*, 393-401.

Meinsma, G. (1985). Thou shalt not steal. *Security Management, 29*, 35-37.

Mikulay, S.M., & Goffin, R.D. (1998). Measuring and predicting counterproductivity in the laboratory using personality and integrity testing. *Educational and Psychological Measurement, 58*, 765-787.

Murphy, K.R. (1993). *Honesty in the workplace*. Pacific Grove, CA: Brooks/Cole.

Newton, T.J. (1989). Occupational stress and coping with stress: A critique. *Human Relations, 42*, 441-461.

Ones, D.S., Viswesvaran, C., & Schmidt, F.L. (1993). Comprehensive meta-analysis of integrity test validities: Findings and implications for personnel selection and theories of job performance. *Journal of Applied Psychology, 78*, 679-703.

Peterson, N. & Gonzalez, R. (2000). *The role of work in people's lives*. Belmont: Brooks/Cole.

Pizam, A. (1999). Life and tourism in the year 2050. *Hospitality Management, 18*, 331-343.

Reynolds, D., & Tabbachi, M. (1993). Burnout in full-service restaurants. *Cornell Hotel, Restaurant and Administration Quarterly, April*, 27-36.

Ross, G.F. (1993a). Type, severity and incidence of work stressors among Australian hospitality industry employees. *Australian Journal of Leisure and Recreation, 3*, 5-12.

Ross, G.F. (1993b). Help-seeking responses to work stress among rural and regional hospitality industry workers. *Regional Journal of Social Issues, 27*, 92-98.

Ross, G.F. (1995a). Work stress and personality measures among hospitality industry employees. *International Journal of Contemporary Hospitality Management, 7,* 9-13.

Ross, G.F. (1995b). Interpersonal stress reactions and service quality responses among hospitality industry employees. *Service Industries Journal, 15,* 314-331.

Ross, G.F. (1997). Career stress responses among hospitality employees. *Annals of Tourism Research, 21,* 41-49.

Ross, G.F. (2003). Workstress response perceptions among potential employees: The influence of ethics and trust. *Tourism Review, 58,* 25-33.

Sahdev, K. (2004). Revisiting the survivor syndrome: The role of leadership in implementing downsizing. *European Journal of Work and Organizational Psychology, 13,* 165-196.

Sarabakhash, M., Carson, D., & Lundgren, E. (1989). The personal cost of hospitality management. *Cornell Hotel, Restaurant and Administration Quarterly, 30,* 72.

Schabracq, M.J., Winnubst, J.A.M., & Cooper, C.L. (2003). *The handbook of work and health psychology.* Chichester: Wiley.

Schultz, D.P., & Schultz, S.E. (2002). *Psychology and work.* Upper Saddle River, NJ: Prentice-Hall.

Scott, B. (1998). Workplace violence in the UK hospitality industry: Impacts and recommendations. *Progress in Tourism and Hospitality Research, 4,* 337-347.

Simons, T. (2002). Behavioral integrity: The perceived alignment between managers' words and deeds as a research focus. *Organizational Science, 13,* 18-35.

Slora, K. (1989). An empirical approach to determining employee deviance base rates. *Journal of Business and Psychology, 4,* 199-219.

Smith, B. (1993). The evolution of Pinkerton. *Management Review, September,* 54-58.

Smithers, J.W., Reilly, R.R., Millsap, R.E., Perlman, K., & Stoffey, R.W. (1993). Applicant reactions to selection procedures. *Personnel Psychology, 46,* 49-77.

Springer, S. (2000, November 30th). Why should the hotel industry be concerned about accessibility? Retrieved from *www.hospitalitynet.org/news/All_Latest_News/4010284.*

Tabacchi, M., Krone, C., & Farber, B. (1991). Workplace and social support in ameliorating managerial burnout in the food and beverage industry. *Hospitality Research Journal, 14,* 553-560.

Tharenou, P. (2001). Managerial Career Advancement. In C. Cooper & I. Robertson (Eds.), *Organizational psychology and development.* Chichester: Wiley.

Thibaut, J., & Walker, L. (1975). *Procedural justice: A psychological analysis.* Hillsdale, NY: Erlbaum.

Townsend, J.W. (1992). Is integrity testing useful? *HRM Magazine, 37,* 96-98.

Tredennick, H. (1976). (trans.). *The ethics of Aristotle–The Nicomachean ethics.* London: Penguin.

Vallen, G.K. (1993). Organizational climate and burnout. *Cornell Hotel, Restaurant and Administration Quarterly, 34,* 54-60.

Van Hoof, H.B., McDonald, M.E., Yu, L., & Vallen, G.K. (1996). *A host of opportunities: An introduction to hospitality management.* Chicago: Irwin.

Warr, P. (1987). *Work, unemployment and mental health.* Oxford: OUP.

Warr, P. (1995). Age and work. In. P. Collett & A. Furnham (Eds.), *Social psychology and work.* London: Routledge.

Wimbush, J.C., & Dalton, D.R. (1997). Base rate for employee theft: Convergence multiple methods. *Journal of Applied Psychology, 82,* 756-763.

Wong, S., & Pang, L. (2003a). Barriers to creativity in the hotel industry–perspectives of managers and supervisors. *International Journal of Contemporary Hospitality Management, 15,* 29-37.

Wong, S., & Pang, L. (2003b). Motivators to creativity in the hotel industry–perspectives of managers and supervisors. *Tourism Management, 24,* 551-559.

Wood, R.C. (1994). *Organizational behaviour for hospitality management.* Oxford: Butterworth-Heinemann.

Woods, R.H. (1999). Predicting is difficult, especially about the future: Human resources in the new millennium. *Hospitality Management, 18,* 443-456.

Zohar, D. (1994). Analysis of job stress profile in the hotel industry. *International Journal of Hospitality Management, 13,* 219-231.

Tourism Crises and Disasters:
Enhancing Understanding of System Effects

Noel Scott

Eric Laws

SUMMARY. This paper examines the definitions and conceptual foundations of crises and distinguishes between crises and disasters. It takes a systems view of these concepts and uses the perspective of systems as organizational networks to examine implications for tourism managers. A tourism destination is perceived as consisting of a network of interacting organizations. This perspective questions the boundaries that should be used to study crisis and disasters. The paper also discusses the possibility of a crisis having a positive outcome for a destination. *[Article copies available for a fee from The Haworth Document Delivery Service: 1-800-HAWORTH. E-mail address: <docdelivery@haworthpress.com> Website: <http://www.HaworthPress.com> © 2005 by The Haworth Press, Inc. All rights reserved.]*

KEYWORDS. Crisis, disaster, normality, crisis management, social network analysis

INTRODUCTION

Crises and disasters attract attention by their unusual, unexpected or severe nature. News of a plane crash or terrorist attack becomes front-page headlines in newspapers around the world, and may be discussed in company board rooms and by government agencies concerned to avoid or minimise similar occurrences. Typically, a response is developed to the particular crisis, and it passes. Viewing a crisis in this manner leads to a focus in policy making literature on the randomness of crises and disasters and the need therefore to develop plans to better manage these unpredictable events.

It is argued here that this focus on the crisis phenomena is often to the exclusion of attention to the effects on the "system." By this we mean that, following the ideas of systems theory (Von Bertalanffy, 1950; Carlson, 1999; Scott & Laws, 2004), tourism activity involves the interactions of organizations, people and events in a variety of subsystems. By better defining and conceptualizing these interactions, it may be possible to better deal with the apparent randomness of individual events through an analysis of the comparable effects of a range of crises. To better examine this idea, there is a need to examine the systemic effects of these events as well as the phenomenon of the crises and disasters themselves.

Noel Scott is affiliated with the School of Tourism and Leisure Management, University of Queensland, Ipswich, Australia (E-mail: noel.scott@uq.edu.au). Eric Laws is Visiting Professor of Tourism in the School of Business Tourism Department, James Cook University (E-mail: e.laws@runbox.com).

[Haworth co-indexing entry note]: "Tourism Crises and Disasters: Enhancing Understanding of System Effects." Scott, Noel, and Eric Laws. Co-published simultaneously in *Journal of Travel & Tourism Marketing* (The Haworth Hospitality Press, an imprint of The Haworth Press, Inc.) Vol. 19, No. 2/3, 2005, pp. 149-158; and: *Tourism Crises: Management Responses and Theoretical Insight* (ed: Eric Laws, and Bruce Prideaux) The Haworth Hospitality Press, an imprint of The Haworth Press, Inc., 2005, pp. 149-158. Single or multiple copies of this article are available for a fee from The Haworth Document Delivery Service [1-800-HAWORTH, 9:00 a.m. - 5:00 p.m. (EST). E-mail address: docdelivery@ haworthpress.com].

Crisis events such as SARS, September 11 and the Gulf War are now global phenomena. The implications and effects of such crises go well beyond the immediate impact of the crisis. This is a result of increasingly integrated global communications and the interdependence of tourism companies, transport systems, and is now an accepted part of people's perceptions of the world around them. As a result, this paper explores an emergent perspective on crises that may help analysts examine and understand these "external" interactions and effects.

This perspective of focusing on system effects is considered useful as it highlights another range of effects or impacts of crises that have not been sufficiently recognised within the tourism literature. These include the idea of system resilience, of change in system states and in improvements or degeneration in the overall system of tourism as a result of a crisis. These ideas were identified and explored in the work of the late Bill Faulkner, particularly in a paper using floods in Katherine Gorge, Australia as a case study examining how a disaster may lead to a positive change in a destination's tourism (Faulkner & Vikulov, 2001).

The present paper examines the concept of system effects and change in system states. It provides a characterization of the literature of crises and disasters in tourism and these sets this literature within the theory of systems. It then examines a number of concepts and ideas that are derived from this strategic and systemic perspective. Such a systems approach is distinct from a number of the other disciplinary approaches that have been used, as will be discussed below.

THEORETICAL PERSPECTIVES ON CRISES

One of the reasons so little progress has been made in the advancing of our understanding of tourism disasters is the limited development of the theoretical and conceptual frameworks required to underpin the analysis of this phenomena. (Faulkner, 2001:136)

The current literature on crises is characterised by a number of disciplinary approaches (Pearson & Clair, 1998). These include the psychological, socio-political and technological-structural perspectives. The first two of these perspectives focus on the individual or social elements of a crisis. In the tourism literature examples are the management of crises through communication (Henderson, 2003) or the differences in perceptions of hotel managers and guests (Drabek, 2000).

The third, technological-structural, perspective is based on the idea of socio-technical systems. Here, technology and social systems (regulations, procedures, norms) are seen to interact to create complexity that may increase (or decrease) the probability of a crisis or disaster (Perrow, 1984). Characteristics of the system as a whole such as "tight coupling" of subsystems and interactive complexity are considered to increase the probability of a crisis. Examples include the interaction of two failures in a complex situation such as in the Challenger Space Shuttle disaster. Here a technical failure was compounded by the social norms and values within the management.

In these approaches, the crisis itself is seen as the unit of analysis. The focus is on the events leading up the crisis which then results in a perturbation of the normal state, followed by a restoration of the "normal" situation. For example, Pearson and Clair (1998:6), in their review of different perspectives on the study of crises and development of propositions for further study, discuss the outcome of a crisis as a system being restored to its normal state In particular the socio-technical perspective on crises views the crisis as distinct from the remainder of the environment.

An alternative analysis views the crisis situation as set within a wider system and uses this wider system as the unit of analysis. Here the system is seen in dynamic balance. Any effect on one part of the system may have an effect on other parts. This perspective is evident in the analysis of tourism distribution channels (Laws & Cooper, 1998; Buhalis, 2000). Here the interdependencies of organizations along a distribution chain have been examined. For example, a National Tourist Organisation might benefit from tour operator or airline advertising which feature it as a destination. Similarly, a tour operator often requires the travel retailers with which it trades to have staff trained in its systems and products so that the majority of client inquiries can be handled at the agency level, rather than by the tour operator's staff; this also encourages agency staff to sell a particular operator's products as they are more familiar with both its holidays and its reservations procedures.

Similarly, Britton (Britton & Clarke, 1987: 132-134) draws on dependency theory to examine the "influence that metropolitan based corporations exert over the nature of tourism development in small Pacific island nations." He documented how they are "emeshed in a global tourism system over which they have little or no influence . . . advertising strategies shape tourist expectations–leading visitors to seek the types of experiences and facilities associated with mass tourism . . . (small government) turn to companies to provide the necessary capital to finance large scale hotels and train staff. The ability of these to offer large commissions to overseas tour operators also enables them to gain control over various sectors of tourist industries. Profits often flow to overseas corporations and local elites. Small scale, locally owned enterprises are either relegated to activities which lie beyond the immediate interests of larger corporations, or find roles as subcontractors. The final outcome is a form of tourism that primarily satisfies the commercial interests of overseas concerns and only partially meets local development needs."

This perspective focuses attention on the politics of networks and relative power. It suggests the formation of alliances to avoid or address problems. From this perspective the outcome of a crisis may not be a return to a normal situation, or, even if the particular component of the system that experiences a crisis does return to normal, other parts of the system may have changed. Within the tourism literature one example of such a result is given by Dombey (2003) who notes the effects of the SARS crisis has led to changes in the travel behaviour of the Chinese population.

A related systemic approach is to compare the effect of different crises (McKercher & Chon, 2004). Here the system as the unit of analysis allows the comparison of various shocks (SARS, Y2K) in terms of their effect on tourism in Hong Kong. In this alternative systems perspective, change in a system may be expected and crises are one way for a system to change. As a consequence, the idea that things return to normal after a crisis is not a given.

DISCUSSION OF THE DIFFERENCE BETWEEN CRISIS AND DISASTER

In order to pursue the idea of an alternative theoretical approach to crisis situations this paper will now examine the definitions of the terms crisis and disaster. A clear distinction between crisis and disaster will highlight the theoretical concepts underpinning these terms and hence allow alternatives to be more easily understood. In addition, the recent usage of the terms crisis and disasters in tourism have varied somewhat from prior literature and the next section will attempt to provide a basis for a consensus on a typology for future researchers.

Recently, crisis and disasters have been examined and defined by Faulkner (Faulkner, 2001). He considers a crisis as an event where the root cause of the situation is "to some extent self-inflicted through problems such as inept management structures and practices or a failure to adapt to change." A disaster refers "to situations where an enterprise (or collection of enterprises in the case of a tourist destination) is confronted with sudden unpredictable and catastrophic change over which it has little control."

Faulkner's definitions of crisis and disaster are based on the idea of non-adaptation to change and random events, a view consistent with related work on "triggers" and chaos (Russell & Faulkner, 1999; Faulkner & Russell, 2001; Faulkner & Vikulov, 2001). The definition of crisis implies interaction of a human entity (person, organization or society) with an event. This appears consistent with the view of other authors where all definitions shown in Table 1 relate an event to an organization. Similarly, his definition of disaster is similar to that of most other authors. There is some disagreement in the literature though with the definition of a disaster as a "collective stress situation" (Quarantelli, 1988) stressing the human perception dimension rather than the magnitude of impact of the event. Importantly, this definition does not define disasters in terms of natural events but rather in terms of its catastrophic nature. The former idea of defining disasters in terms of natural disasters has been attributed to government concern and initiatives (Murphy & Bayley, 1989). While it may be more likely that a natural event is a disaster, as has been noted above, events such as the Chernobyl reactor meltdown or a terrorist bombing may be considered disasters.

As a result of this discussion, the usage in this paper of the terms crisis and disaster are as follows. The term crisis refers to a human view of a shock event. This event may be positive or negative in effect on a system. A positive event is an opportunity for the organisa- tion or destination, while a negative event is an immediate threat. A disaster is a negative cata- strophic event that affects a system. Shock events (but especially disasters) are managed using crisis management techniques (Barton, 1994). There are different types of disasters such as conflict and consensus types of disas- ters (Quarantelli, 1988). A conflict type of di- saster is one where no collective response to the event is possible (i.e., a transport strike), whereas a consensus disaster may be a natural disaster.

These concepts are illustrated in the follow- ing figure. In Figure 1, a system path mea- sured on some variable shown on the vertical

TABLE 1. Definitions of Terms Crisis and Disaster

Term	Definition	Source
Crisis	an event where the root cause of the situation is to some extent self-inflicted through problems such as inept management struc- tures and practices or a failure to adapt to change	(Faulkner, 2001)
	crises are the possible but unexpected result of management fail- ures that are concerned with the future course of events set in motion by human action or inaction precipitating the event	(Prideaux et al., 2003)
	a low probability high impact event that threatens the viability of the (entity) and is characterised by ambiguity of cause, effect and means of resolution as well as by the belief that decisions need to be made quickly	(Pearson & Clair, 1998)
	crises are disruptive situations affecting an organization or given system as a whole and challenging previously held basis assump- tions; they often require urgent and novel decisions and actions, leading potentially to a later restructuring of both the affected sys- tem and the basic assumptions made by the system's members	(Pauchant & Douville, 1993)
	a situation which is harmful and disruptive (versus a turning point or an opportunity); is of high magnitude (versus a threat or a prob- lem); is sudden, acute and demands a timely response (versus decline) and is outside the firm's typical operating frameworks (versus routine such as fire to firefighters)	(Reilly, 1993)
	an organizationally based disaster	(Preble, 1997)
	any action or failure to act that interferes with an (organisation's) ongoing functions, the acceptable attainment of its objectives, its viability or survival, or that has a detrimental personal effect as perceived by the majority of its employees, clients or constituents	Selbst (1978) discussed in (Faulkner, 2001)
Disaster	situations where an enterprise (or collection of enterprises in the case of a tourist destination) is confronted with sudden unpredict- able a catastrophic change over which it has little control	(Faulkner, 2001)
	disasters are unpredictable catastrophic change that can normally only be responded to after the event, either by deploying contin- gency plans already in place or through reactive response	(Prideaux et al., 2003)
	an event, natural or man-made, sudden or progressive, which im- pacts with such severity that the affected community has to re- spond by taking exceptional measures	(Carter, 1991)
	a collective stress situation	(Quarantelli, 1988)
	any sudden, random or great misfortune	(Murphy & Bayley, 1989)

Source: Various authors.

FIGURE 1. Illustration of Concepts Related to Crises and Disasters

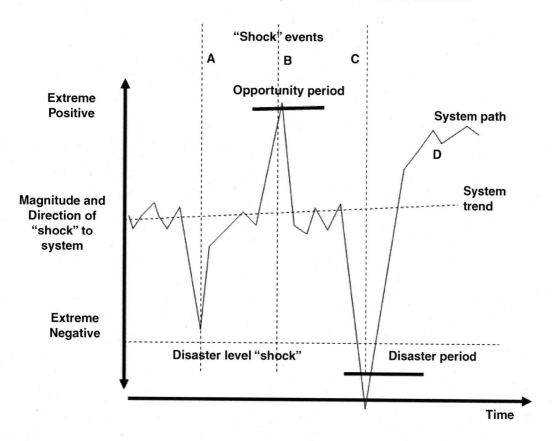

axis (say destination visitor numbers) is traced with the solid line over time (horizontal axis). The system is subject to three shock events (A, B and C). The system follows a trend line marked as a dotted line. Event A is a negative shock event while B is a positive shock event. After both A and B the system returns to its initial trend line. At C, the system is subject to a disaster and a crisis period ensues. The system returns to a new level (D) that is above the trend line.

DELINEATION OF A CRISIS AND NORMALITY

General theories of crisis management assume that events move through a series of stages (pre-crisis, crisis and post-crisis) with action sometimes possible to avert a final crisis (Henderson, 2003). Turner (1976) identifies six such stages, commencing with a *notionally normal starting point* that has two significant characteristics. These are culturally shared beliefs about the world and its hazards, and associated precautionary norms enshrined in laws and codes of practice. Events for which accepted beliefs about hazards and the norms for their avoidance cannot cope with occur during a crisis *incubation period*. The third stage is a *precipitating event* which transforms general perceptions and leads to *crisis onset*. At this stage, the immediate consequences of the collapse of cultural precautions become apparent. Recovery from the crisis occurs in two further stages in Turner's model. During *rescue and salvage* the immediate post-collapse problems are recognized in ad hoc adjustments which permit the work of rescue and salvage to be started. The sixth stage is *full cultural readjustment*: during this stage, "an inquiry or assessment is carried out and beliefs and precautionary norms are adjusted to fit the newly gained understanding of the world" (Turner,1976, p. 381).

This idea of stages follows from the view of the crisis as dividing time into a before and after. Huang and Min (2002), for example, indicate that government intervention led to the rapid recovery in tourism numbers from an earthquake in Taiwan. This perspective appears associated with the idea of the crisis having a distinct start and finish and the end of the crisis is defined by a return to normality. Here normality means a return to the state prior to the crisis.

The alternative systems perspective is based on the idea of an evolving system where (gradual) change is endemic and a crisis may lead to fundamentally different states and a return to normality is not necessarily the required (or even desired) endpoint. Here a crisis is seen as the result of one form of change and the effects of a crisis are not confined only to its immediate temporal or geographical vicinity. These changes may be positive or negative but certainly the subsequent system may be different from the preceding one, and importantly, the changes were not planned in the strategic management of the organisation. In these terms the effect of a disaster as a catastrophic change event is much more likely to trigger a change of state than other "lesser" events. This perspective is presented in the case study of a flooding disaster in Katherine Gorge in the Northern Territory of Australia (Faulkner & Vikulov, 2001) previously referred to. Here the disaster is seen as leading to the opportunity to change the quality of accommodation and other infrastructure in the tourism sector. Similarly, Burstein (1991) has also noted the focusing effect of a crisis on government agenda and resultant post-crisis opportunities in a study of policy agenda setting.

CRISIS MANAGEMENT

Following the convention and style employed in Figure 1, the effect of crisis management is illustrated in Figure 2. In this illustration, a disaster level shock event is experienced by the system and various outcomes are shown by paths A-D. In A the path experienced by the system without active management is shown. The system returns to equilibrium after a short period. In B the system is actively managed and as a result

the overall magnitude of the system effect is lessened. However, in C and D the effect of active management is to worsen the crisis leading to extension of the deviation from the trend line for the system path.

An example is the serious reduction in visitor arrivals often experienced by destinations following an economic crisis in the origin country, which happened as the Asian Economic meltdown of the late 1990s deepened and spread. However, in Queensland, Australia this prompted the Government of the day to become more involved in tourism. If this had not occurred then the effect on tourism of the Asian Crisis may have been more profound (line C or D). Instead, additional funding and a refocusing of efforts led to development of new markets and stimulation of traditional ones (line B).

ORGANIZATIONAL NETWORK DIMENSION OF CRISES AND DISASTERS

Given this conceptualization of crises and disasters in terms of a systems view, we are now in a position to consider the implications of viewing tourism networks as systems. An organizational network is a set of interacting organizations that exchange information, share customers, or exchange resources. Tourism involves many companies involved in transport, accommodation, attractions, etc., working together to produce a product. This view of tourism views tourism destinations as involving interacting networks of suppliers of services (Scott & Laws, 2004) that change over time. The achievement of an entrepreneur for example can be understood as creating new networks of organizations that service a new product market or niche within a destination.

The concept of organizational networks originated in the early sociological writings of Simmel (1908) and social anthropological work of Radcliffe Brown (1935). These writers developed a structural view on social interaction which highlights the importance of social organizations, relationships and interactions in influencing individual decisions. Structures are recurring patterns of social relations (Thatcher, 1998). This view may be contrasted with a rationalist perspective that focuses on the attributes and actions of individu-

FIGURE 2. Illustration of Different Outcomes from Management of Crises

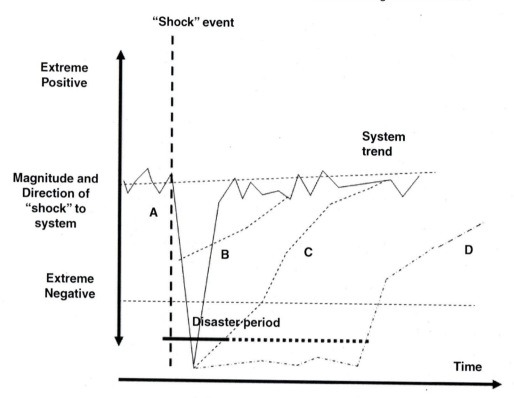

als or organizations (Brinton Milward & Provan, 1998).

Social network analysis seeks to define and quantify these relationships. The work of Moreno (1934) indicated that social configurations had definite structures which could be described in "sociograms" to visualise the flow of information between organizations or the friendships between individuals. This led to the development of graph theory where the relationships between individuals in groups are represented as points and lines and the resulting patterns are described. Later developments led to the identification of groups of individuals with similar patterns of relationships (blockmodels) and to the use of statistical methods such as multidimensional scaling to transform relationships into social distance and map them in social space. Social network analysis relates the relationships of the individual to the pattern of the network, and provides insight into the interactions between the two (Stokman, 2002). Social network analysis is philosophically related to systems theory (Boulding, 1956), where the properties of the system are derived from the interaction of many components.

Social network analysis delivers a number of useful outcomes. It provides a means of visualizing complex sets of relationships and simplifying them and is therefore useful in promoting effective collaboration within a group, supporting critical junctures in networks that cross functional, hierarchical, or geographic boundaries; and ensuring integration within groups following strategic restructuring initiatives (Cross et al., 2002). The use of standard methods and questions enables networks of relationships to be compared between regions or over time, thus allowing the study of dynamic situations. A more ambitious aim of is to offer a structural analysis and suggestions for improving network characteristics such as communication flows. As a result, social network analysis overlaps and informs the study of inter-organizational collaboration and cooperation, networks and strategic alliances. It has been used in studies of inter-organizational relationships and in the development of policy (Tyler & Dinan, 2001; Coleman, 2002; Pforr, 2002). A social network has been defined as a specific set of linkages among a defined set of persons, with

the additional property that the characteristics of these linkages as a whole may be used to interpret the social behaviour of the persons involved (Mitchell, 1969).

From this social network perspective, the tourism system is a network of organizations and the effect of a disaster is to place stress on these relationships. This stress is also systemic to some extent such that impact of a disaster on one organization or destination may in turn lead to a knock-on effect on others. One reason for this is that competition between companies and destinations is intense and the effect of disaster in one destination will have an effect on related destinations. Thus the effect of SARS on Australian tourism destinations was to reduce international visitor numbers but to boost domestic visitors to the Gold Coast. As a result, some operators on the Gold Coast experienced a bumper Christmas holiday period. A number of authors have examined the effect of a crisis on organizations outside the initial crisis area. Litvin and Alderson (2003), for example, examine the effect of the 9/11 crisis on the Charleston Convention and Visitors Bureau. Here effective management was able to avert the full extent of the impact by switching promotion expenditure to different markets.

This view of the effect of a crisis on the destination conceptualized as a network of organizations is shown in Figure 3. Here a crisis leads a set of organizations with existing relationships to become more networked.

A related view is that the nature of other relationship types such as cooperation and alliances between stakeholders is important in minimizing or averting the effects of a disaster through better crisis management (Pearson & Clair, 1998). This view is related to a management approach of scanning for problems and avoiding or minimizing their impact. But it is also related to the idea that a network of organizations that cooperate together may be able to better manage the effects of a crisis. This approach, similar to the socio-technical systems perspective, has been examined in a study of social networks and a crisis in the construction sector (Loosemore, 1998).

FIGURE 3. Conceptualization of the Effect of a Crisis on a Destination System

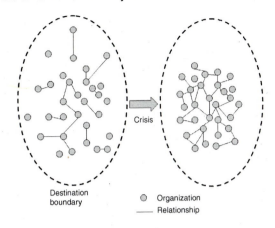

Destination boundary

○ Organization

—— Relationship

IMPLICATIONS FOR STUDYING CRISES AND DISASTERS

The above discussion has conceptualized the study of crises and disasters firstly by examining their definitions and secondly by using a view of tourism systems as networks of organizations. Three implications of this are discussed here. Firstly, this systems view questions the boundaries that should be used to study crisis and disasters. Secondly, a social networks view provides a different perspective of the effect of crises and disasters by focusing on the interactions between organizations. Thirdly, the idea of a positive effect of a crisis is discussed.

The first implication is that the effects of a crisis may be transferred across system boundaries by organizational relationships. For example a baggage strike at one airport may delay passengers, lead to costs to airlines in accommodating passengers and moving luggage and rescheduling flights, lead to extra stress for airport staff, local congestion. However, it may also have knock on effects at distant airports and lead to a loss of business to hotels in that destination.

Here, systems perspectives can help identify the range of stakeholders involved, and lead to a study of factors influencing speed of recovery, the intensity of effects and the factors causing breadth of effect (i.e., on other stakeholders).

Finally, the effects of a crisis may be to produce an altered trend path. Destinations as networks of stakeholders may be reconfigured into more efficient structures by a crisis. This is slightly different to the view of Faulkner and Vikulov (2001), who suggested a disaster may have a positive outcome but this was primarily due to new infrastructure. However, crises may also lead to more cohesive industry wide or community wide response mechanisms, better information flows and indeed the development of new organizational structures (Quarantelli, 1988). This emphasises the flow of information as a critical issue in crisis management and leads to the idea of social network analysis as a means of analysing the structure of this "flow."

DISCUSSION AND CONCLUSIONS

This paper has examined the concept of crises and disasters from a systems theory perspective. This view differs from the majority of prior literature in that it emphasises interconnection, dynamic disequilibrium and change rather than an internal/external "return to normal" perspective. It is similar to the socio-technical perspective on crises but changes the focus to the system as the unit of analysis.

This perspective appears useful in tourism which is an interconnected and systemic phenomenon. It focuses attention on understanding the potential positive and negative effects of crises beyond the focal area. This may help destinations consider risks and potential of various possible crises.

It also focuses attention on the need to develop more effective theoretical tools for examination of crises, and to adopt more precise terminology in describing crisis events. One concept that may be useful in exploring crises and disasters is that of resilience. An interesting feature of modern tourism is that reports of its death has been somewhat exaggerated. Mass tourism is alive and well, surviving many disasters and crises. It may be useful to study the reasons for this resilience and it is suggested here that organizational network analysis may be a useful approach.

REFERENCES

Barton, L. (1994). Crisis Management: Preparing for and managing disasters. *Cornell Hotel and Restaurant Administration Quarterly, 35*(2), 59-65.

Boulding, K. E. (1956). General Systems Theory; the skeleton of science. *Management Science, 2*(3), 56-68.

Brinton Milward, H., & Provan, K. G. (1998). Measuring network structure. *Public Administration, 76,* 387-407.

Britton, S., & Clarke, W. (Eds.). (1987). *Ambiguous alternative: Tourism in small developing countries.* Suva, Fiji: University of the South Pacific.

Buhalis, D. (2000). Marketing the competitive destination of the future. *Tourism Management, 21*(1), 97-116.

Burstein, P. (1991). Policy domains: Organization, culture and policy outcomes. *Annual Review of Sociology, 17,* 327-350.

Carlson, J. (1999). A systems approach to island tourism destination management. *Systems Research and Behavioral Science, 16*(4), 321.

Carter, W. N. (1991). *Disaster management: A disaster manager's handbook.* Manila: Asian Development Bank.

Coleman, W. D. (2002). Policy Networks. In *International Encyclopedia of the Social & Behavioral Sciences.*

Cross, R., Borgatti, S. P., & Parker, A. (2002). Making invisible work visible: Using social network analysis to support strategic collaboration. *California Management Review, 44*(2), 25-46.

Dombey, O. (2003). The effect of SARS on the Chinese Tourism Industry. *Journal of Vacation Marketing, 10*(1), 4-10.

Drabek, T. E. (2000). Disaster evacuations: Tourist-business managers rarely act as customers expect. *Cornell Hotel and Restaurant Administration Quarterly, 41*(4), 48-57.

Faulkner, B. (2001). Towards a framework for tourism disaster management. *Tourism Management, 22*(2), 135-147.

Faulkner, B., & Russell, R. (2001). Turbulence, chaos and complexity in tourism systems: A research direction for the new millennium. In B. Faulkner, G. Moscardo & E. Laws (Eds.), *Tourism in the 21st Century: Lessons from Experience* (pp. 328-349). London: Continuum.

Faulkner, B., & Vikulov, L. (2001). Katherine, washed out one day, back on track the next: A post-mortem of a tourism disaster. *Tourism Management, 22*(4), 331-344.

Henderson, J. (2003). Communicating in a crisis: flight SQ 006. *Tourism Management, 24*(3), 279-287.

Huang, J. H., & Min, J. C. H. (2002). Earthquake devastation and recovery in tourism: The Taiwan case. *Tourism Management, 23*(2), 145-154.

Laws, E., & Cooper, C. (1998). Inclusive tours and commodification: The marketing constraints for mass-market resorts. *Journal of Vacation Marketing, 4*(4), 337-352.

Litvin, S. W., & Alderson, L. L. (2003). How Charleston got her groove back: A Convention and Visitors Bureau's response to 9/11. *Journal of Vacation Marketing, 9*(2), 188-197.

Loosemore, M. (1998). Social network analysis: Using a quantitative tool within an interpretitive context to explore the management of construction crises. *Engineering, Construction and Architectural Management, 5*(4), 315-326.

McKercher, B., & Chon, K. (2004). The Over-Reaction to SARS and the Collapse of Asian Tourism. *Annals of Tourism Research, 31*(3), 716-719.

Mitchell, J. C. (1969). The concept and use of social networks. In J. C. Mitchell (Ed.), *Social networks in urban situations.* Manchester: University of Manchester Press.

Moreno, J. (1934). *Who Shall Survive?* New York: Beacon Press.

Murphy, P. E., & Bayley, R. (1989). Tourism and disaster planning. *Geographical Review, 79*(1), 36-46.

Pauchant, T., & Douville, R. (1993). Recent research in crisis management: A study of 24 authors' publications from 1986 to 1991. *Industrial and Environmental Crisis Quarterly, 7*(1), 43-63.

Pearson, C. M., & Clair, J. A. (1998). Reframing crisis management. *Academy of Management Review, 23*(1), 59-76.

Perrow, C. (1984). *Normal Accidents: Living with High Risk Technologies.* New York: Basic Books.

Pforr, C. (2002). The 'makers and shapers' of tourism policy in the Northern Territory of Australia: A policy network analysis of actors and their relational constellations. *Journal of Hospitality and Tourism Research, 9*(2), 134-151.

Preble, J. F. (1997). Integrating the crisis management perspective into the strategic management process. *Journal of Management Studies, 34*(5), 769-791.

Prideaux, B., Laws, E., & Faulkner, B. (2003). Events in Indonesia: Exploring the limits to formal tourism trends forecasting methods in complex crisis situations. *Tourism Management, 24*(4), 475-487.

Quarantelli, E. L. (1988). Disaster crisis management–a summary of research findings. *Journal of Management Studies, 25*(4), 373-385.

Radcliffe-Brown, A. R. (1935). On the concept of function in social science. *American Anthropologist, 37*(3), 394-402.

Reilly, A. (1993). Preparing for the worst: The process of effective crisis management. *Industrial and Environmental Crisis Quarterly, 7*(2), 115-143.

Russell, R., & Faulkner, B. (1999). Movers and shakers: Chaos makers in tourism development. *Tourism Management, 20*(4), 411-423.

Scott, N., & Laws, E. (2004). *Stimulants and inhibitors in the development of niche markets–The whale's tale.* Paper presented at the CAUTHE 2004, Brisbane.

Scott, N., & Laws, E. (2004). Whale watching–the roles of small firms in the evolution of a new Australian niche market. In R. Thomas (Ed.), *Small Firms in Tourism: International Perspectives* (pp. 153-166). London: Elsevier.

Simmel, G. (1908). *Soziologie* (1968 edition). Berlin: Dunker and Humblot.

Stokman, F. N. (2002). Networks: Social. In *International Encyclopedia of the Social & Behavioral Sciences.*

Thatcher, M. (1998). The development of policy network analyses from modest origins to overarching frameworks. *Journal of Theoretical Politics, 10*(4), 389-416.

Turner, B. A. (1976). The organizational and inter-organizational development of disasters. *Administrative Science Quarterly, 21*, 378-397.

Tyler, D., & Dinan, C. (2001). The role of interested groups in England's emerging tourism policy network. *Current Issues in Tourism, 4*(2-4), 210-252.

Von Bertalanffy, L. (1950). The Theory of Open Systems in Physics and Biology. *Science, 111*, 23-29.

Index

BOOK ORDER FORM!

Order a copy of this book with this form or online at:
http://www.haworthpress.com/store/product.asp?sku= 5788

Tourism Crises
Management Responses and Theoretical Insight

_____ in softbound at $29.95 ISBN-13: 978-0-7890-3208-9 / ISBN-10: 0-7890-3208-2.

COST OF BOOKS _____

POSTAGE & HANDLING _____
US: $4.00 for first book & $1.50
for each additional book
Outside US: $5.00 for first book
& $2.00 for each additional book.

SUBTOTAL _____
In Canada: add 7% GST. _____

STATE TAX _____
CA, IL, IN, MN, NJ, NY, OH, PA & SD residents
please add appropriate local sales tax.

FINAL TOTAL _____
If paying in Canadian funds, convert
using the current exchange rate,
UNESCO coupons welcome.

❑**BILL ME LATER:**
Bill-me option is good on US/Canada/
Mexico orders only; not good to jobbers,
wholesalers, or subscription agencies.

❑**Signature** _____

Payment Enclosed: $ _____

❑ **PLEASE CHARGE TO MY CREDIT CARD:**
❑Visa ❑MasterCard ❑AmEx ❑Discover
❑Diner's Club ❑Eurocard ❑JCB

Account #_____

Exp Date _____

Signature _____
(Prices in US dollars and subject to change without notice.)

PLEASE PRINT ALL INFORMATION OR ATTACH YOUR BUSINESS CARD

Name

Address

City   State/Province   Zip/Postal Code

Country

Tel   Fax

May we use your e-mail address for confirmations and other types of information? ❑Yes ❑No We appreciate receiving
your e-mail address. Haworth would like to e-mail special discount offers to you, as a preferred customer.
We will never share, rent, or exchange your e-mail address. We regard such actions as an invasion of your privacy.

Order from your **local bookstore** or directly from
The Haworth Press, Inc. 10 Alice Street, Binghamton, New York 13904-1580 • USA
Call our toll-free number (1-800-429-6784) / Outside US/Canada: (607) 722-5857
Fax: 1-800-895-0582 / Outside US/Canada: (607) 771-0012
E-mail your order to us: orders@haworthpress.com

For orders outside US and Canada, you may wish to order through your local
sales representative, distributor, or bookseller.
For information, see http://haworthpress.com/distributors

(Discounts are available for individual orders in US and Canada only, not booksellers/distributors.)

Please photocopy this form for your personal use.
www.HaworthPress.com

BOF06